Class, Race, Disability and Mental Health in Higher Education

Also Available from Bloomsbury

Community-Based Transformational Learning, *edited by
Christian Winterbottom, Jody S. Nicholson and F. Dan Richard*
The Roma in European Higher Education, *edited by Louise Morley,
Andrzej Mirga and Nadir Redzepi*
Locating Social Justice in Higher Education Research, *edited by
Jan McArthur and Paul Ashwin*
Migration Narratives, *Stanton Wortham, Briana Nichols,
Katherine Clonan-Roy and Catherine Rhodes*
Austerity and the Remaking of European Education, *edited by
Anna Traianou and Ken Jones*
Transnational Perspectives on Democracy, Citizenship, Human Rights and
Peace Education, *edited by Mary Drinkwater, Fazal Rizvi and Karen Edge*
Education and Disability in the Global South, *edited by Nidhi Singal,
Paul Lynch and Shruti Taneja Johansson*
Dominant Discourses in Higher Education, *Ian M. Kinchin and
Karen Gravett*
Decolonizing University Teaching and Learning, *D. Tran*
Social Theory and the Politics of Higher Education, *edited by Mark Murphy,
Ciaran Burke, Cristina Costa and Rille Raaper*
Changing Higher Education for a Changing World, *edited by
Claire Callender, William Locke and Simon Marginson*
Hopeful Pedagogies in Higher Education, *edited by Mike Seal*

Class, Race, Disability and Mental Health in Higher Education

Questioning the Access, Success and Progression of Disadvantaged Students

Mike Seal

BLOOMSBURY ACADEMIC
LONDON • NEW YORK • OXFORD • NEW DELHI • SYDNEY

BLOOMSBURY ACADEMIC
Bloomsbury Publishing Plc
50 Bedford Square, London, WC1B 3DP, UK
1385 Broadway, New York, NY 10018, USA
29 Earlsfort Terrace, Dublin 2, Ireland

BLOOMSBURY, BLOOMSBURY ACADEMIC and the Diana logo are trademarks of Bloomsbury Publishing Plc

First published in Great Britain 2022
This paperback edition published 2024

Copyright © Mike Seal, 2022

Mike Seal has asserted his right under the Copyright, Designs and Patents Act, 1988, to be identified as Author of this work.

Cover design by Jade Barnett
Cover image © Jose A. Bernat Bacete/Getty Images

All rights reserved. No part of this publication may be reproduced or transmitted in any form or by any means, electronic or mechanical, including photocopying, recording, or any information storage or retrieval system, without prior permission in writing from the publishers.

Bloomsbury Publishing Plc does not have any control over, or responsibility for, any third-party websites referred to or in this book. All internet addresses given in this book were correct at the time of going to press. The author and publisher regret any inconvenience caused if addresses have changed or sites have ceased to exist, but can accept no responsibility for any such changes.

A catalogue record for this book is available from the British Library.

A catalog record for this book is available from the Library of Congress.

ISBN: HB: 978-1-3502-4738-3
PB: 978-1-3502-4742-0
ePDF: 978-1-3502-4739-0
eBook: 978-1-3502-4740-6

Typeset by Integra Software Services Pvt. Ltd.

To find out more about our authors and books visit www.bloomsbury.com and sign up for our newsletters.

Contents

Introduction: Questioning the Access, Success and Progression of Disadvantaged Students in Higher Education 1

1 Theoretical Perspectives on Widening Participation 19
2 Social and Higher Education Policy and Widening Participation 37
3 Access, Success and Progression of Disadvantaged Students: Case Study of the UK 53
4 Working-Class Students, the Politics of Social Mobility Denied 71
5 Global Majority Students: The Politics of Denial 99
6 Student with Disabilities: The Politics of Marginalization 127
7 Students with Mental Health Issues: The Politics of Complicity 157

Conclusion: Setting a Realistic Goal for the Access, Success and Progression of Disadvantaged Students in Higher Education 185

References 193
Index 243

Introduction: Questioning the Access, Success and Progression of Disadvantaged Students in Higher Education

Introduction

I agree with Garritzmann (2017) that higher education has a potential to be both a progressive and a regressive force for social justice, social mobility and knowledge creation, and inevitably does both. The question is whether the balance is right – I think that it is not, and needs to change, and this is why I wrote this book. One of the fundamental questions we need to ask about higher education, and the policies around it, is whose interests do they serve. As Hinton-Smith says, *'the potential of education to empower depends fundamentally on the motivations behind processes of inclusion; informing the importance of interrogating the lived reality of participants, underlying rhetoric of educational opportunities'* (Hinton-Smith et al., 2018, p812).

Therefore, before we enact yet another initiative to widen participation, we need to examine the conflicting motivations and policy drivers behind them and, as importantly, look at the lived experience of those who choose to, and choose not to, go through higher education. The importance of the latter is reiterated by Freire below, who recognizes that education should reflect the worldview, experiences and cultures of all students. Freire would also ask us to recognize that on another level higher education already reflects the worldview, experiences and cultures of *some* students – it reflects the culture of those students who thrive in it – students from elite backgrounds. As he says, 'one cannot expect positive results from an educational or political action program which fails to respect the particular view of the world held by the people. Such a program constitutes cultural invasion, good intentions notwithstanding' (Freire, 1996, p93).

I am a working-class, queer professor with dyslexia, dyspraxia and attention-deficit hyperactivity disorder. I have never felt I belonged the entire time I have worked in academia, which is now over twenty years. However, I recognize this reaction for being the working-class doubt it is. I remember sitting in my doctoral viva, which is a space that has little room for self-doubt and for me is the epitome of privilege. I have known many middle-class people who did not find it an intimidating space, having been encultured to believe in themselves. I heard the two examiners talking and was convinced they were wondering how I had even dared to submit this thesis – it was so bad. Had my supervisor not been with me I would have walked. I thought I had learned how to 'pass' in that I could fake confidence and self-assurance. I realized at that point that it is not as easy as that.

Class bit again when I was trying to become a professor. I remember coming back from another failed professorial interview and talking the experience over with a colleague who was a professor. His advice was very veiled and telling. He made comments like 'I had not developed the authority', 'I did not carry myself like a professor' and 'I did not speak like a professor'. These thoughts resonated, but the class-based assumptions underpinning them were revealed when I pressed for what the phrases really meant, and what I could do – fundamentally I was not one of them, I could not pass. It took a post like professor of social mobility for me to be allowed in, and I know I am a token working-class person. At the same time, I am a white CIS gendered male who has no doubt felt the benefit of privilege in higher education on many occasions. I am acutely aware that there are a tiny percentage of professors who are Black, and even fewer Black women – I have privilege.

Widening participation in higher education has been high on the agenda for governments worldwide for over twenty-five years, with a recognition that higher education fails disadvantaged students, although this is frequently couched as these students failing to meet the standards and demands of higher education. While there have been some surface improvements, on many levels, initiatives have systematically failed, with disadvantaged students still not accessing universities, and when they do, rarely the elite universities. They have higher rates of dropping out, lower grades, progress onto lower-paying jobs, if at all, and rarely undertake further postgraduate study compared to their peers. The initiatives we have undertaken to address these phenomena, as Younger et al. (2019) note below, have not been robustly evaluated, so we do not even know why they have failed on this meta-level.

> This systematic review found no robust evaluations of UK-based interventions. …. There is a pressing need for evidence on widening participation interventions in the UK context, and nuanced interpretation and development is required to ensure that HEIs develop interventions appropriate to their own context.
>
> (Younger et al., 2019, p775)

Yet at conferences and meetings I consistently hear calls for action over research (which always sounds seductive). We are pushed to be 'pragmatic' and look at 'what works', when we have rarely established what we are even talking about. Such calls for pragmatism are ideological in themselves, as we shall explore later.

Context

In the UK, widening participation has been a major focus of both Advance HE (formerly the Higher Education Academy), the British Education Research Association (BERA) and the Society for Research into Higher Education (SRHE) for some years, and is likely to remain so. It is a priority in most countries in the world. Atherton et al. (2016) in 'Charting Equity in Higher Education: Drawing the Global Access Map' showed that in 90 per cent of countries across the world access to higher education is unequal and in the remaining 10 per cent evidence is not available. In Europe the Bologna Process obliges countries to develop widening access strategies: augmented by the Open Method of Coordination (OMC), a soft form of governance, adopted by the EU. The Yerevan Communiqué focuses on four key policy areas for higher education and widening participation: implementation of key commitments; learning and teaching; employability; and social inclusion.

Australia and the United States both have government-funded access initiatives. In Australia, there is the Higher Education Participation and Partnership Programme (HEPPP) which began in 2011. It allocates funding directly to higher education providers to support work to address inequalities across the student lifecycle. There is a focus on regional partnerships delivering a range of outreach and school capacity-building work similar to that in England. There is evidence to show that regional partnerships have had a significant impact on higher education participation for students from lower socio-economic groups. In the United States, the major government-funded widening access programme is not delivered regionally but via the national TRiO programme. (TRiO is a set of federally funded college opportunity programmes that motivate and support students from disadvantaged backgrounds in their pursuit of a college degree.)

My theoretical framework

It seems pertinent to outline the theoretical influences I bring to bear in this book as they both frame my argument and foreground the lens I am bringing to the analysis. This includes what I have selected in and out in terms of the literature.

The influences on this perspective include:

Critical pedagogy

I am a critical pedagogue in that I believe that education is one of the major mechanisms through which elites preserve their power and privilege. In this sense, I come down fairly hard, initially, on the side of seeing higher education as a site of regression and retrenchment, the antithesis of social mobility. However, as mentioned before, it does not have to be this way; it has the potential to be progressive. Freire, the father of critical pedagogy, emphasizes the importance of cultivating hope. Conversely, I have catalogued elsewhere (Seal, 2021a, b) how many authors who advocate critical pedagogues (Cowden and Singh, 2013, Cooper, 2015) have understandably given up on higher education as a site for liberation of those who are traditionally disadvantaged by it. This is not a view I hold, but for higher education to be transformative higher education has some soul searching to do and a number of things need to be in place, which hopefully this book will outline.

As a critical pedagogue, the book argues from the premise that contemporary international HE reproduces existing privileges, and goes on to argue that widening participation agendas should recognize the changing nature of academic life through a more inclusive, holistic approach: one that includes an informed understanding of how students position themselves in academia and how their identity and academic status are enabled and developed with the support of the university. In order to do this, universities need to redefine their purpose and the nature of their relationships with the communities they purport to serve.

It proposes that to close the gap, which has remained despite widening participation having been a policy goal of successive governments for twenty-five years, universities need to interrogate, expose and deconstruct the cultures they re-inscribe of what a university is, who it is for and what it is to strive at university. Furthermore, universities need to redefine their civic purpose and engage communities proactively. Higher education needs to change to meet communities and the economy's needs. This will entail a different kind of partnership, pedagogic approach and conceptualization of what constitutes legitimate knowledge creation.

Critical realism, structure and agency

For me a balance needs to be struck between structure and agency. It is all too easy to give present structural constructions of higher education as inescapable monoliths. Individuals do have agency and come together and make a difference. The 'Black Lives Matter', 'Rhodes Must Fall' and 'Why Is My Curriculum White' movements have come from the ground and are starting to have a discernible impact. At the same time, we do not want to descend into individualism and underestimate the power of structural forces.

I am a critical realist. This means that ontologically there is a world outside of my and others construction of it and forces independent of us. However, our understanding of this world will always be partial, contingent and evolving. Critical realism allows for agency. If structural force's constructions of higher education go too far outside of disadvantaged people's ontologies, they will feel it and react, as these movements named in the previous paragraph exemplify. These transfactual (Martinez et al., 2014) experiences and feelings give people room to operate outside higher education's hegemony, and therefore they have the potential to challenge the social constructions they are subject to.

I agree with Herz and Johansson (2015) in that 'people's everyday life, agency, and the social practices where they act, need to be the starting point of analysis' (p.1019). For this reason, particularly in looking at interventions, I focus on the interface of disadvantaged students and the institution as this is the place where change can start. One of the other advantages of a critical realist approach is that it allows for analysis of the interplay between structure and agency. Authors such as Giddens talk about 'structuration' (Giddens, 1984) whereby agency and structure are inseparable and mutually informing. This is problematic when it comes to analysis, and particularly when looking at interventions. Critical realists such as Archer (2010) conversely see agency and structure as distinct entities, while recognizing that there is an interaction. Separating them allows for their interaction to be analysed and potentially understood, calling this the 'morphogenetic approach'.

Archer (2012) adds a temporal distinction to the 'morphogenetic approach' saying that current social and cultural structures are a result of past social interactions, which condition the current context within which social agents operate. How agents react to their current conditioning will, over time, change these social and cultural structures which will set the conditions for future social actors and so on. Structure and agency being distinct, and operating in different temporal spheres, make it possible to unpick them analytically. Firstly, we need to isolate and analyse how structural and/or cultural factors provide a context of action for agents. It is then possible to investigate how those factors shape the subsequent interactions of agents and how those interactions in turn reproduce or transform the initial context.

Change is needed at a structural and social policy level, but to say this should happen first is politically naive (Archer, 2012). I have therefore not stressed what I think should change at a governmental structural level as I do not think an academic making such pronouncements is particularly useful, or how change will come about. Politicians represent their constituents at best, and more realistically their class interests. Politicians have largely abandoned a supposedly fact-based 'what works' approach, which was not neutral either

(Seal, 2009), to conviction politics. Elsewhere (Seal, 2009, 2018) I trace the shift from evidence-based policy in government, with policy supposedly based on evidence, to principles-based policy, where policy is based on the principles and convictions of those in government. In the UK, we have had forms of conservative government for eleven years, and I will argue that they have represented middle- and upper-class interests entrenching and widening class divisions in higher education.

We will explore later how the tripling of university fees led to the impoverishment of disadvantaged students, while at the same time the loans for them are a source of cheap investment for already-privileged parents. Blatant class discrimination was attempted in summer 2020 with an attempted introduction of an OFQUAL algorithm that meant if you came from a state school from a poor your pre-degree qualifications were graded down, while if you came from a private school you were graded up. In higher education, there has been privatization, with legislation and finance to support the setting up of private universities.

There are also narratives that making higher education more universal was a mistake as it is not what the 'economy needs'. These narratives saw we need to concentrate on STEM and not have 'useless' social science degrees. Tories in parliament have expressed sentiments such as there being too many universities anyway, and that they are bastions of liberalism where too many quasi-Marxists have influence. There have been backlashes to the 'Black Lives Matter' and 'why is my curriculum white' narratives with parliamentary talk about 'War on Woke', statements that there is no structural racism in education, drafting of policy that will give racists a platform in universities under the guise of free speech, and statements that say talk of white privilege is not 'helpful'. Progressive educators need to create a counter-narrative, and seek alliances for it, particularly with disadvantaged students and communities, and eventually progressive political forces and policymakers. What will form, sustain and further these narratives are interactions at the university level and then the building of alliances and communities of practice beyond this.

Intersectionality, primary issues, standpoint epistemologies and responsibility

I also draw on intersectional approaches (Davis, 2008, Crenshaw, 2017, Collins, 2020) and other conceptualizations such as 'simultaneity' (Carastathis, 2016) and Kyriarchy (Fiorenza, 1993). Albeit from different value bases, all of these approaches foreground a recognition that people can simultaneously have privilege and be oppressed, that these processes interact and that multiple oppressions can compound each other. Crenshaw (1991) and Collins (2020) had a particular focus on race and gender, recognizing that women can be subject to multiple oppressions that amplify each another. Intersectionality also recognizes that these processes operate at individual, structural, political and representational level, and are fluid, contested and dependent on context. I do not think it is helpful to talk about what issue(s) have primacy. I agree with Gillborn (2015), who argues for the primacy of race in a situation, but also what has primacy will be contextual and situational, and is dependent on the relative position, and political motivation, of the author. It is entirely legitimate for a researcher to focus on issues of race, or any other issues, particularly as such scholarship needs to be foregrounded. To accuse those focusing on race of forgetting class, or vice versa, sets us up against each other, as long as dialogue is maintained.

I also question the usefulness of holding a standpoint epistemology, be that for race, gender, sexuality or anything else, whereby the oppressed is best placed to understand their own oppression in a way that the non-oppressed could not, concurrently with placing the responsibility for understanding oppression solely on the non-oppressed hegemonic majorities. While both positions are understandable, and may well be right, I do not think they are useful. If a majority group has the responsibility for exploring an issue, but whatever they conclude will be judged as inherently misplaced, this just makes for frustration.

I am also not making a case for white, male, able bodied or heterosexual fragility. I think dominant majority groups should feel uncomfortable for their inevitable complicity in oppression, and the responsibility for learning should remain with them. However, there needs to be space for learning and developing of mutual understanding and alliance making, however shifting, fragile and contextual. I think approaches like Critical Race Theory are to be embraced as they are not divisive. However, I have been subject to people who do not understand the approach properly that have been divisive and they need to be countered. I found Anuj Kapilashrami's (2021) *Intersectionality-informed Framework for Tackling Racism and Embedding Inclusion and*

Diversity in Teaching & Learning particularly useful in that it dovetails with critical pedagogy's desire to unearth and articulate indigenous knowledge, avoid siloing and essentialism and locate change in the everyday practices of higher education, while acknowledging and accounting for wider structural issues.

The need for a whole institutional approach, not just training

Both OFFA (2017) and the Office for Students (OfS, 2021) suggest taking a whole institutional approach to working with disadvantaged students. What is less clear is how this should come about and what is meant by an institutional approach. Is it about doing some liberal tinkering, or is it about enacting deep fundamental change and focus? Advance HE in the UK advocate taking a whole-institutional approach, 'bringing together, strong leadership, an enabling infrastructure, relevant and practical policies and processes, supportive quality assurance and enhancement mechanisms, enhanced staff capacity and motivation, effective reward and recognition, and a collaboration with students as both partners and producers' (Advance HE, 2016, p12). In 2020, they further recommended recognizing that any initiatives or actions are likely to take time to have any significant impact. Positively they say that action needs to focus on institutional barriers and inequalities, rather than 'improving' or 'fixing' the student, and a change of focus from the underachievement or lack of attainment of students to a focus on the institutional culture, curriculum and pedagogy. However, the way these ideas are expressed could mean tinkering or undertaking a wholesale change.

A classic example of a tinkering approach is focusing on training. Almost ubiquitous in the literature, for countering discrimination against disadvantaged students, is a call for training (Advance HE, 2016, Stevenson et al, 2019, OfS, 2020). Training is therefore an essential aspect of a strategic approach. However, I am concerned that training often becomes the strategy, rather than being seen as an element of it. In isolation, training on inclusion is in danger of falling into Kumashiro (2002) category of 'training about the other'.

The book's themes

All UK universities have to produce plans to eliminate the gaps in access, success and participation of disadvantaged students in higher education. They are set targets with regard to Global Majority, working-class and disabled students, as well as students with mental health conditions. This book takes each of the four groups of students for which universities are set targets, Global Majority, disabled, working class and those with mental health conditions, and examines the terminology, theoretical debates and positions, possible causes of gaps, and evaluates proposed initiatives. The book has a number of themes that thread through it.

1. There is still an assumption by higher education institutions that they are progressive forces for social good, justice and mobility, rather than that they re-inscribe elite privileged power bases. The author feels that higher education has the potential to be both, but has historically been the latter.
2. Consequent initiatives and strategies for addressing disadvantaged students have focused on the individual changing over the institution, which has made progress and systemic change negligible.
3. There is a concurrent unexamined assumption that higher education is a 'good thing' materially and intellectually for students. This social construction demonizes those for who this is questionable, and perpetuates a simplistic deficit view of disadvantaged students that they do not understand higher education but and once educated, they will come.
4. There is continuing nuanced structural and individual discrimination in terms of class, race and disability. Higher education institutions have denied their structural classism, racism and ableism and they can be a cause of mental health issues and negative well-being.
5. Initiatives and strategies for addressing disadvantage consequently continue to focus on the individual changing over the institution, which has made progress and systemic change negligible.
6. There is an unexamined 'assimilation' model that expects these students to abandon their culture and communities, despite students wanting to give back to these communities being a major extrinsic motivation, and

embrace a culture that will rarely embrace them. Terms like cultural and social capital are masks for the operation of raw privilege, evidenced by disadvantaged students not being systematically able to gain such capital.
7. Behind this assimilation model is an again unacknowledged archetypical ideal student around which structures and services within higher education are designed. This archetype also informs concepts such as 'engagement' and 'participation' in higher education. The model is of an eighteen-year-old male, white, middle-class, able-bodied student who is living away from home.
8. There is a need for change at a whole institutional level, with champions throughout the institution and mechanisms of accountability.

Intended audience

The primary market for this book is academic development professionals, widening participation teams and lecturers in higher education institutions across the Globe. It will also be highly relevant for support professional, careers and business/community engagement and outreach teams. A secondary market is education studies academics and in particular those designing postgraduate qualifying courses for lecturers. Another secondary market is those professional associations which endorse courses such as social work, youth work and health professions, which often recruit students from the named widening participation backgrounds. While the structure of access, success and progression will speak to the policy framework in the UK, other countries and regions' systems have similar language and structures. The examples drawn on are global, indeed for Global Majority groups the literature from the states is highly pertinent and, in terms of disability, Australia is often leading the way.

How the book fits into and complements the existing literature

There are several books that look at the different groups of disadvantaged students in higher education in specific detail. Bhambra, G. K., Gebrial, D. and Nişancıoğlu, K. (2018). *Decolonizing the University* and Arday, J. and

Mirza, H. S. (2018); *Dismantling Race in Higher Education: Racism, Whiteness and Decolonising the Academy*, both examine the nature of structural racism limiting social mobility and equality within Britain for Global Majority students and academics in its inherently white Higher Education institutions. Bhambra also offers resources for students and academics to challenge and resist colonialism inside and outside the classroom. Both focus on why British racial equality legislation has failed to address racism and explores what the Black student movement is doing about this.

Similarly, in terms of class, Reay, D. (2017). *Miseducation: Inequality, Education and the Working Classes* (1st ed.) Bristol: Policy Press brings Brian Jackson and Dennis Marsden's pioneering Education and the Working Class from 1962 up to date for the twenty-first century. It looks at class identity, the inadequate sticking plaster of social mobility, and the effects of wider economic and social-class relationships on working-class educational experiences. The book addresses the question of why the working classes still fare so much worse than the upper and middle classes in education. It reveals how we have ended up with an educational system that still educates the different social classes in fundamentally different ways.

Riddell, Wilson and Tinklin's (2005) *Disabled Students in Higher Education: Perspectives on Widening Access and Changing Policy* for Routledge and Beauchamp-Pryor's (2013) *Disabled Students in Welsh Higher Education: A Framework for Equality and Inclusion* for Sense do similarly in terms of disability, although Riddell et al. are somewhat old and Beauchamp-Prior is specifically within a Welsh context. Stones and Glazzard's (2019) *Supporting Student Mental Health in Higher Education* for Critical Publishing is closest to this volume in its treatment of mental health issues. All three recommend whole institutional approaches, which this publication builds upon. While not published commercially, Stevenson, J. and Lang, M. (2010). *Social Class and Higher Education: A Synthesis of Research* and Singh, G. (2011). *Black and Minority Ethnic (BME) Students' Participation in Higher Education: Improving Retention and Success* are synthesis of research evidence, both published by the Higher Education Academy, are closest of all to this publication. They both give policy implications, implications for stakeholder groups and practice implications, citing a number of case studies. However, both are again singles issue and are somewhat old now.

This book builds on and cites all of these publications extensively and I will recommend reader go to these publications if they want an in-depth coverage of a particular disadvantaged group. However, the book differs in scope and aims from these publications, and adds to the literature in a number of significant other ways. Firstly, while all these other publications are excellent at looking at social policy in respect of their group, none look across the spectrum of widening participation policy as a whole. Secondly, none look at all the core groups and seek to find the commonalities between them, which will be foregrounded in this book. Finally, none of these books uses the framework of access, success and participation, which directly speaks to higher education institutions and government policy in the UK and have significant reach in the rest of the world.

The structure of the rest of the book

The book has two sections. The first explores theories of social policy towards and key studies on widening participation in higher education. The second explores terminological debates, theoretical perspectives, contrasting views on what the issues are for Global Majority, working-class, disabled students and students with mental health conditions, perceived causes of the issues, suggested interventions and further research needed.

Section one: Key debates and literature, theoretical perspectives and social policy on widening participation

1. Theoretical perspectives on widening participation

This chapter explores theoretical perspectives on widening participation in higher education, starting with the premise that contemporary international HE reproduces existing privileges (Waters and Brooks, 2010) and amplifies inequalities (Stitch, 2012). A historical overview is given of the theoretical perspectives on widening participation from early functional analysis to the present-day dominance of Bourdieu. The rest of the chapter will explore underlying narratives and debates around widening participation in higher education including the poverty of aspirations narrative, the university-is-good-for-you narrative, a certain take on the integration/assimilation narrative, inside, outsides agency narratives, encouraging sense of belonging narratives and narratives on the importance of transition, continuation and engagement. It will also de-construct the language of widening participation, as Taylor and Costas (2019) note, where positioning students as 'non-traditional' can encourage a deficit perspective (Field and Morgan-Klien, 2010) and labelling students as 'disadvantaged' may strengthen stereotypes (Smit, 2012) rather than contest them. This 'othering' of students from non-traditional backgrounds may well be internalized by students. A similar examination is undertaken on how words such as widening participation and social mobility re-inscribe similar deficit models.

2. Social and higher education policy and widening participation

This chapter begins by tracing how the Widening Participation (WP) Agenda in higher education (HE) has been a mantra of successive governments for twenty-five years. Following the Dearing Report (NCIHE, 1997) recommendations that the government should develop strategies to support students from disadvantaged backgrounds to gain access to HE, New Labour pledged that 50 per cent of adults aged eighteen to thirty years would be actively participating in HE by 2010 (Department for Education and Skills, 2002). Fifteen years later, the challenges of increasing access to HE for those from disadvantaged backgrounds are still being felt (Hillman and Corral, 2017, Augar et al., 2019). The chapter will trace policy development aimed at widening participation in the UK, Europe and the United States, unearthing the ideologies that have driven this policy development. It will examine the Bologna Process, the Open Method of Coordination (OMC) and the Yerevan Communiqué in Europe, the HEPP programme in Australia and the Trio programmes in the States. In doing so, this chapter will look at how higher education has been seen as a tool of social mobility in the case of working-class students, integration and social mobility in terms of Global Majority students. The chapter also traces how, in terms of social policy, disabled students and students with mental health issues, by contrast, are curiously absent in government's social goals, extenuating the invisibility of disability in higher education.

3. Access, success and participation of disadvantaged students

This chapter begins by outlining in Britain universities are expected to develop access and participation plans that set out how they will improve equal opportunities for underrepresented groups and close the attainment and participation gap. Universities and colleges set their own targets working towards the OfS national targets, the threat being taking away the right to set higher charges, and ultimately lowering the fees a university can charge. The chapter argues that these initiatives are largely premised on the assumption that change need to happen at an individual rather than structural level, with universities having initiatives to support individuals. The chapter will follow the argument of Hinton et al. (2018) that narratives emphasizing individual responsibility problematize the marginalized for their own exclusion, and obscure and negate responsibility for the development of policies at the International, state and individual HEI levels to develop policies fostering more inclusive learning. This chapter then traces how the APP agenda, with particular definitions of BAME and working class, distorts the agenda of widening participation for these groups in its narrowing of the agenda and encourages HEIs to game their data collection. In terms of disability data collection is also distorting, particularly so in the case of mental health, where its conflation with well-being often renders those with diagnosed mental health issues invisible.

Section two: The politics of working-class, Global Majority and disabled students, including those with mental health conditions

4. Working-class students: The politics of social mobility denied

This chapter will explore the existing data, showing that working-class students are still not proportionately represented at university, and while working-class participation rates have gone up, middle-class rates have gone up even higher, and the later have disproportionately gone to the elite institutions, squeezing out their working-class peers. Secondly, when it comes to continuation and attainment, working-class students leave more often, and attain lower degrees. They are also more likely to get less well-paying jobs; even in the long term, they are also less likely to go into postgraduate study. Even if they achieve a doctorate, they are less likely to go on to enter academia. The chapter then explores how deficit narratives around working-class students persist, despite the evidence. The assimilation/integration model is examined in some depth. Expectations of students, in terms of attitudes, behaviour and ways of being constructed, are classed in ways that the working-class student will anyways fall short. The chapter argues that the interventions that are needed are primarily cultural in nature rather than individual. There is a concurrent need to deconstruct and reconstruct the non-neutrality of higher education and widening participation initiatives. Interventions explored in the chapter include outreach activities, foundation years and the first-year experience, with an emphasis on critical approaches that actively deconstruct and reconstruct working-class experiences of education to date. Recommendations around further research including looking at working class experience of postgraduate education.

5. Global Majority students: The politics of denial

This chapter begins by exploring the theoretical perspectives that seek to explain the relative disadvantage of Global Majority students, in particular anti-oppressive practice, critical race theory and intersectionality, within the context of the themes of the book. It will then consider the importance of taking a whole institutional approach. It will assess the empirical evidence arguing that Global Majority students are subject to structural racism. They undertake certain courses, go to certain institutions, drop out more, achieve less and, even when their qualifications are comparable with white students, go onto less well-paying jobs and rarely further study, particularly doctoral study. The chapter concurrently considers initiatives and approaches to outreach and access, retention attainment and progression, evaluating peer approaches, developing senses of belonging and the importance of a representative staff force. It will also focus on how Global Majority staff are marginalized with higher education and have their labour exploited. The rest of the chapter will consider some of the debates and evolving knowledge base around decolonizing and liberating the curriculum, assessment, epistemology and pedagogy. It argues that we need to go far beyond what gets onto reading lists, and contest the epistemological and pedagogical bases of the cannon, including who gets to create that cannon and unearth hidden, unfairly discredited and denied knowledge bases.

6. Student with disabilities: The politics of marginalization

This chapter explores discourses around disability in higher education. It covers aspects relating, at different times, to physical disabilities such as hearing and sight, cognitive disabilities such as dyslexia, dyspraxia and ADHD, and non-neuro-typical disabilities such as autism. The examples are therefore intended to be illustrative rather than definitive. This chapter will consider barriers such as finance and the politics of disclosure, linked to theoretical debates around stigma, self-determination, self-advocacy and identity. It will then explore theoretical models, noting that they are underdeveloped in higher education, starting with a brief overview of the overall medical, social and critical models of disability, making a case to adopting the latter. It then explores specific models of disability that may be applicable to the higher education context including Weidman's (1989) Conceptual Model of Undergraduate Socialization, Perna's (2006) Conceptual Model of College Choice, Hurtado et al.'s (2012) Multi-contextual Model for Diverse Learning Environments and Hewett et al.'s (2017) Bioecological Model. Concurrently, the chapter will consider issues and interventions focusing on access, success and progression for these different groups. The chapter will also focus, again, on the importance of taking a whole institutional approach, the need for training, nuanced support, changing our approach to teaching, assessment and pedagogic approach, including personal tutoring. It advocates Universal Design for Learning, which recognizes that many of the issues may equally apply to non-disabled students, and we should focus on learning, assessment and curriculum design that works for all.

7. Students with mental health issues: The politics of complicity

The chapter will consider four dimensions to mental health issues in higher education: the experiences of those who come to university with a diagnosed mental health issue, the experiences of those who develop mental health issues while at university, the impact that university has on a person's mental health and the wider issues of student and staff well-being. The chapter argues that higher education providers are often guilty of not facing up to the extent of poor mental health in their institutions, and particularly of not recognizing their own culpability and how they exacerbate it. The chapter will critically explore statistics around the access, success and progression of students with mental health issues and theoretical themes such as the politics of disclosure, transitions to universities, staff, student and employer's view of mental health and their impacts on the university experience of those with mental health conditions. In terms of interventions, we will consider ways of developing social capital for those who have developed or are developing conditions, as well as managing transitions, into, during and out of higher education. The chapter will also consider the key debates within providing mental health services, particularly how we should interact with statutory mental health services. The chapter will also consider the degree to which we should embed issues around mental health within the curriculum, learning, teaching and assessment including psychoeducational approaches. Finally, the chapter will look at issues of progression, in particular the importance of working with employers and of recognizing and ameliorating mental health issues within doctoral study.

Conclusion: Setting a realistic goal for the access, success and progression of disadvantaged students in higher education

As I have stated elsewhere, 'commitment to social mobility in the guise of widening participation is espoused by most universities and governments, though increasingly not in the form of giving it resources' (Seal, 2021, p156). However, social mobility is more than a moral imperative for a modern university; it is what is needed for our economy to thrive. This conclusion argues that in order to do this universities need to redefine what they are there for and the nature of their relationships with the communities they profess to serve. I argue that higher education institutions have a civic responsibility to do so because engagement with the community is also a necessary part of effective research and pedagogy. They concurrently need to change their pedagogic approach and notion of what constitutes legitimate knowledge creation and dissemination. Finally, universities need to interrogate, expose and deconstruct the cultures we re-inscribe of what a university is, who it is for and what it is to strive at university.

1
Theoretical Perspectives on Widening Participation

Introduction

Higher education is not neutral in what is taught there, who goes there, which institutions groups of students attend, who thrives and what is re-inscribed. Freire sees it as a source of indoctrination *'Education .... functions as an instrument which is used to facilitate integration of the younger generation into the logic of the present system and bring about conformity'* (Freire, 2000, p34). Positively he also sees it as having potential to be *'the practice of freedom, the means by which men and women deal critically and creatively with reality and discover how to participate in the transformation of their world'* (Freire, 2000, p34). Other authors, such as Hinton-Smith (2018), see the neo-liberal university as promoting the image on an economically solvent, individually orientated, internationally mobile student that *positions the marginalized student as deficit, in receipt of an education 'gift', and consequently as one who should demonstrate gratitude* (Hinton-Smith et al., 2018).

Theories of widening participation should not be neutral and need to have a perspective on higher education and those students who are disadvantaged within it. They also, crucially, need to articulate what needs to change, in policy and on the ground, and have a sound theoretical base. Taking this further, Boeren and James (2017) feel widening participation theories need to be explicit about the theoretical positions that underpin them, as they are often ideologically, and all too frequently ideologically conservative. This chapter will explore these perspectives and the difference debates and narratives of widening participation in higher education.

A historical perspective

Kettley (2007) examines the historical development of widening participation in higher education in the UK comprehensively. He states that educational research was, after 1945, dominated by structural functionalism and social-class analysis. Functionalism also flourished in the United States until the 1970s. Class analysis or educability studies predominated in the British sociology of education until the 1960s. Functionalist approaches tended to view working-class culture as 'unsuited' to higher education, and blamed working-class communities and families for this (Kelly, 2007). As Kelly says, 'this approach to access is inadequate because it dichotomised material and cultural experiences, depicted working-class culture as pathological and tended to ignore social processes within education' (Kettley, 2007, p339).

Class-based approaches saw education, including higher education, as a way of controlling or placating the working class. Elsewhere I have traced this Marxist account of education, and how progressive forces have responded in turn (Seal, 2021, Seal and Smith, 2021). I outline a series of turns in the process – the first turn being denial of education to the working class, epitomized by the MPs speech against developing elemental education for them in 1807.

> It would teach them to despise their lot in life, instead of making them good servants in agriculture, and other laborious employments to which their rank in society had destined them; instead of teaching then subordination, it would render them factious and refractory,... it would enable them to read seditious pamphlets, vicious books, and publications against Christianity; it would render them insolent to their superiors.
>
> (Giddy, 1807, p798)

The progressive reaction was to fight for at least elementary education for the working class, while concurrently creating alternate modes of education for the working classes such as the Workers Educational Association and the Mechanics Institute. The second turn was ruling elites' acceptance that minimal education for the working class was necessary to improve the economy through skilled labour, but that it should be set to a minimum. Education was to reinforce social distinction and separation, later expressed through private, grammar and secondary modern schools. The progressive response was to demand comprehensive education to degree level for the working classes, although private education and grammar schools for the middle classes were never eliminated.

Ruling elites' reaction to comprehensive education constituted a third turn in their construction of education for the working classes. It was to 'manufacture their inabilities' (Tomlinson, 2017). Education became sedentary in nature, convincing the working classes that education was boring, not for them. It was to be vocational and technical, a transference of set knowledge, rather than seeing students as partners in the creation of it. Education that encouraged true learning was the preserve of private, public and some grammar schools, where students were encultured into the values needed for higher education. Working-class people were encultured into working-class employment, not higher education. Perhaps the most famous account of this is in Willis's Learning to Labour in 1977, subtitled 'How Working-class Kids Get Working-class Jobs'.

Policy-wise, the report of the Robbins Committee (1963) was a sea-changing, if not radical, document. It exposed how members of the professional class were thirty-three times more likely to enter HE than their counterparts from semi-skilled and unskilled backgrounds. This difference was explained in terms of familial, educational and socio-economic processes, although gender and race were notably absent in its analysis. Moore (1996) in the UK and Bowles, Gintis and Meyer (1975) in the States track the growing post-Robbins influence of neo-Marxist, phenomenological, feminist and ethnographic approaches. Phenomenologists were primarily interested in exploring the stratification of knowledge, knowledge production and de-constructing the curriculum, neo-Marxists with the reproduction of existing class relations, feminists with the reproduction of patriarchy and ethnographers with the exploration of student life.

Concurrently critical pedagogy grew in Latin America. Its ideas and approaches were first articulated by Paulo Freire (1972) and since developed by authors such as Henry Giroux, Ira Shor, Michael Apple, Joe L. Kincheloe, Shirley R. Steinberg and Peter Maclaren. It grew out of a concern amongst educationalists with how education was being used as a method to re-inscribe power relations in society, to create a 'common sense' that re-inscribed dominant elites' social positions as 'natural and inevitable' and, rather than to develop enquiring minds, to shut them down and make exclusive knowledge creation. However critical pedagogy has rarely flourished in higher education (Cowden and Singh, 2013, Giroux, 2017, Seal et al., 2021) apart from being taught as a mode of education on some of the more radical education studies and youth and community work courses. It has certainly rarely featured in any higher education institution's approach to widening participations, with the exception of the 'student as producer' movement that came out of Lincoln University (Neary, 2016).

Since 1997 there has been a massification of higher education. However, as we shall see, this expansion has not been even across institutions for disadvantaged groups. The old universities, and particularly the Russell Group institutions, remain the privilege of the elites with a smattering of working-class and disadvantaged students to maintain the illusion of meritocracy. Disadvantaged students go to post-1992 universities, which are the higher education equivalent to comprehensive schools. The educational experience is also different. The Oxbridge and Durham models of one-to-one teaching do not prevail in new universities. Instead, lecturer halls of up to 500 students are the norm where critical engagement is not possible. Education is again transference of elite knowledge, with an emphasis on the technical and vocational.

While some post-1992 universities are committed to widening participation (they will all say they are), many would rather have more 'traditional' students as widening participation students affect their retention rates negatively, and therefore their position in the leagues tables echoing Parkes et al.'s (2014) analysis that success in higher education, particularly retention, has historically been seen as attributable to entry characteristics such as family, class, race, academic aptitude and economic status alongside the level of student involvement in social and academic activities (Goodenow and Grady, 1993, Walker et al., 2004). This ignores more recent studies that show retention is a much more complex social and cultural picture (Quinn, 2004, Walker et al., 2004) and 'though many of the aforementioned student characteristics play a part, student persistence is further influenced by the interaction between individuals, institutions and wider society' (Parkes, 2014, p4).

Kelly and Cook (2007) argue that modern research on widening participation, a field they trace back to the 1980s, has reflected the three distinct and separate strands: a focus on the analysis of rights to education and contestation of policies and constructions of inclusion and exclusion; a focus on social causation, often through measuring participation and quantitative analysis of the barriers to learning; and a focus on social formation through analysing the constructions and meaning of student experiences. Since that article the research base has been extended by a plethora of governmental, managerial and monitoring studies of widening participation as well as more theoretical, ethnographic, feminist and post-modern research and studies of access discourses (Burke, 2002). Kelly (2007) makes a call for research that conjoins exploration of social formation and social causation.

Many contemporary theorists on widening participation use a Bourdieuan analysis, particularly utilizing the concepts of 'field', 'habitus' and 'capital'. The field is the social environment, such as university, in which individuals operate. It has its own culture and rules, often not explicit, which, nevertheless, need to be learnt. Bourdieu also saw it as a battlefield, where vested interests may be right for resources, in this case academic achievement and progression, particularly pertinent in days of perpetual accusations of grade inflation. Field is also not neutral. The field invests in certain beliefs, types of behaviour and rituals with the aim of reinforcing a stable relationship between a dominant form of agency and the structure in which it operates. It perpetuates a dominant culture through the 'orchestration of habitus' (Bourdieu, 2000, p146). As Bennet et al. (2009) expand, this habitus may not be conscious; indeed higher education often makes a point of its neutrality and seems surprised when those othered have difficulties 'adapting'.

> Authorized/institutionalized knowledge(s), are built up through communal banks of know-how and contain self-celebratory discourses of belonging and surreptitious exclusionary discourses of an Otherness that does not share those views/that knowledge/the specific values contained within them – the largely incognizant 'rituals of cultural consensus' – will simply join in and conform.
>
> (Bennet et al., 2009, p251)

Parkes (2014) talks about 'institutional habitus, which is' ' ... the impact of a cultural group or social class on an individual's behaviour as it is mediated through an organisation in turn, determining ... the way in which difference is dealt with, and thus the way students encountering difference for the first time react' (Thomas, 2002, p439). Institutional structures and attributes can either perpetuate or deconstruct (Seal and Parkes, 2019) the dominant cultures in society through pedagogy and process that socialize and reinforce societal status (Thomas, 2002, Quinn, 2004). Organizational attributes of institutions that go on to influence student persistence should be considered when discussing student retention (Berger and Lyon, 2005, Kuh et al., 2005, Tinto, 2006, James et al., 2016).

Bourdieu believed different levels of access to various forms of capital are the root causes of social inequality, something perhaps magnified in higher education. For Bourdieu 'capital' is not just economic, it is cultural and social. He saw a person's knowledge and tastes as a form of cultural capital, which is 'institutionalized in the form of educational qualifications' (Bourdieu, 1986, p245). Social capital is more difficult to define. Bourdieu (2000, p28) described it as 'the aggregate of the actual or potential resources which are linked to possession of a durable network of more or less institutionalized relationships of mutual acquaintance and recognition'. Or, to put it in more common parlance, 'it's not what you know, it's who you know'.

Social capital is an important factor shaping an individual's understanding of the world, what Bourdieu called 'habitus' and which can be defined as a framework of skills, knowledge and expectations that guide behaviour. Habitus is heavily influenced by personal experiences from upbringing and schooling from an early age. Broadly speaking, if no one in a young person's family or social circle has been to university, they are less likely to go themselves or feel they fit when they do go exemplified in the phrase 'it isn't for the likes of me'. Universities' middle-class image culture conflicts with a working-class identity.

On a deeper level, one's habitus has a major influence on the way one performs and situates oneself in the field of higher education. Not knowing the rules that govern the field of action means students cannot situate themselves in the playing field as agents with relative authority. Many authors (Burnell, 2015, Reay, Crozier, and Clayton, 2010) have reported how the habitus of widening participation students is at odds with the activities that direct the field of higher education and which conflict with persisting culture in academia.

Other perspectives have emerged, such as critical race theory, that, similarly to Marxist approaches, see higher education, at least to date, as largely an instrument of control, oppression and social reproduction. Walmington (2020) notes its success in re-igniting the race debate in higher education and that it has helped 'shape many of the current youthful movements to dismantle racism in higher education, such as 'Decolonising the University' and "Why Is my Curriculum White?"' (Walmington, 2020, p25). We will explore this approach in more detail in Chapter 6.

Underlying narratives and debates around widening participation in higher education

Throughout the literature, there seem to be a number of ongoing debates and narratives around widening participation which need examining. The debates are overt and the narratives less so. Underpinning them, and the different versions of them, are the theoretical wider perspectives mentioned above. It seems sensible to talk about the narratives first, as the debates are, at least in part, attempts to resolve and ameliorate some of these underlying narratives.

The poverty of aspirations narrative

Raising the aspirations of under-achieving young people from deprived backgrounds has been a cornerstone of widening participation policy (Sinclair, McKendrick and Scott, 2010).

As Sinclair et al. (2010) indicate, the concept of aspirations is a key driver in widening participation policy. The 'poverty of aspirations' narrative broadly holds that people from deprived communities do not successfully participate in university that they have low aspirations. Interventions should therefore concentrate on raising their aspirations. Behind this is an assumption of the neo-liberal construct of meritocracy, whereby 'aiming higher' and working hard will result in economic rewards (Spohrer, 2015, Zipin et al., 2015). Failure to aspire is attributed as the failing of an individual, rather than a structural condition (Bauman, 1998, Archer, 2007). Shildrick, MacDonald and Furlong (2016) link such thinking to the 'failing families' agenda and notions of an 'underclass' (Murray, 2003). In the next chapter we will explore how this thesis has historically informed much widening participation policy and continues to do so.

It is not that aspirations do not play their part. Gutman and Akerman (2008) and Copestake and Camfield (2010) postulate that there are correlations between low aspirations and low educational achievement, with parental and community influence a key factor (HM Treasury, 2007). However, this is contested. Gutman and Akerman (2008) argue that although constraints have a major impact on aspirations, these do not materialize until the post-school years (between the ages of eighteen and twenty-one). Even if aspirations do play a part, are they truly lower in disadvantaged communities? Cuthbert and Hatch's (2009) longitudinal case study concluded that almost all parents projected positive aspirations for their children regardless of their social position, contradicting the evidence which suggests that low parental aspirations will lead to low aspirations for children. Cummings et al. (2012) found that most people have high aspirations and attach great importance to education and want to go to university or to attain professional jobs irrespective of barriers and constraints they may face.

Even where aspirations do wain in disadvantaged communities, we need to ask why. Robers and Atherton (2011) reported that at the age of twelve, disadvantaged young people have high aspirations. As we shall explore later, with Global Majority students, why aspirations wain at a certain point is a fundamental question. Several authors (Campbell and McKendrick, 2017, St Clair and Benjamin, 2011) argue that even if aspirations are an issue, individualized solutions are not the solution. Both authors argue that aspirations are embedded within social contexts and are therefore influenced by structural constraints as well as social expectations. Other authors (Hutchings and Archer, 2001, Reay, Crozier and Clayton, 2010) see cultural constraints such as lack of confidence and self-efficacy can result in disadvantaged young people forming low aspirations. We will explore this in more depth in the third narrative. What the aspiration thesis does not take account of is that many from disadvantaged communities may not be suffering from low aspirations but are making a cost–benefit analysis of university and concluding that it is not worth it, either economically or more generally in terms of well-being. These phenomena are explored in more detail in the working-class and Global Majority chapters.

Higher education as inherently 'good for you' narrative

> HE study and the accumulation of intellectual and social capitals is constructed as an inherent good, linked to individual benefits including higher earnings, increased employability, better health and greater life satisfaction (Naidoo and Callender 2000, BIS, 2013a, Brown, 2013, Purcell et al., 2013). However, existing research into equity and access demonstrates that HE's 'premium' is neither available equally to all, nor experienced uniformly. Indeed, despite expansion and 'democratisation' narratives, the opportunities of contemporary international HE are seen to reproduce existing privileges (Waters and Brooks, 2010) and amplify inequalities.
>
> (Hinton-Smith et al., 2018, p23)

Shah, Bennett and Southgate (2015, p227) would concur with Hinton-Smith (2018) saying 'the narrative of a "good," educated citizen is that of participation and success in higher education'. Several authors (Brennan and Naidoo, 2008, Callender, 2011, Brown, 2013, Purcell et al., 2013, Hinton-Smith et al., 2018) note how HE study is constructed as an inherent good, linked to individual benefits including higher earnings, increased employability, better health and greater life satisfaction, as well as the accumulation of social, cultural and intellectual capital. Southgate and Bennet (2014), critiquing the narrative of choice in higher education, say that the policy narrative in both the UK and the United States is that to be a good citizen is to be an educated one, and this means going to university, with the implication that bad citizens have 'chosen' not to educate themselves.

Hinton-Smith et al. (2018) similarly note that access to internationalized HE is similarly promoted as being of perceived benefit to all – in relation to cultural enrichment, developing mutual understanding, personal development and well-being, academic quality enhancement, technological innovation and economic growth (Altbach, 2013). However, existing research into equity and access demonstrates that HE's 'premium' is neither available equally to all nor experienced uniformly. Rather it reproduces existing privileges (Waters and Brooks, 2010) and amplifies inequalities (Stitch, 2012). We will come back to the myth of higher education as a tool or mechanism for social mobility in the next chapter. Of course, there are many other ways of measuring and evaluating weather higher education is good for you, but as we can see in the next chapter, this is questionable as well.

A certain take on the student integration narrative

> The goal of such orchestration is that of aligning habitus with field. The more aligned the two are, the more indistinct they will become, and the more likely individuals who internalise the rules of the field as their habitus are to succeed. It is therefore not surprising that students from widening participation backgrounds are more likely to feel outcasts on the inside (Redmond, 2006) than they are to feel included, because they are more likely to experience the existence of a 'cleft habitus'.
>
> (Bourdieu, 1990a)

Tinto's (1975, 2006) theory of student integration has been the mainstay of student retention for forty years (Thomas, 2012), believing that student needs to be integrated pedagogically, socially and institutionally, and that there is responsibility on both sides to make this happen. What the model does not ask is what culture people are being integrated into, and what cultures they are being expected to move away from. For disadvantaged groups this model seems to have taken an insidious turn, particularly for BAME and working-class students.

These students are expected to abandon their culture and communities, which are demonized as not being supportive and a negative influence. The tension of doing this is compounded by the fact that a major extrinsic motivation for them being to give back to these communities (Guiffrida et al., 2018a). Disadvantaged students also experience an additional pressure from a concurrent contradictory narrative as higher education is predicated on an assumption that parents and communities will support students through university, financially, emotionally and culturally, meaning they need to 'Stand Alone'. They are then expected to embrace a culture that is rarely articulated, but certainly felt, in that it will rarely embrace them (Costas et al., 2020, Scharp and Dorrance-Hall, 2017).

Probably most insidiously, even when widening participation students try and assimilate and integrate, they will not be accepted. Some of the reasons behind this are unchallenged assumptions about them. McKay and Devlin (2018) talk about a persistent myth in higher education that letting in certain groups of students, particularly working-class student, will lower standards. However, on a deeper level we need to examine the model of student that they are being asked to assimilate into. Ives and Castillo-Montoya's (2020) recent systematic review illuminates the process of constructions of an ideal student archetype that working-class students are expected to assimilate into. It is a middle-class, white, male, heteronormative construction that assumes the supposed cultural values of someone eighteen, straight from school and living away from home (Tomlinson, 2018).

This has important implications. Most indicators around social mobility say that it is very difficult to achieve class assimilation – people are generally stuck in the same social class of their parents (Major and Machin, 2018). Higher education re-enforces and re-inscribes this rather than alleviates it. Throughout this book we will see that all too often higher education is a force for social stratification, rather than social mobility. When higher education was the preserve of the elite, it could afford to 'let in' some from lower socio-economic backgrounds as it preserved the illusion of a meritocracy. However, when there was a desire for mass higher education, the class barriers snapped back-up.

Insider/outsider structural/agency debates

Bernstein (1975, 1996) also makes a useful distinction between whether solutions or changes need to happen primarily at the institutional level, or at the level of the individual or community. This is certainly a debate underpinning the poverty of aspiration narrative. Hinton-Smith et al. (2018) are quite clear that most institutions put the need to change within the individual and the communities they come from.

> Too often, how to promote inclusion is decided by those in relatively powerful positions with insufficient consultation of the marginalised, in doing so leaving relations of unequal privilege unchallenged, and empowering potential short-changed. There is a vital need to engage with, hear and respond to voices of educationally marginalised groups ... to continue to identify both persistent and newly emerging inequalities, and responses to these at individual and collective levels.
>
> (Hinton-Smith et al., 2018, p32)

They issue a further challenge.

> We need to continue to work to both imagine and create more democratic and empowering spaces in education by engaging in direct dialogue between the marginalised and majority, by increasing the influence of marginalised groups within powerful institutions while continuing to problematise the inadequacies of these institutions, and by recognising the complexity of the relationship between individual agency and institutional responsibility as a means for tackling persistent inequality.
>
> (Hinton-Smith et al., 2018, p34)

Such positionings work at a linguistic level, including the language of widening participation itself. As Taylor and Costa (2019) and Taylor and Goodfellow (2020) note, positioning students as 'non-traditional' can encourage a deficit perspective (Field and Morgan-Klien, 2010) and labelling students as 'disadvantaged' may strengthen stereotypes (Hinton-Smith, 2012) rather than contest them. Even at widening participation institutions, where the norm is actually non-traditional students, the measures, systems and structures students are subject to are predicated on norms of an archetype of an eighteen-year-old full-time student, living away from home.

Whether this is determined by wider higher education or societal structures, or universities not challenging their own constructions is a moot point. At my last institution 'commuter students' (those whose home address is the same as their term time address, with large demographics of being older working class – widening participation students) made up of 90 per cent of students yet were still talked about as exceptions to the norm. They were to be catered for, rather than an acknowledgement they were the norm and that structures should be built around their lived realities rather than an imaged archetype of an ideal student. I have worked at two new universities which only became universities in the last decade. They had the opportunity to develop different structures, approaches and mechanisms without the weight of history. Yet, sadly, they largely aped imagined processes of established universities. While there are undoubtedly quality-assurance process that dictated elements of this, a distinct lack of imagination was also at play, though an institutional desire to be seen as 'proper'.

This 'othering' of students from non-traditional backgrounds may well encourage a sense of difference among students themselves (Blake and Illingsworth, 2015). Members of the foundation Year network have talked about a common conception amongst their students of their 'difference' and how other students construct them in a negative way, which is mirrored in lecturer's perceptions that they are the less able students, and should be grateful for their second chance at education. We will encounter multiple examples of such othering throughout the other chapters.

Hinton et al. (2018) argue that the narratives and realities of aspiration and individual responsibility underpinning academic success and failure in HE 'arguably problematise the marginalised for their own exclusion'. Bennet et al. concur:

> The freedom to choose (the luxury of choice) is socially stratified, unequally distributed and hidden from view within dominant discourses that carry the individual consumerist myth of the freedom to choose one's lifestyle and future.
>
> (Bennet et al., 2009, p249)

Reay, Crozier and Clayton (2010) note that without targeted parental investment of economic and cultural capitals, underprivileged students have to struggle to get to university, requiring a strong self-reliance. Hinton-Smith et al. (2018) think this resonates with criticisms of much of the wider discourse of widening participation in HE over recent decades (Hinton-Smith, 2012). For example, O'Shea (2016) argues that an effect of approaches to university transition for marginalized students has been to negatively position such students as deficit or replete as a result of their background. Such emphasis on individual deficit obscures the persistence of structural inequality and negates responsibility for the development of policies at the European, state and individual HEI levels. Actively promoting institutional responsibility acknowledges and addresses the pervasive messages that 'you are not from here' (Ahmed, 2012, p179) that can all too often be experienced by marginalized 'non-traditional' students.

Ahmed (2012) reads these experiences of educational participation/ exclusion as producing insiders/outsiders in the academy. For example, educational participation/exclusion can be experienced at the level of affect, whereby the processes by which 'the inhabiting of different spaces by bodies engenders feelings either of being at home, or becoming a stranger … of becoming noticeable, of not passing through or passing by, of being stopped, or held up' (Ahmed, 2012, p3). Such internalization of responsibility for not feeling 'at home' in HE resonates with Morrice's work on refugee UK university students who, like Roma, are frequently international yet marginalized students. Here, feelings of shame, embarrassment and inferiority are identified as products of symbolic domination active in experiences of HE transition (Morrice, 2013).

Encouraging senses of belonging narratives

Parkes (2014) notes that one of the key factors in student retention is the successful generation of a sense of belonging within students (Osterman, 2000, Krause, 2005, Thomas, 2012). Building on Goodenow (1993) she defines this as 'a students' sense of being accepted, valued, included, and encouraged by others in the academic setting and involves supporting and respecting the personal autonomy of the student as an individual' (Goodenow, 1993, p25, Parkes, 2014). This sense of belonging is fostered during interactions within the social, academic and professional services spheres of a student's experience. The success of such activity is underpinned by ensuring that student and staff capacity is built and supported across the student lifecycle from pre-entry to employment.

Thomas (2012) developed a 'Student Engagement to Improve Student Retention and Success' model that encompasses a set of key characteristics, underpinning principles and features of a wider institutional culture that intends to foster student belonging (Thomas, 2012). This sense of student belonging is achieved through: ' ... supportive peer relations; meaningful interaction between staff and students; developing knowledge, confidence and identity as successful HE learners and providing a HE experience relevant to students' interests and future goals' (Thomas, 2012, p55). The model reflects findings from a UK national longitudinal study that suggest activities across all institutional domains: the academic, social and professional service spheres (Thomas, 2012) foster student engagement that promotes student retention and success.

Narratives on the importance of transition, continuation and engagement

Several authors (Thomas, 2012, Parkes et al., 2019, Seal and Parkes, 2019) emphasize transition rather than engagement, continuation or belonging for a number of reasons. Firstly, to do so questions looking for a discrete moment of change that enables a student to continue or engage. Transition instead implies a state of perpetual movement that occurs amidst 'irreducible difference' (Osberg, 2015, p25) and secondly it potentially recognizes that the university should also be in transition as a learning institution. Gale and Parker's (2014) approach of transition-as-becoming (TAB) emphasizes the complexities of life and the interdependence of the institution and its stakeholders to be in a perpetual state of transition (Gale and Parker, 2014, p744). This is distinct from other approaches such as Transition-As-Induction (TAI) and Transition-As-Development (TAD). TAI is linear, where students go through a number of 'phases' or pathways of inculcation such as the HEFCE Student Lifecycle model (see Morgan, 2011). TAD represents 'qualitatively distinct stages of maturation involving trajectories of transformation, from one student/community and/or career identity to another from one life stage to another' (Gale and Parker, 2014, p738).

TAB with its 'creative chaos' (Braidotti, 2016, p172) of flows, energies, movements and capacities (Grosz, 2020) constructs possible futures (Braidotti, 2016). For example, non-completion of university study can be seen as part of a complex cultural and social picture, rather than an individual failure (Quinn, 2004). TAB is relational (Barad, 2007) which necessitates a 'process of perpetual inward institutional reflection on our pedagogies and institutional processes' (Parkes et al., 2014, p8). Rather than simply generating institutional spaces for different kinds of students, TAB 'values the diverse knowledge and ways of knowing' (Gale and Parker, 2014, p741) of students and co-creates a space and transitions that are also mutual, with the university equally in transition with the students (Seal and Parkes, 2020).

Conclusion

> Widening participation agendas should be looking to recognise the changing nature of academic life through a more inclusive, holistic approach: one that includes an informed understanding of how students position themselves in academia and how their identity and academic status is enabled and developed with the support of the university.
>
> (Taylor and Costa, Taylor and Goodfellow, 2020, p12)

Even Marxist, Critical pedagogues and Critical Race theorists, those most critical of the motivations of universities widening participation agendas, do not write off Higher education as a cite of resistance or change, although there may be a sense of pessimism about the chances of this happening. I have written elsewhere about the hopeful possibilities for higher education (Seal, 2020) in that unlike in schools higher education staff award our own degrees, devise admissions criterion, develop the curriculum, devise the teaching, learning and assessment strategy, quality-assure and assess the courses. We also have the ability and permission to write, proclaim and research with relative academic freedom. This is done relatively close to the ground, at lecturing team and programme manager level. We do not do this in a vacuum and the next chapter will explore the limitations and constraints on all of this. Nevertheless it is a luxury, indeed privilege, other education sectors do not have.

To undertake widening participation effectively we need to examine the philosophical and theoretical underpinning of any strategy and initiatives we initiate – it is not enough to go with 'what works', for such reductive agendas are ideological in themselves and have been show not to 'work', as we shall explore in the next chapter. We also look at ourselves and who we are, checking our privileges. We should also explore the life world experiences of our students, not only regarding entry into academia, but also, and especially, in relation to students' trajectories through and out of the higher education system (see Burke, 2015). This raises related questions on the role of education in supporting the acquisition and development of capitals as part of students' experiences (Costa and Gilliland, 2017), as well as the role of educational policies in the development of inclusive practices.

2

Social and Higher Education Policy and Widening Participation

Introduction

As Shah et al. (2015) note, governments have seen widening participation in higher education as a priority for a long time. They have also had a variety of espoused motivations for this, from recognizing the changing economy and the consequent need for a more highly trained and specialised workforce, to using it as a driver of a social mobility agenda, particularly in the New Labour/Cameron period in the UK. In the United States the economy has similarly been a primary driver of the structure of higher education, as the Department of Treasury said in 2012, *'Higher Education is a critical mechanism for individual socioeconomic advancement and an important driver of economic mobility. Moreover, a well-educated workforce is vital to our nation's economic growth'* (US Department of the Treasury, 2012, p5). In Europe it is driven by both economic and social drivers, particularly for European integration (Weedon and Riddell, 2016).

Neo-liberalism has permeated higher education thoroughly over the last forty years (Seal and Smith, 2021) and as a driver for widening participation has not delivered the goods. Commenting on the New Labour/Cameron Social Market model's impact on higher education, Bennet et al. comment: *'Massification and marketization have delivered the most benefits for the most advantaged in society, and it is the challenge of equity practitioners, researchers and policy makers to challenge 'taken for granted' assumptions and aspects* (Bennet et al., 2015, p248). This dominant ideology has in turn had other consequences and impacts, including what research on widening participation in higher education is conducted and why. As Ketley expands,

> The agenda of current widening participation research is, primarily, a product of the macro-economic and social policy objectives of the New Right and New Labour. Successive governments have tried to manage human capital and achieve economic growth by expanding HE.. it has produced a reactive widening participation research agenda focused on narrow issues, discrete aspects of learning and a lack of awareness of prior studies.
>
> (Kettley, 2007, p334)

The Dearing Report (NCIHE, 1997) recommended that government should develop strategies to support students from disadvantaged backgrounds to gain access to HE. Over twenty years later, the challenges of increasing access to HE for those from disadvantaged backgrounds are still being felt (Hillman, 2017, Augar et al., 2019). Those targeted continue to be cast as having low aspirations, albeit with little supporting evidence (Whitty et al., 2015). Specifically, this chapter will look at how higher education has been seen as a tool of social mobility in the case of working-class students, integration and social mobility in terms of Global Majority students. It will also trace how, in terms of social policy, disabled students and students with mental health issues, by contrast, are curiously absent in using education as a policy driver for social goals, extenuating the invisibility of disability in higher education.

Historical developments in the UK

As Kettley indicates, we need to start by looking historically at higher education structures and orientation. He traces how for the first 700 years of higher education it was exclusively done in elite institutions for the elite, those from private schools, and until the industrial revolution, the gentry. The expansion of universities in the last half of the nineteenth century mirrored the expansion of the middle classes, and the demand for education was for their children to be able to attend university. It was only in the twentieth century that the demand arose for highly able students from disadvantaged backgrounds to enter university (Cole, 1955, p115). Kettley also explores how demands from progressives focused on access to higher education until the Second World War. It was some time after the subsequent expansion of higher education for all those people started to examine the student experience.

As talked about in the previous chapter, the sea change for higher education, and its shift from being elite to being 'mass', or certainly larger, was the Robbins report in 1963, concurring soon afterwards with the expansion of plate glass universities and conversion of technological colleges into universities. Anthony Crosland in his Woolwich speech two years later introduced the binary system of universities doing traditional education (largely for the elites) and polytechnics for advanced vocational higher education (largely from those state schools). This divide has been traditionally seen as a betrayal of Robbins, although Scott et al. (2013) say this has been exaggerated and such an initiative, while not named, was in keeping with Robbins thinking. Such policy changes did not happen in the UK alone (Scott, 2014). There were parallel developments such as the Californian mater plan (which popularized the similarly binary system of state universities and community colleges) and similar developments in France (Patterson, 1976), and in Australia, as a consequence of the Murray report (Scott, 2014).

Changes in the UK in the 1970s and 1980s were largely about cuts in funding and working conditions, such as the 1988 Education Reform Act. This abolished tenure in the universities and replaced the University Grants Committee with a funding council, leading to a concurrent expansion of university numbers and institutions. In 1992, the Conservative government's Education Act paved the way for polytechnics and colleges of higher education to become universities, supposedly putting all institutions on an equal footing. Tellingly, the rapid expansion of university places was concentrated in the post-1992 universities, and there is plenty of debate about how the divide still exists between universities, with more groupings, Oxford and Cambridge, the rest of Russell Group, non-Russell but pre-1992 institutions and post-1992 institutions (which also has several divisions).

However, what is starkly noticeable in terms of widening participation is that those from working class and Global Majority backgrounds have largely gone to post-1992 institutions, with a minimal rise in them going to non-Russell pre-1992 institutions and negligible change in them accessing Russell Group universities (Raffe and Croxford, 2015). Tellingly when reporting figures 'Old Institutions' when talking about state schools mean Grammar schools and 'good' comprehensive schools (Bennet et al., 2015). The middle class have certainly accessed the old institutions in greater numbers and are one of the prime beneficiaries on most widening participation initiatives (Bennet et al., 2015, Hinton-Smith et al., 2018).

The modern era of interest in access to higher education in England arguably begins with the publication of the Dearing Review in 1997 (National Committee of Inquiry into Higher Education [NCIHE], 1997) and *From Elitism to Inclusion: Good Practice in Widening Access to Higher Education* (Woodrow et al., 1998). These reports put the many inequalities in participation into a sharper statistical focus than had previously been possible. This coincided with the election of a Labour government who responded in contradictory ways. They pledged that 50 per cent of adults aged eighteen to thirty years would be actively participating in HE by 2010 (Department for Education and Skills, 2002), something it was close to having achieved. It also pledged to close the 'social class gap' in admissions, especially to elite universities where it was most marked, something it systematically failed to do.

At the same time, Teaching and Higher Education Act (1998) and the Higher Education Act (2004) cemented student loans, brought in student contribution to tuition fees and, subsequently, variable top-up fees, all of which impacted on widening participation students the hardest (Callender and Jackson, 2008). The main manifestation of the new policy direction was the Aim Higher programme, which ran from 2004 to 2011 with an overall expenditure in the region of £650 million (Moore and Dunworth, 2011, Doyle and Griffin, 2012, Harrison, 2012). This initiative was firmly wedded to the Poverty of Aspiration narrative.

Aim Higher included universal elements, such as summer schools and mentoring of school/college students by higher education students, called Aim Higher Associates, often from disadvantaged backgrounds themselves. Other activity was developed at the local level, though common approaches included higher education students and staff visiting schools and colleges to deliver a range of activities: non-residential visits by school/college students; subject enrichment programmes; master classes or revision courses; and IAG publications and events. Thomas (2012) found that there was very little research, just two small-scale studies (Blicharski, 1999, Walker et al., 2004b), that explicitly examines the impact of pre-entry interventions on student retention and success in higher education.

In the last twelve years the UK higher education landscape has experienced significant changes (Hordósy and Clark, 2018, Harrison, 2020). In 2008, the UK government acknowledged that aspirations among young people from different socio-economic backgrounds were, in fact, similar. '[D]isadvantaged young people do not have fundamentally different aspirations from their more adapted peers' (Social Exclusion Task Force 2008, 10). However, the following year in a report to the Cabinet Office, the focus of the same Taskforce reverts back to raising aspirations: '[U]ltimately, it is the aspirations people have to better themselves that drives social progress' (Millburn, 2012, p6).

The framing of aspirations remains a key driver of political agenda and policy, despite a growing body of literature demonstrating high aspirations among disadvantaged young people (Cuthbert and Hatch, 2009). The National Collaborative Outreach Programme has established partnerships between universities and colleges to create higher education outreach programmes for widening participation, building on the previous National Networks for Collaborative Outreach and Aim Higher initiatives, although again the emphasis is on raising aspirations. Increases in sixth-form college attendance and Business and Technology Education Council Level 3 qualifications (Smith, Joslin, and Jameson, 2015) have had effects on participation and attainment in higher education. At the same time, tuition fees in England have dramatically risen, strongly impacting the experiences of lower-income students in particular (Hordósy and Clark, 2018).

In October 2011, the Government set up a review of higher education funding and student finance – the Browne Review. The Review Report said: *'There has been less progress in widening access to the most selective institutions for students from lower income backgrounds despite efforts by these institutions to improve the situation'* (Browne Review, 2011, p2). It called for removing the cap on higher education tuition fees and, conversely, extra support for students from families with an income below £60,000. It was followed by the 2011 White paper, *Higher Education: Students at the Heart of the System*. Chapter 5 of the paper 'Improved social mobility through fairer access' outlined a new framework for widening participation and fair access.

The paper announced the introduction of the National Scholarship Programme (NSP) to help individual students from low-income backgrounds as they entered higher education. The programme closed in 2015. The White paper also strengthened the role of the Office for Fair Access (OFFA). In 2014, the Higher Education Funding Council for England (HEFCE) and OFFA published a shared strategy on higher education access and student success called the national strategy for access and student success in higher education. It was the first time that an emphasis was placed on the whole student lifecycle, including how disadvantaged students did at university and where they progressed onto. Previous to this the emphasis was very much on gaining access for disadvantaged students.

The 2017 White paper *Success as a Knowledge Economy Teaching Excellence, Student Mobility and Student Choice* set targets to double the number of disadvantaged students accessing higher education and increase access by 20 per cent by 2020 (this was not achieved). It also obliged universities to keep demographic data on its students, link the new Teaching Excellence Framework (TEF) to widening participation students and keep data on progression through their attainment of 'graduate employment'. Later in 2017 the government also published the action plan 'Unlocking Talent, Fulfilling Potential', making a link between future funding and the access and participation plans universities would need to produce, placing an emphasis on data gathering, and that initiative was research and evidence based and 'properly' evaluated. The Office for Student was established by the Higher Education and Research Act 2017, came into existence on 1 January 2018, merging the Higher Education Funding Council for England and the Office for Fair Access. The OfS inherited HEFCE's funding responsibilities (aside from those for research which passed to United Kingdom Research and Innovation) and OFFA's responsibility for promoting fair access to higher education.

Reflecting in January 2020 on twenty years of editing the journal *Widening Participation and Lifelong Learning*, Dr John Butcher, Associate Director at The Open University, felt there are still gaps in the extent to which students from the most disadvantaged backgrounds persist and succeed in their higher education studies; there are still potential students excluded from learning in universities because of inflexible institutional systems; there are still university teachers who resist the implications of teaching a more diverse student body; and there are still students who are forced to bend themselves to fit archaic university systems because institutions are unwilling or unable to become more inclusive.

Social policy on widening participation in the United States

> Despite structural, socio-cultural and economic differences between the case study nations (Australia, Ireland, the Netherlands, Norway, South Africa, and the US and England), there are clear similarities in the way in which the education systems are organized and the factors which have been identified as inhibiting or facilitating educational attainment and progression to HE. Many of the systemic factors linked to participation in HE are, therefore, also shared.
>
> (Bennett et al., 2013m, para. 1.4)

As Bennett et al. (2013) note above, the issues around widening participation and higher education, and the underpinning philosophies of social policy outside of the UK are often similar, but like most things the differences are nuanced and thus worth exploring. Challan (2013) notes that post-war the major vehicles that policymakers in the United States have used to expand college access have underpinned their strategies with three approaches: (1) increasing the number of college enrolment places available; (2) provision of financial aid; and (3) provision of pre-college academic and motivational preparation support services and continued support services during college. These drivers are most recently expressed in the *No Child Left Behind* (NCLB) strategy that 'provided much stronger focus on academic achievement goals and on accountability provisions' (p30). The law requires states, local districts, higher education institutions and schools to set academic achievement goals and submit plans with an aim to have 100 per cent of students reach 'proficiency' by 2014. Similarly in the UK disadvantaged students are broken down by ethnic groupings and targets are set for each.

Finance for WP students is regulated by the Higher Education Opportunity Act (HEOA) of 1965 which has been re-authorized by Congress six times, most recently in 2008 and is going through senate as I write. There are three types of Federal student aid: (a) grants, (b) loans and (c) work study. Federal Pell Grants (received by about 45 per cent of students) are provided based on financial need and are awards up to $5,500 per year. Federal loans are received by about 60 per cent of all enrolled. The act also provides support for students prior to college (from middle school onwards), during college and latterly, afterwards. Collectively these are known as the 'TRIO' as there were originally three programmes – now there are eight.

Kemp et al. (2013, p31) note that 'the characteristics of the various Federal programs reflect the times in which they were initiated by Congress in their major features'. The middle and high school programmes are Talent Search (TS), Upward Bound (UB), Upward Bound Math Science (UBMS) and GEAR UP. The programmes to encourage success once in college are: Student Support Services (SSS), Child Care Access Means Parents in School (CCAMPIS) and the McNair programme to increase graduate school entrance and completion. In addition, high schools and Minority serving institutions (MSIs) serving those populations can get state aid. The United States has a tradition of having specific school and institutions that serve ethnic communities. In 2013, Hispanic-serving institutions and Black-serving (non-HBCUs) accounted for 27 per cent and 16 per cent respectively of MSIs followed by Asian serving (8 per cent), HBCUs (5 per cent), and American Indian-serving institutions (1 per cent).

Kemp et al. (2013) go on to critique these approaches, particularly for not challenging the cultures at elite institutions and having no notion of contextual admissions. They see them as again being about upskilling disadvantaged students to achieve the necessary grades, rather than challenging the way that grades are constructed and measured. Kamatuka (2016), using the concept of 'College Fit' (p33), explains why access does not guarantee success and can be another form of segregation. He also describes those without cultural capital are 'unsophisticated consumers', who are then targeted by private providers who offer condensed programmes and promise employment outcomes.

Europe

The European agenda for modernizing higher education is economically driven and concerns jobs and growth with a secondary emphasis on social cohesion, social equity and active citizenship (European Commission, 2011). Weedon and Riddell (2016) note that there is a permanent tension between the primary and secondary objectives, with neo-liberal economic approaches often being incompatible with goals of social mobility, equity and cohesion. Economic priorities normally prevail (Weedon and Ridell, 2016). The Bologna process in the 1980s aimed to harmonize higher education structures and allow for free movement of student with the European Community. Riddell et al. (2014, p15) feel that there was an agenda also to create a global higher education system 'based on European ideals and economic interests'. The Open Method of Communication (OMC) is a 'soft governance' mechanism intended to harmonize social policy across Europe (Riddell and Weedon, 2014). In relation to higher education, it is envisaged as the means of achieving the social inclusion goals of the Bologna Process. At an earlier stage, the Council of Europe included a definition in its recommendation on Access to Higher Education stating that countries should adopt

> [a] policy that aims both at the widening of participation in higher education to all sections of society, and at ensuring that this participation is effective (that is, in conditions which ensure that personal effort will lead to successful completion).
>
> (Council of Europe, 1998)

However, a recent report from Eurydice (Crosier et al., 2015), pessimistically reporting on access, retention and employability, notes that in most European countries there are few or no targets, and limited data gathering in relation to student characteristics beyond gender and age. Eurostat confirms that whilst all countries have made progress on increasing participation, this has varied greatly and 'it will be some time before policy and practice are harmonized across European countries'. As Riddel and Weedon (2014) expand in relation to widening participation in higher education,

> the OMC has been only moderately effective in promoting widening access for under-represented groups, since in the field of higher education there is lack of accord between the policy priorities of the EU and individual member states. Financial retrenchment across Europe is likely to have a negative impact on opportunities for under-represented groups in higher education.
>
> (Riddell and Weedon, 2014, p26)

Riddel and Weedon (2014) go on to note in 2016 that there has been no shared definition of disadvantaged or non-traditional students, and countries have identified very different groups (or failed to identify any at all), as they conclude, somewhat pessimistically:

> In the wake of the economic crash of 2007, slow progress on widening access may be linked to reductions in educational spending which have a disproportionately adverse effect on students from poorer backgrounds. In addition, middle class anxiety over uncertain future economic prospects in countries such as Sweden may have contributed to the de-prioritization of the widening access agenda.
>
> (Weedon and Riddel, 2016, p14)

Higher education, social policy, Global Majority, low socio-economic status and students with mental health issues and disabilities

Social mobility

If we look across history and different countries and contexts, higher education has been seen as a tool of, or mechanism for, social mobility for the working classes, and integration and social mobility in terms of Global Majority students. Adnett (2016) successfully questions this narrative below. Generally social mobility may happen within a social class, working-class students with degrees do better than those without, and higher education does not achieve mobility across social classes.

> Underrepresented groups are on average likely to receive higher lifetime earnings if they graduate. However, these returns are uncertain and are likely to be, on average, significantly lower than those received by over-represented student groups ... In particular, the economic and social benefits received by nontraditional HE entrants seem to be smaller and are crucially dependent on the particular higher education institution attended.
>
> (Adnett, 2016, pp219 & 221)

This is in a context where, as the aforementioned literature shows, the expansion of participation students has been predominantly within the new universities. Gaskell and Linwood (2019) talk about a tautology whereby students have less 'recognized' degrees from less prestige universities, with lower grades, even if these are for the structural reasons discussed. They are individually judged as having not shown communication, networking and resilience, the skills many employers talk about looking for.

Depressingly, plenty of studies have shown that students from low socio-economic backgrounds are less likely to get top jobs than those from affluent backgrounds, even with the same degree, university and grade (Social Market Foundation, 2018, Thomas, 2015). Even more starkly, recent research by Friedman and Laurison (2020) found that if you're a working-class graduate with a first-class degree, you are less likely to land an elite job than a middle-class graduate with a 2:2. Even when individuals from working-class backgrounds are successful in entering the country's elite occupations, they go on to earn, on average, 16 per cent less than colleagues from more privileged backgrounds, or in the case of Black British working-class women £20,000 less per year.

Similarly in the United States, those with class privilege and who are white continue to be advantaged in terms of academic achievement and attainment (Coleman, 1966, Gamoran, 2001), university entrance and graduation (Melguizo, 2008, Bowen, Chingos, and McPherson, 2009, Bailey and Dynarski, 2011, Bastedo and Jaquette, 2011), short- and long-term employment prospects and income (Jencks et al., 1972, Grodsky and Pager, 2001, Huffman and Cohen, 2004). In the case of class inequalities, the academic achievement gap and income between children of low- and high-income families have widened substantially over the past fifty years (Reardon, 2011).

In a way seeing higher education as a tool for social mobility, as well as ignoring structural issues and class stratification outside of the academy (Reay, 2021), ignores the function of higher education in maintaining social stratification (Giroux, 2017). University education has long been a gatekeeper to well-paying professional jobs meant for the upper middle classes (Seal, 2021). Having a degree as a marker maintained the illusion of social mobility ignoring the fact that only a small percentage of working-class people went to university, but just enough to sustain an illusion of meritocracy. Did those masterminding the expansion of higher education under New Labour its equivalents in the States and Europe seriously believe that expanding the number going to university from 5 to 50 per cent would concurrently expand the amount of degree level jobs there were to go round? As we have seen, it is your contacts made at university, and increasingly your parents' contacts that determine the job you will get. Social mobility through higher education is bound to fail, purely on economic grounds.

Integration and social cohesion

As Kantzara (2011) says,

> Education is considered the institutional means through which to accomplish the integration of newly arrived or newly born members of society. In this function, schooling operates as a 'melting pot', while it cultivates tolerance and understanding among segments of the population; at the same time, it provides a valuable recourse to new members accentuating and promoting citizenship and the sense of belonging.
>
> (Kantzara, 2011, p37)

Kantzara (2011) goes on to illustrate how higher education serves social cohesion in a number of ways: (a) providing social involvement and participation; (b) allowing group to preserve or better their social position; (c) as an institutional means for governments to manage and control society from a distance; (d) as a means to control and mitigate social conflicts relating to accessing a valuable resource; (e) cultivating interdependence of individuals in the society of which they aspire to be part; and (f) carrying and transmitting different meanings and valuable ideals, among others the sense of commitment, belonging and solidarity together with a vision of a more just society.

However, Faine et al. (2016) discuss how globalization and the neo-liberal construction and operationalization of universities have eroded the potential of enacting such values. Going down Kantzara's typography, university offers less change for social involvement and mixing, with huge class sizes and lately a move to online working under Covid, which will undoubtedly further effect teaching, and is disproportionately bad for widening participation students (Montacute and Holt-White, 2020). The expansion of higher education for widening participation was similarly highly racialized, with Global Majority group predominantly being in new universities, and still not succeeding at them or, even when they do succeed, not progressing onto 'graduate employment' or further study, even compared to the white student at their own institution, let alone predominantly white students at elite institutions where the majority of doctoral study happens. We should also not forget, particularly in the United States, that structurally universities were sites of physical racial segregation, not integration and this is still maintained today (Singh, 2011).

Disability and mental health

In terms of social policy, disabled students and students with mental health issues, by contrast, are curiously absent in government's using higher education as a policy driver for its social goals, extenuating the invisibility of disability in higher education. Barnes (2007) notes that until the 1990s, most British universities were virtually inaccessible to disabled students and staff (Leicester and Lovell, 1994, Barnes, 2006). Beachamp-Prior (2012) found that disabled students in higher education were rarely involved, or even consulted, about policy and practice (Hurst, 1993, Hall and Tinklin, 1998, Borland and James, 1999, Riddell, Tinklin and Wilson, 2005). It was better in the states where the Rehabilitation Act of 1973 and the American Disablement Act of 1990 enshrined the rights of disabled people to education including higher education and illegality of discrimination.

In the UK, since 2001, universities and colleges have had a legal requirement to make 'reasonable adjustments' for disabled students. Under the Equality Act 2010, universities and colleges have a duty to ensure equality of opportunity for disabled students by changing rules or practices, altering or removing physical barriers and providing support services or devices. However, in 2015 the government changed the criteria for DSA in 2015, meaning that non-medical help such as note-takers would no longer be covered, expecting universities and colleges would meet the shortfall by extending adjustments for individual students into more sustainable inclusive practices across the board, rather than seeing a decline in provision for disabled students. Higher Education Funding Council for England (HEFCE) and more recently the OfS have been distributing an increased level of funding, rising from £20 million in 2015 to £40 million annually from 2016 onwards. The funding was allocated explicitly to support providers to develop inclusive teaching practices and further the adoption of the social model of disability (see below).

Since 2015 to claim assistive technology, students have had to pay the first £200 themselves. In 2015, there was an 18 per cent fall in the number of students receiving funding for assistive technology compared with 2014. While some of this fall can be attributed to students already owning a laptop, others say they cannot afford it. The uptake of DSA overall has declined from a high of 7.3 per cent of UK students studying in England claiming it in 2014–15, reversing an upward trend of more than a decade. Now 6.8 per cent of students cannot receive DSA to help them complete their course. Not all disabled students studying in England can apply for DSA. International students cannot claim the benefit. Students undertaking degree apprenticeships are not eligible, as their employer is responsible for making reasonable adjustments. At postgraduate level, the maximum support a student can claim is lower by a third than that available at undergraduate level. Other trends include providers' interaction with external agencies increasing.

A greater proportion of providers now buy disability services from external suppliers, particularly non-medical helper (NMH) support. Only one in ten providers now provides all services inhouse (Williams et al., 2019). In 2018, the largest amount of compensation recommended by the Office of the Independent Adjudicator was to a disabled student who complained about the non-medical support they received from their provider. This type of action does, however, place the onus on the student to challenge their university or college, which takes time and can be stressful. The Office for Students (OfS), disabled students and the National Union of Students (NUS) raised issues around the reforms to the Disabled Student Allowance, availability and suitability of assistive technology, and the provision of support services, especially for mental health (NUS, 2019, Weale, 2019). Responding to these concerns, in June 2019, the government announced the establishment of a Disabled Students' Commission, which first reported in 2021.

Conclusion

> Diversification of the higher education system has taken place in the context of deeply rooted historical inequalities.
>
> (Burke and Hayton, 2012)

As Ozga famously said, policymaking is a political not a rational process (Ozga, 1999). There is always an ideology behind any social policy initiative, which has generally reflected the ideology of the government of the time (Balchin, 2013). Higher education is often seen as a panacea that can bring people together, build social and cultural capital and cure economic and social injustices – it cannot and should not be expected to. However, this does not mean that those in higher education have no responsibility. As Naylor and James indicate, universities would do well to remember what we can do, and which side we are on.

> Pragmatically, universities have two roles in social inclusion. First, they must ensure that their policies and practices ameliorate rather than enhance existing inequities ... Secondly, academics and administrators must ensure that what resources are available – university or otherwise – are deployed in as effective a manner as possible.
>
> (Naylor and James, 2016, pp11–12)

However, we should not forget that while many formations of social policy are government-driven, and often central government-driven, the impetus for them can come from below. As Gale and Hodge (2014) and Watson (2013) critique, widening participation has not resulted in 'under-represented' student transformation, but student frustration and significant dropout rates, that has then led to student action independent of any state initiative. Students will get angry and they see they are being controlled and paying a lot of money for a deception of social mobility that could exacerbate, not ameliorate, social conflict. As we will explore, many groups do not feel a sense of belonging at university; instead, they feel isolation, socially distanced and other. Positively, it is students directly that have pushed for increased inclusivity and diversity in higher education curricula, such as the National Union of Students' 'Why

Is My Curriculum White?' campaign, which has been running since 2015 and the 'Why Rhodes Must Fall' protests.

As Adnett (2016) indicates below, students can have impact and hopefully we have sometimes provided the critical space, not necessarily to become socially mobile and cohesive, but to articulate and act on the lack of social mobility and prevalence of unresolved social conflict that they are subject to and the inadequacy of higher education to provide and resolve these things, and in turn how neo-liberalist approaches to social policy are not going to work either.

> Effective social movements – and most importantly the Black Movement – can pressure the state and interact with various levels of government to convert their claims into policies and interventions. Countering this positive dynamic is the continuing strength of the business sector driving for the growth of private institutions, a force still beyond the regulatory power of the state ….
>
> (Adnett, 2016, pp65 & 78)

3

Access, Success and Progression of Disadvantaged Students: Case Study of the UK

Introduction

In the UK, widening participation practitioners tend to talk about the access, success and progression of students. This is largely because it is the language of the regulatory body of the Office for Students (OfS) that monitors universities' 'progress' in terms of widening participation in higher education. Access is broadly about students getting into university, and often covers issues such as outreach and transition programmes, but also expectations and admissions processes. Success firstly covers continuation, i.e. that people finish their programmes, and includes students who interrupt or repeat, which is almost universally seen as a bad thing. Success also covers attainment, i.e. the grade that people obtain at the end of their course. Progression is what graduates go onto once they complete, and is measured by the OfS in terms of employment and further study, although they do not differentiate between the two in their data gathering.

Before the Office for Students was created, higher education access regulation was the responsibility of the Office for Fair Access (OFFA). Higher education providers that wanted to charge more than a certain level of tuition fees were required to have 'access agreements' approved by OFFA, which set out how the provider planned to sustain or improve access, student success and progression among people from underrepresented and disadvantaged groups. OFFA monitored the implementation of these agreements and took action if agreements were breached. This function was taken over by the OfS in 2018 and universities are expected to develop access and participation plans (APPs) that set out how they will improve equal opportunities for underrepresented groups and close the attainment and participation gaps. In theory, universities and colleges set their own targets working towards the OfS national targets, the threat being taking away the right to set higher fees for course. In reality the OfS heavily monitors what targets are set and they have to show a trajectory of ending gaps within five years. Important differences between APPs and access agreements are firstly that APPs cover the whole life cycle of a student including success and progression. Second difference is that there is an emphasis on any initiatives being undertaken needing to be 'research informed' and 'properly' evaluated, although, as we shall see, there is a politics around both of these extensions in how they are conceptualized and theorized.

The chapter argues that APPs and their initiatives are largely premised on the assumption that change needs to happen at an individual rather than structural level, with universities developing initiatives to support individuals. The chapter will follow the argument of Hinton et al. (2018) that these narratives in emphasizing individual responsibility problematize the marginalized for their own exclusion. In doing so they also obscure and negate responsibility for the development of policies at the European, state and individual HEI levels to develop policies fostering more inclusive learning. This chapter will then examine how the OfS's conceptualization of evaluation was initially, and to a large degree still is, neo-liberal and pseudo-scientific (Crockford, 2020). I then trace how the APP agenda, with particular definitions of BAME, working class, distorts the agenda of widening participation for these groups in its narrowing of focus and encouragement of HEIs to game their data collection. In terms of disability data, collection is also distorting, particularly so in the case of mental health, where its conflation with well-being agendas often renders those with diagnosed mental health issues invisible. Before all that it seems worth exploring in some detail what the state of play is presently for the access, success and progression of working class, Global Majority and student with disability and mental health conditions in higher education.

Access

We will explore the facts around disadvantaged students in more detail in the dedicated chapters. Suffice to say, as we have already explored in previous chapters, despite widening participation being a high priority for the previous twenty-five years, those from working-class backgrounds and some from Global Majority communities are still less likely to apply and progress to higher education (Gorard et al., 2012; Younger et al., 2019). Even with the same grades as middle-class children, working-class students still apply to university less often, and to Russell Group universities especially less often (Anders, 2012). UCAS (2018) found that those from the least deprived areas were 2.3 times more likely to enter higher education by age twenty than those in the most deprived area. This gap is even wider at the most selective universities, to which students from the least deprived areas are 5.7 times more likely to progress compared to their counterparts from more deprived areas (UCAS, 2018). Global Majority students are less likely to receive an offer to study at a Russell Group institution even if they have the same qualifications and grades as other applicants (Boliver, 2013).

According to the OfS (2019c), they cannot measure whether disabled young people are entering higher education at a lower rate than their non-disabled peers. There are small-scale studies which suggest this might be the case. The National Deaf Society (2018) found that Deaf children are 50 per cent less likely to go to Russell Group universities. The number of new entrants with a disability (i.e. first-year disabled students) has grown from 68,000 in 2013/14 to over 94,000 in 2017/18 – an increase of 38 per cent. The most commonly reported disability is a specific learning difficulty (SpLD), followed by a mental health condition (Williams et al., 2019). According to Higher Education Statistics Agency (HESA) in 2018/19, 308,000 students said they had a disability of some kind – this was 16.2 per cent of all home students. Within this, 82,000 said they had a mental health condition: 4.3 per cent of all home students. Thorney (2017) found that mental health conditions account for an increasing proportion of all disability disclosed by first-year students (17 per cent in 2015/16 compared to 5 per cent in 2006/7).

Success

While widening participation policies in higher education have contributed to an increase in student numbers from non-traditional, diverse backgrounds, with the goal of creating a more equitable HE system, research has shown that 'broadening entry points does not necessarily ensure inclusion or positive experience for these students'.

(Meuleman, Garrett, Wrench and King, 2015, p503)

The OfS (2020) found that for 2017–18 entrants (not including mature students), the continuation rate of students who were eligible to receive free meals whilst at school was 5.4 percentage points lower than those who were not. For qualifiers in 2018–19, the rate of achieving a first- or upper-second-class degree was 13.0 percentage points lower for students who were eligible for free school meals compared to those who were not. The OfS (2020) found that for 2017–18 entrants, the continuation rate of students whose parents do not have a higher education qualification was 3.1 percentage points lower than the continuation rates of students whose parents do. Qualifiers in 2018–19 whose parents do not have a higher education qualification had a rate of achieving a first- or upper-second-class degree that was 5.7 percentage points lower than students whose parents do.

In terms of Global Majority, the most recent Office for Students (2020) data found a continuation gap for all groups compared with white students that has steadily increased over the last five years (Black, 4.1–6.6; mixed, 1.9–2.1; Asian, 0.2–1.2; other, 1.6–3.5). The same date found that attainment has decreased slightly with Black students (24.6–22.1) and remained the same for others (14.3), mixed (4.8) and Asian (10.8). It remains true that graduates from ethnic minority backgrounds are less likely to be awarded good degrees than their white counterparts (Richardson, 2018, 2020). Across all ethnic minority groups, the odds of a student obtaining a good degree are roughly half those of a white student obtaining a good degree, and this situation has not changed over the last twenty years (Richardson, 2018, 2020). The HEFCE (2018) data analysis found that in 2016–17, 82 per cent of white graduates had been awarded good degrees. As many as 75 per cent from mixed backgrounds were awarded good degrees; 72 per cent of Asian students and 60 per cent of Black students. Black students are more likely to be mature students than other ethnic groups and less likely to enter HE with A-levels. The attainment gap for mature BME students has traditionally been higher than for young BME students.

According to the OfS students who report a disability have lower degree results overall (OfS, 2019b). The OfS (2019c) found that undergraduate disabled students are doing less well than non-disabled students in terms of continuation (0.9 percentage points), degree attainment (2.8 percentage points) and progression onto highly skilled employment or postgraduate study (1.8 percentage points). The pattern is also uneven: 54 per cent of universities and colleges had a gap of less than 2.5 percentage points (either positive or negative) between the continuation rate for their non-disabled and disabled students. In rates of attainment and progression, 33 per cent and 41 per cent of providers respectively achieve figures within this range. However, there is a marked difference between different disabilities. Those with cognitive or learning difficulties had higher continuation rates (91.4 per cent) than non-disabled students (90.3 per cent). The biggest difference is for those with mental health issues (see separate literature review). Between 2009 and 2013, students with a declared disability had a consistently lower than average overall satisfaction rate. This result persists even when other factors (such as choice of subject, gender and ethnicity) were taken into account (HEFCE, 2018). Disabled students are less satisfied with their professional placements and report more difficulties with them than non-disabled students (Hill and Roger, 2016).

Researchers have found that students with mental health problems receive lower grades and experience higher rates of educational attrition than their peers (Hysenbegasi, Hass and Rowland, 2005, Kessler et al., 1997). OfS (2019) found that for all full-time undergraduate students starting in 2015–16, the continuation rate was 90.3 per cent. For part-time students, it was 63.4 per cent. Continuation rates were significantly lower for both full-time and part-time students who had reported having a mental health condition, when compared with the continuation rate across the whole sector, though the gap has narrowed slightly since 2012–13. 20. In 2015–16, full-time students who reported having a mental health condition had a continuation rate of 86.6 per cent. According to the OfS (2020) for those students with mental health conditions graduating in 2017–18, the attainment rate was 78.3 per cent for full-time students and 54.6 per cent for part-time students. The proportion of students receiving a first or 2:1 is marginally lower among those with a reported mental health condition. In 2017–18, 77.3 per cent of full-time students and 53.2 per cent of part-time students with a reported mental health condition received a first or 2:1. Across all ethnic groups, full-time students were less likely to receive a first or 2:1 if they reported having a mental health condition. Black full-time students had the largest attainment gap of any ethnicity group; Black full-time students with a reported mental health condition had an attainment rate 5.8 percentage points below that of all Black full-time students.

Progression

> Progression, particularly into graduate employment and postgraduate study has received the least attention … Graduates from nontraditional backgrounds do less well in the labor market and access to postgraduate study, even when other variables such as entry qualifications, institution attended, subject studied and degree classification are controlled for.
>
> (Thomas, 2015, pp138 & 139)

The OfS in May 2020 found that progression rates (a distinction is not made between progression to further study or employment) have decreased for all BAME students (Black, 7.9–4.7; Asian, 6.9–3.8; other, 5.5–3.9) in the last five years, apart from mixed students where it has been static (2.9). In earlier analysis, the OfS (2018) notes that disadvantage also persists beyond higher education for some ethnic groups. There are unexplained disparities in the progression of different ethnic groups from undergraduate study to employment (including professional employment) and further study. Regardless of entry qualifications, subjects studied, degree outcomes and other socio-demographic characteristics, differences in employment outcomes between white and BME graduates persist even three years after graduation. The Equality challenge Unit (2017) found that 7.8 per cent of BME leavers were unemployed six months after qualifying compared with 4.3 per cent of white leavers, and six months after qualifying, 61.2 per cent white leavers were in full-time work compared with 54.8 per cent of BME leavers.

The OfS (2020) found for qualifiers in 2016–17 (not including mature students), the rate of progression into highly skilled employment or further study was 4.8 percentage points lower for students who were eligible to receive free meals whilst at school when compared to those who were not. This progression data is only available for one year of qualifiers for a reduced student population and more data is required to determine how free school meal eligibility is related to progression rates. They also found that for qualifiers in 2016–17 the rate of progression into highly skilled employment or further study at a higher level was 2.6 percentage points lower for students whose parents do not have a higher education qualification compared to students whose parents do (not including mature students).

Powell and Pfahl (2019) found that disabled people with a degree have employment rates of 74 per cent, compared with 49 per cent for those disabled people whose highest qualifications are at GCSE level. While there is still a substantial employment rate gap between disabled and non-disabled graduates, it is smaller than for other qualification levels, but is still 15 per cent (OfS, 2019b). There are again differences between different disabilities. For full-time undergraduates who graduated in 2016–17, only 61.8 per cent of those with a social or communication impairment had progressed into highly skilled work or postgraduate study after six months compared with 73.3 per cent of their non-disabled peers (HEFCE, 2018).

The OfS (2019) reports that progression rates were lower throughout the period 2012–13 than 2016–17 among students who had reported having a mental health condition. For example, in 2016–17, full-time students were 4.0 percentage points less likely to enter into skilled work or further study if they had reported having a mental health condition (progression rates were 73.1 per cent and 69.2 per cent respectively for full-time students and full-time students who had reported having a mental health condition). The same pattern is observed for students completing part-time study, with the participation rate for all part-time students being 73.4 per cent and 61.6 per cent for those who reported having a mental health condition among those leaving higher education in 2016–17.

For full-time students aged twenty-one and over, progression rates were 10.4 percentage points lower in 2012–13 for students who had reported having a mental health condition, falling to just 2.8 percentage points in 2016–17. The gap in progression rates between full-time students with a reported mental health condition and all full-time students within the same ethnic group is greatest for white students (4.5 percentage points in 2016–17), closely followed by Black students (4.4 percentage points in 2016–17). The report does not make any distinction between progression onto further study or employment.

Individualization

The process of individualization is never simple, and all stakeholders will make noise about not ignoring the structural and the need for institutional change. In the case of access and participation plans, as with many monitoring regimes, the devil is in the detail, and it happens in stages. The higher education sector is asked to make widening participation happen, and the emphasis is firmly on what higher education institutions can do. Structural dimensions like loans structure, DSA or HE funding are not acknowledged. Wider structural issues like the rest of the education sector housing, poverty, health, mental health services, private and public sector employers are firmly off limits. The only thing HEIs can change is themselves. Inevitably APP targets are set by individual institutions, rather than tacking issues across institutions and regions. HEIs are again in competition with each other.

Targets are annual and institutions need to show how they are having incremental impact through their initiatives. Therefore, HEIs are compelled to be short term and reductive. De-colonizing the curriculum may well have longer-term effects, but is harder to demonstrate, and may even had adverse effects in the short term, as students get angry when they realize that the curriculum can be changed, but has not been. As we shall see, much of the literature calls for cultural and fundamental change at an institutional level and most higher education institutions make noises about understanding the need for cultural sea changes and paradigm shifts. In reality, such cultural changes take a long time, need to be embedded and are hard to prove in the pseudo-scientific way that the Office for Students demands.

Worried that they will not be able to meet their short-term specific targets HEIs look for quick wins with the promise of cultural change to come, which it rarely does as the short-term imperative never goes away. It is a lot easier to try and tinker with individual assessments, reading lists and 'giving more support' than undertake the hard slog of challenging established norms, overcoming institutional inertia and facing some of the uncomfortable realities of who higher education institutions have traditional favoured, the narratives they have re-inscribed and the blatant discrimination they have covered up. Such dynamics do not take account of the fact that many institutions are still not really prepared to look at themselves and make the changes needed. It is far easier to re-inscribe the deficit narrative that it is the student who needs to change, but we are prepared to 'support' them in their endeavours. We will explore this dynamic in greater depth later in individual chapters as we will find that it is repeated over and over in relation to the different constituent groups.

It would be all too easy to just blame senior management. Williams et al. (2019) note that the attitudes of senior staff are a key factor, as he states in the context of disability.

> Senior leadership is pivotal, particularly where there are multiple agendas and competing demands. Where senior leaders prioritise support for disabled students, signal their commitment to a wider culture of inclusivity, and are actively working to integrate it across their institution, there is likely to be a better chance of success in bringing about the shifts required.
> (Williams et al., 2019, p12)

It would take a brave vice chancellor to truly embrace this when they are subject to a plethora of short-term reductive targets and knowing that the real change needs to happen at a far more structural level than their individual institution.

Pseudo-scientific evaluation

Crockford (2020) notes that many commentators on the evaluation of widening participation initiatives in higher education, such as researchers for the Sutton Trust (Torgerson, Gascoine, Heaps, Menzies and Younger, 2014) and the Education Policy Institute (Robinson and Salvestrini, 2020), come from a distinctly positivistic perspective. As Gorard and Smith (2006) state, evaluations lacked 'controlled interventions' or 'suitable comparators even in passive designs'. The ideal model exemplified by the OfS is the 'What Works Network', launched 'to develop a robust evidence base for policymakers' through 'randomised controlled trials (RCTs) and the more systematic analysis of what is working where, and why'.

Such positivistic tyrannies have a long history in UK policymaking, going back to the emergence and subsequent dominance of evidence-based practice in the Blair years (Seal, 2009). Borrowed from medical practice and transferred to social and educational contexts, such approaches were self-portrayed as being ideology free, but were really theory light. There was an emphasis on 'practice', 'what works' and 'measurable impact'. These are all seductive terms from a seductive narrative, but in reality, evidence-based practice then and the what works agenda now are anything but ideology free. It sees higher education and social policy in general, as being neutral, which means that the existing hegemonies behind these supposed neutralities are again buried and re-inscribed. Concurrently, as described, these agendas also re-inscribed positivistic approaches. In turn these agendas have made policymakers and initiative designers make spurious claims for having 'evidenced impact' and claim correlations, wanting to make generalizible claims from small-scale specific studies (sometimes hidden in phrases like 'scaling up'). As Crockford notes,

> Policymakers tend to prefer 'robust' evaluation and a clear narrative. They are also concerned with value for money, underpinned by a questionable assumption about the generalisability of individual activities.

The OfS see three approaches to evaluation within APPs.

Narrative evaluation

Existing evidence provides a narrative and a coherent theory of change to motivate selection of activities. Evidence of impact is from elsewhere and/or in the research literature on A&P activity effectiveness.

Local empirical evaluation

Empirical work is needed where there are gaps in the research or where the local context needs exploring. Quantitative and qualitative evidences may be needed of the difference made by an initiative, demonstrating empirically that interventions are associated with beneficial results.

Causal research

This is where there is little larger-scale empirical evidence, and where a causal relationship can be established, associated with larger data sets, experiments where there is a control group who did not get the intervention and the effects of the intervention can be isolated and demonstrated.

OfS has a positivist stance. While it says it values 'local empirical work' and 'qualitative approaches', it still sees quantitative large-scale causal research as the 'gold standard' and implies that where there is a gap in the literature, this is the approach that should be taken. Equally constraining is the OfS instance on a 'theory of change' underpinning the plans. It is good to have an end goal in mind, and to know the trajectory you are going in and the nature of the claims you are making. However, there is a danger in that such an approach mitigates against exploratory research which tries to understand a phenomenon in favour of action. While action might have a supposedly tangible result, even if we do not know why it works, we miss some of the wider picture. If a suggested initiative or research is not clear about where it sits in the 'outcome chain', a model predicated on huge assumptions of literality and demonstratable causality, it will be sidelined. I have experienced this a number of times where initiatives focusing on cultural change, relationship building or exploring perceptions have been criticized as being 'too academic', 'too wooly' or being unclear about how they will 'directly lead to change', and are postponed in favour of quick wins.

Williams et al. (2019) also note that HEIs are continuing to evaluate the effectiveness of the support they provide, or commission from an external provider, with a shift towards using hard outcome measures of effectiveness in line with developments in the Teaching Excellence and Student Outcomes Framework (TEF) and the new requirements around access and participation plans (APPs). They (2019) note that while these shifts can act as drivers for positive change, the value of qualitative evaluative feedback to aid understanding of the issues and support future developments was frequently noted, and is in danger of being marginalized.

The devil is in the data and definition

Working-class students

Several authors (Gaskell and Linwood, 2019, Richardson et al., 2020) note that while a variety of measures have been used to classify social class in the UK, each is problematic in different ways.

> *A Classification of Residential Neighbourhoods (ACORN)*: A postcode-based tool that categorizes the UK's population by level of socio-economic advantage.
>
> *Free school meals (FSM)*: A means-tested benefit to show income background (as measured by whether a person was in receipt of free school meals, a means-tested benefit while at school). Household salary: A measure of the combined incomes of all people sharing a particular household or place of residence.
>
> *Income deprivation affecting children index (IDACI)*: Measures in a local area the proportion of children under the age of sixteen that live in low-income households.
>
> *Multiple equality measure (MEM)*: UCAS-developed principal measure of equality, which brings together information on several equality dimensions for which large differences in the probability of progression into higher education exist. These equality dimensions include sex, ethnic group, POLAR3 and FSM.
>
> *Parental education:* Records information about whether an entrant's parents have higher education qualification.
>
> *Participation of local areas (POLAR)*: The POLAR4 classification is formed by ranking five groups from quintile 1 areas, with the lowest young participation (most disadvantaged), up to quintile 5

areas with the highest rates (most advantaged), each representing 20 per cent of the UK young cohort. Students have been allocated to the neighbourhoods based on their postcode. Those students whose postcode falls within middle-layer super-output areas with the lowest participation (quintile 1) are denoted as being from a low-participation neighbourhood.

Socio-economic classification (SEC): HESA collects the socio-economic classification of students participating in higher education if aged twenty-one or over at the start of their course or parental classification if under twenty-one.

School type: HESA collects information about whether the student went to a state school or private school.

Traditionally, the classification of social class for students domiciled in the UK was based on the occupations of their parents (UK Registrar General). Since 2005, an alternative classification has been based on Participation of Local Areas (POLAR) and this is used by the Office for Students. This estimates the proportion of young people within a particular geographical area who proceed to higher education by the age of nineteen. However, there are a variety of problems with POLAR data (Harrison and McCaig, 2015, Boliver, Gorard, and Siddiqui, 2019, pp5–6). Some disadvantaged families live outside the areas that are designated as disadvantaged, while some families who live in such areas are not themselves disadvantaged. Moreover, when using POLAR as a proxy for social class, it becomes circular to maintain that participation in higher education is higher in people from a middle-class background than in people from a working-class background. I use the term working class unless citing an author who uses a specific term.

Global Majority

In the UK, the umbrella term 'black and minority ethnic' (BME or less often BaME) or Black, Asian and Minority Ethnic (BAME) are the terms most commonly used to describe all those who are non-white British, and thus may also include those who describe themselves as 'white other' (Stevenson et al., 2019). Key higher education (HE) policymaking organizations including the

Higher Education Funding Council for England (HEFCE), the Office for Fair Access (OFFA), and the Office for Students and Advance HE use the acronym BME whilst simultaneously recognizing the problematic nature of using a reductionist term to describe a population that is highly diverse not just in terms of ethnic or racial background but also by dint of socio-economic status, religion and gender amongst others. BAME students are not a homogeneous group (Singh, 2011, Miller, 2016) and while it is useful to look at commonalities within all BAME students, it is also sometimes necessary to analyse data by relevant sub-groups. Many are starting to use the term Global Majority in recognition that white people are, in fact, not the demographic majority of humans on the planet; white is not 'majority' and people who do not identify as white are not 'minority'.

BAME can be difficult to break down data into sub-groups as the dataset can become too small to be of statistical significance. Conversely, to not disaggregate data, and portray it as a simple black/white binary is simplistic and can be statistically deceiving, as Demack notes:

> It is possible for analyses of aggregated data to completely contradict that of disaggregated data, meaning that BME classification can be used to show a declining pattern of white advantage when, in reality, across more defined groups it increases. This has serious implications for attempts to evaluate the impact of any BME-focussed action on degree attainment.
>
> (Demack, 2020, p22)

Miller (2016) also notes that there is significant overlap between BME students and students from WP backgrounds, suggesting that any future interventions to address differential attainment should be mindful of Intersectional issues. Miller (2016) also highlights ethical concerns about what, when and whether to tell students about the attainment gap, bearing in mind there is a risk of students internalizing the issue and performing less well as a result. The OfS (2018) says providers should disaggregate BME students into different ethnicities and consider how students' ethnic backgrounds may intersect with other characteristics, such as low household income or coming from a low participation area. I use the term Global Majority unless citing an author who uses a specific term.

Disability and mental heath

Under the Equality Act 2010, a person has a disability 'if they have a physical or mental impairment, and the impairment has a substantial and long-term adverse effect on his or her ability to carry out normal day-to-day activities'. 'Substantial' is defined by the Act as 'more than minor or trivial'.

An impairment is considered to have a long-term effect if:

- it has lasted for at least twelve months;
- it is likely to last for at least twelve months; or
- it is likely to last for the rest of the life of the person.

OfS (2019) notes the most common type of disability is a cognitive or learning difficulty, such as dyslexia, dyspraxia or attention-deficit hyperactivity disorder (5 per cent of students in 2017–18). Disabilities may include:

- specific learning differences, such as dyslexia or attention deficit hyperactivity disorder;
- mental health conditions, including anxiety, anorexia or depression (covered in a separate literature review);
- physical disabilities affecting mobility or dexterity;
- sensory impairments such as deafness or severe sight loss;
- social or communication impairments, such as Asperger's syndrome or another autistic spectrum disorder; and
- long-term health conditions, including cancer, Crohn's disease or HIV.

Hugues and Spanner's (2019) mental health charter for universities gives a good overview of common terms in usage. However, many terms and definitions around mental health evolve, are contested and must be treated as contextual.

Mental health refers to a full spectrum of experience ranging from good mental health to mental illness. Good mental health means more than the absence of illness (Keynes, 2005). It will refer to a dynamic state of internal equilibrium (Galderisi et al., 2015) in which an individual experiences regular enduring positive feelings, thoughts and behaviours, can respond appropriately to normal negative emotions and situations and is able to make a positive contribution to their community.

Mental illness means a condition and experience, involving thoughts, feelings, symptoms and/or behaviours, that causes distress and reduces functioning, impacting negatively on an individual's day-to-day experience, and which may receive or be eligible to receive a clinical diagnosis.

Mental health problems or poor mental health refers to a broader range of individuals experiencing levels of emotional and/or psychological distress beyond normal experience and beyond their current ability to effectively manage. It will include those who are experiencing mental illness and those whose experiences fall below this threshold, but whose mental health is not good.

Well-being encompasses a wider framework, of which mental health is an integral part, but which also includes physical and social well-being. This uses a model provided by Richard Kraut (2009), in which optimum well-being is defined by the ability of an individual to fully exercise their cognitive, emotional, physical and social powers, leading to flourishing.

Student well-being adopts the general definition of well-being above, but we recognize that in addition, students' engagement with academic learning is a key component part of their experience and makes a significant contribution to their well-being (Hugues and Wilson, 2017).

Hewitt (2019) feels that conflating mental health and well-being can be damaging to individuals and the provision of support services. The Office for Student conflates the issues often. While the targets HEI's are judged on relate to students with specific mental health conditions, the literature that informs and is produced from the OfS often talks in terms of students well-being, and presents it on a spectrum with specific mental health conditions at one end of it. Advance HE used the two-continuum model to further explain this, demonstrating that mental health and well-being are not necessarily interrelated.

Conclusion

The OfS and access and participation plans are here to stay in the UK, at least for the foreseeable future. Whether they have an impact on widening participation is to be determined. As I said at the beginning, HEIs were meant to set their own targets, but when they did, and if they were not 'ambitious' enough, they were 'encouraged' to do them again. Essentially, they all had to say that within five years they would eliminate the attainment gaps for all groups. Asking HEIs to achieve in five years what has not been achieved by policy or HEI's in thirty years is setting institutions up to fail. No account was taken of the wider structural issues and forces at play. HEIs are expected to achieve these targets alone. I am sure some good initiatives will happen, and they will be better researched and evaluated and may even go some way to challenging the culture and structural forces at play that re-inscribe these groups oppression.

However, when the elimination of the gaps does not happen, and targets are missed by most, as seems extremely likely, will the APP monitoring system collapse under the weight of its own irrationality? Are the government really going to fine and restrict the fees that HEIs can charge, knowing that they are not going to make up for the shortfall, for this vast majority of institutions, including most of the elite ones? Perhaps the APP is another way of putting a straight-jacket on institutions, or certain institutions, up until that point, as is often the case the NSS, TEF, KEF, etc. Even if the APP structure lasts its planned five years, I am sure it will be re-invented as another widening participation initiative that will set slightly different targets but may will not get to the routes of the cultural and structural forces at play in higher education, let alone address some of the wider social and economic forces that set the context within which higher education operates. As Grange et al. (2020) say below, we need to think differently and outside of the neo-liberal nexus that has dominated for so long that it often seems the only way to structure things – it is not and there are no alternatives. These other approaches must be embraced and those trying to truly widening participation must learn to articulate them, and build for a time when different discourses can be heard above the ever-failing ones we are currently subject to.

> A more flexible higher education system needs to be conceptualized, one that is not specifically drawn on a business model of inputs, processes, and outputs, but one that would allow for students to enter and exit the higher education system based on students' personal circumstances and needs.
>
> (Grange et al., 2020, p208)

4

Working-Class Students, the Politics of Social Mobility Denied

Introduction

The expansion of working-class participation in higher education has been partial and particular and perversely, as Cote and Furlon note, has *'resulted in a steeply hierarchical and stratified system with working class students, for the most part, clustered in the low status, poorly resourced institutions'* (Cote and Furlon, 2016, p2). This chapter will affirm this by exploring the existing data, showing that working-class students are still not proportionately represented at university, and while working-class participation rates have gone up, middle-class rates have gone up even higher, and the latter have disproportionately gone to the elite institutions, squeezing out their working-class peers. Secondly, when it comes to continuation and attainment, working-class students leave more often and attain lower degrees. They are also more likely to get less well-paying jobs, even in the long term, and even with commensurate degrees or better as their middle-class counterparts. They are also less likely to go into postgraduate study, are less likely again to undertake doctoral study and are more likely to drop out. Even if they achieve a doctorate, they are less likely to go on to enter academia.

The chapter then explores how deficit narratives around working-class students persist, despite the evidence. Poor aspirational narratives prevail, as do judgements about their academic entrance grades and readiness to study. A middle-class social and transformational capital is expected from working-class students, and when not experienced by university structures, working-class students are excluded, considered 'other' and blamed for not engaging and participating in particular prescribed ways. The assimilation/integration model is examined in some depth. Expectations of students, in terms of attitudes, behaviour and ways of being, are constructed and classed in ways that the working-class students will anyways fall short. A call is made for the recognition of working-class skills, knowledge, autonomy and ways of learning, and that such acknowledgement may give us a blueprint for a more liberatory view of the 'ideal' student.

> This privileged instrument of the bourgeois sociodicy which confers on the privileged the supreme privilege of not seeing themselves as privileged manages the more easily to convince the disinherited that they owe their scholastic and social destiny to their lack of gifts or merits, because in matters of culture absolute dispossession excludes awareness of being dispossessed.
> (Bourdieu, Passeron and Nice, 1977, p210)

Acknowledging Bourdieu above, the interventions that are needed are primarily cultural in nature rather than individual. There is a concurrent need to deconstruct and reconstruct the non-neutrality of higher education and widening participation initiatives. Interventions explored in the chapter include outreach activities, foundation years and the first-year experience, with an emphasis on critical approaches that actively deconstruct and reconstruct working-class experiences of education to date. Recommendations around further research include looking at working-class experience of postgraduate education.

Theoretical perspectives and causes

In their synthesis of existing research on social class and higher education in 2010, Stevenson and Lang (2010) echo the aspirations and integration themes mentioned in the theoretical themes chapter. They concur that in the policy discourse working-class students are identified as *deficient* (Christie et al., 2007, Leatherwood and O'Connell, 2003, Thomas, 2012) – 'in ability, in aspirations and educational background, and in their (un) willingness to adopt a "student" identity, which is linked to their likelihood of dropping out and in their "unpreparedness" for learning' (Stevenson and Lang, 2010, p23). Similarly, to Global Majority student groups, there are several schools of thought on the low attainment for those students from working-class backgrounds.

Low aspirations narrative for working-class students

The low aspirations narrative (Bruce and Bridgeland, 2014) seems particularly strongly attributed to working-class students. Authors such as Berrington et al. (2016) found that positive aspirations were higher among children from managerial and professional backgrounds than among those from intermediate or routine class backgrounds. This difference in aspirations was larger in boys than in girls, but the interaction between the effects of gender and class was not statistically significant. Conversely, other research (St Clair and Benjamin, 2011, Archer, DeWitt and Wong, 2014, Baker et al., 2012) has indicated that aspirations for higher education and professional occupations are no different for students from more deprived neighbourhoods.

Atherton and Mazhari (2019) challenged the perceived need to 'raise' aspirations that they say has underpinned the rationale for much of the widening access work in the last two decades. Their research affirms findings that parents/carers from lower socio-economic groups do not lack educational aspirations; they just have different types of aspirations. Boliver (2013) found that students from disadvantaged backgrounds (judged by their parents' occupations) were less likely to apply to Russell Group universities than socially advantaged students, even when they held similar qualifications. The middle-class hierarchical aspiration culture, where you aim for Oxbridge, then the Russell Group, then the old universities, then new universities if all else fails, is not always at play in working-class culture. University being the traditional way to leave home, or a continuation of boarding school, may have less resonance for working-class students (Reay et al., 2017). Other considerations, like it being cheaper to study locally, may have greater pull or living in a community that accepts you.

O'Sullivan et al. (2019) feel that aspiration-raising approaches generally have little impact on institutional culture (Bowes et al., 2013) and fail to recognize the complex nature of educational disadvantage, running the risk of raising aspirations without actually affecting academic performance (O'Sullivan et al.,

2019). While attainment and aspiration definitely contribute to inequalities in HE participation, the underlying reasons for these are varied and complex. Bourdieu's (1986) paradigm of cultural reproduction explains inequalities in student mobility (Donnelly and Evans, 2016), highlighting its intersectional nature. According to this paradigm, each class has a different habitus which determines the possession of core values, practices and beliefs that are played out in behaviour and actions; these are 'internalised, "embodied" social structures [which] function below the level of consciousness' (Bourdieu, 1986, p6).

O'Sullivan et al. (2019) also note that often aspiration-raising initiatives actually serve to identify the students with the 'most' potential or the 'most gifted' students, and support them into and through HE, rather than look at the educational achievement of all those disadvantaged (O'Sullivan, 2019). This policy approach, known as 'cream-skimming', does nothing to address the societal and structural barriers which limit progression and aspirations (O'Sullivan et al., 2019). According to Thomas (2012), these activities reinforce cultural and socio-economic divisions based on a deficit model of the potential entrant, placing the responsibility for change on the student in a manner similar to 'victim blaming' (Tight, 1998).

Academic achievement

Other thinkers, particularly in the States (Chowdry et al., 2013), assert that academic achievement is the primary barrier to HE participation, with large disparities observed between the attainment of working-class students and their more affluent counterparts (McKnight et al., 2015). O'Sullivan et al. (2019) believe this approach frames access to HE in terms of human capital – seeing education reform and curriculum changes as preconditions. A practical way of ameliorating for such discrepancies is to make differential offers for working-class students. However, such differentiated offers are often frowned upon (Hannon et al., 2017) and therefore avoided or curtailed, particularly in elite institutions. Mechanisms such as the league table disincentivize universities from lowering their entrance grades as it is one of the metrics they are judged on. However, part of the resistance is attitudinal, as McKay and Devlin describe.

> There exists an assumption that by allowing differently prepared students into university, and thereby improving equity, standards are compromised. This dichotomy is premised on an assumption of deficit in, and inherent lack of respect for, students from working class backgrounds. There is thus a clear need for a purposeful challenge to the equity/standards dichotomy in order to ensure working class students feel respected and empowered to achieve the high standards they want and expect.
>
> (McKay and Devlin, 2015, pp161–2)

They discuss several studies (Vuong et al., 2010, Atherton, 2014, Elliott, 2014, Horowitz, 2017) that show how academics and professional and support staff tend to position first-generation college students as entering higher education already academically behind their continuing-generation peers, not taking account for why their grades may be lower. Reay (2017) described how universities undertake such policies to increase their widening participation performance, rather than a recognition that working-class students often have poorer schooling and that for them to achieve an equivalent grade to a student from a private or 'good' state school is harder. She found that universities currently active in promoting WP under this policy do not concurrently look at subject support, guidance and learning support alongside financial support for these students.

Such approaches do not look at or acknowledge the persistent perception, and deficit view, that is both perpetuated in attitude of staff and operationalized through service design and delivery. As we shall see later, tutors and support staff often consequently treat working-class students more negatively through such attitudes. If they underachieve or start to wobble, it is very quickly highlighted that they came into the institution under a lower offer, rather than looking at more nuanced factors. In a number of pieces of research, I have found that foundation-year students, who undertake a preparatory year through having non-traditional qualifications, often carry stigma throughout their degree, with staff being very quickly remembering that they were foundation-year students if they subsequently struggle.

Double consciousness

Diane Reay (2021) has consistently found that working-class students in general and Global Majority working-class students in particular make choices (and aim low) based on a desire to 'fit in'. Other research relating to retention identifies that those who are seen as 'different' are either forced to adopt middle-class values and practices to survive, which is referred to as turning 'towards the institution' (Hannon et al., 2017). Quinn (2004, p70) and Stevenson and Lang (2010) found that some working-class students actively dropped out 'as resistance to the middle-class hegemony of the university', although the institutions no doubt created a very different narrative about such actions. Stevenson and Lang (2010) talk about how discourses of difference are closely linked to those of identity – in particular the fear of losing identity and that this fear affects working-class students in numerous ways. As they expand,

> The tensions experienced by working-class students in trying to 'find' themselves are also evident in the literature, particularly where this involves changing class and, therefore, identity. In this way, for many learners, 'finding yourself' is mediated by feelings of guilt, particularly for those students who want to 'escape' from their working-class backgrounds.
>
> (Stevenson and Lang, 2010, p28)

Stevenson and Lang also cite Bufton (2006) who argues that the hegonomic 'academic stance', of being measured, impartial, distanced and analytical, mirrors the cultural experience of the privileged classes and is 'less in harmony with the working-class habitus than with the middle-class habitus and, in working-class students, can result in a threat to identity, a betrayal of working-class background and consequent problems in relationships with family and community' (Bufton, 2006, p43). Research suggests such tensions impact on working-class students' decision making about where to study (Ball et al., 2002), whether to stay in HE or leave (Bamber and Tett, 2000), and whether to access HE at all (Archer et al., 2005, Ball et al., 2002).

I am reminded of the Dubosian idea of 'double consciousness' (DU Bois, 1902) where one sees the world through both one's own cultural lens and the oppressors, while the oppressor only sees it through their own lens. Reay

(2017) and Crozier et al. (2008) found working-class students moved in and out of different identity constructions between university and home. Their identities were often fragmented and contradictory as a result, which Du Bois (2006) saw as a consequence of double consciousness. As Reay describes (2017, p45), 'some embraced this change but most dipped in and out, occupying the twilight space of identity, or they are hybrids but this hybridisation is not a bringing together of equal parts. It is the struggle over unequal differences that could often be troubling and disruptive.' There is also a practical element to this. Reay (2017) talks about how working-class students are governed by expediency and 'the logic of necessity' (Bourdieu, 1986) 'in which their learner identities are constantly at risk of being subsumed by their responsibilities and commitments as workers and family members' (Reay, 2017, p46).

However, Orne (2013) argues that there are two interpretations of double consciousness: one where different cultural orientations are in tension and another of it being a positive socio-psychological lens for operating a society characterized by 'liquid modernity' and fragmentation (Baumann, 2006). In this alternate usage, double consciousness is a mechanism through which marginalized people become aware of the worldviews of those in positions of power, whilst holding their own opinions and drawing on their identities as resources to mediate those in power. What is less articulated, and something that we will come back to in the conclusion are what the conditions are for a positive double consciousness to thrive for working-class students, and indeed all disadvantaged students, for double consciousness equally applies to race, disability and the multitude of associated intersections.

Reay et al. (2009) also talk about how working-class students do not always possess the 'navigational capital' (which refers to the students' ability to navigate the complex and unfamiliar university system) to support progression to HE, and they lack experience of the 'norms' associated with HE. Social mobility can, however, be facilitated through the acquisition of certain forms of 'social capital', despite facing significant barriers (Hannon et al., 2017, O'Sullivan et al., 2017, 2019). Putnam's (2000) more contemporary definition provides an explanation of how social capital can facilitate social mobility. He distinguishes between two forms of social capital: bonding and bridging. Bonding social capital occurs when people with similar backgrounds enter into relationships and collaborate to achieve shared goals.

These associations are inward looking and may reinforce stratification by keeping low SES students bonded to beliefs about where they belong in terms of education (O'Sullivan et al., 2019). However, Bourdieu talks about the limits associated with social capital (Bourdioue et al., 1977). This concurs with the themes of this book where terms like cultural and social capital can mask the operation of raw privilege, evidenced by disadvantaged students not being systematically able to gain such capital, or where a few are allowed to do this to give the illusion higher education is a meritocracy.

Beyond the assimilation model

> Once we recognise that excluding behaviour is a consequence of the middle class and upper-class institutional culture in Russell Group universities in the UK rather than being attributable to deficits or self-exclusion in the individual working-class student, it becomes clear that the institution needs to be the focus for radical change rather than the working class individual. Furthermore, the cultural exclusion of the working classes in higher education has deep and enduring roots that implicate wider society not just the field of HE and stem from profound historical class inequalities that have never been addressed and continue to scar English society.
>
> (Reay, 2017, p8)

We noted in the theory chapter that higher education often has an assimilation narrative underpinning it. However, while Tinto's original vision was that this is a two-way process, the reality is often that it is working-class students who are expected to change, and there is no acknowledgement of the class-based assumptions of the ideal student that underpins the assimilation model. As Ives and Castillo-Montiya say in their recent systematic review of working-class higher education students,

> When higher education scholars use frameworks and theories that encourage assimilation of marginalized students, their findings will follow suit. Studying first-generation college students only by what they are not – whether that be their peers or how they do not fit into the dominant culture – frames the field's understanding in problematic ways. Putting

the onus on first-generation college students to change, higher education scholars, teachers, and practitioners are asking them to assimilate to the dominant ways of thinking, being, and doing in academia; and even more, they normalize this ask.

(Ives and Castillo-Montoya, 2020, p163)

Perhaps unsurprisingly they also found that while working-class students want and seek interactions with their tutors, they are less likely to experience quality interactions with them. Concurrently working-class students tend not to seek official assistance (Yee, 2016), speak with faculty or peers for help (Hicks and Wood, 2016) or seek tutoring resources (Lipp and Jones, 2010/2011). They tend, instead, to turn to online sources before turning to people in their network for help (Tsai, 2012). Yee (2016) detects underlying this, different class-based models about responsibility and seeking help, as she expands

First-generation students believed that they would have to be more responsible for themselves. Unlike middle class students who interpreted that responsibility as reaching out to seek help, first-generation students interpreted the responsibility as being on their own to succeed.

(Yee, 2016, p845)

Unfortunately, modern ways of measuring student engagement and participation often use learning analytics measured by students speaking up in class discussions, and engagement with lecturer-led activities, despite the fact this may conflict with the cultural preferences of working-class and Global Majority students (Kim and Sax, 2009, Soria and Stebleton, 2012). As White says, 'the problem with measuring academic engagement through participation is that it neglects the underlying power embedded in assumptions about what academic participation ought to look and sound like' (White, 2011, p32).

White (2011) expands on this dynamic discussing how, in academic spaces, working-class students can feel their own ways of talking and participating may not align with the normative academic discourse. This lack of congruency may sway these students from actively participating in class or seeking out conversations with faculty outside of class. Failure to participate in these expected ways of engaging may lead lecturers to mistakenly interpret the behaviour as 'disrespect for the teacher or the class, disinterest in the subject matter, or apathy in general' (White, 2011, p250).

Ives and Castillo-Montoya (2020) found some authors therefore prescribe adjusted assimilation programmes. Faulkner and Burdenski (2011) found that teaching working-class students how to better identify and act on their needs helped increase their academic self-efficacy and success in developmental mathematics. Nosaka and Novak (2014) noted the benefit of programmes encouraging academic and social integration, resulting in statistically higher retention rates than students outside of the programme. Morales (2014) suggested that lecturers can build students' self-efficacy through realistic appraisals of their strengths and weaknesses and encouraging them to seek help.

However, these approaches again seek to change working-class ways of doing things and expect them to adopt middle-class ways of being. It is also nuanced. While they may not seek support from their general peers in class, they may seek support and aspiration from other working-class students. Stephens et al. (2014) similarly found in a randomized control trial that when college seniors told entering first-year students' stories about the value of diverse backgrounds and the ability of people from different backgrounds to succeed, the gap between first-generation and continuing-generation college students' first-year grades decreased by 63 per cent in the intervention group.

Ives and Castillo-Montoya (2020) distinguish in the literature between assimilation-based programmes that expect working-class students to adopt middle-class ways of learning and being, and other approaches which try and unearth and work with the indigenous working-class ways of knowing and being, and design services around them. Furthermore, they advocate that services should acknowledge the class-based educational experiences they may have had so far.

> We also encourage practitioners to frame their programs for first-generation college students in a way that emphasizes strengths and assets rather than helping 'at risk' students. Validating and affirming students' home cultures, while teaching them how to navigate the academy, can encourage bicultural competence and pride in their first-generation student status.
>
> (Delgado Bernal, 2006)

We will come back to this when looking at how we could design transitional and foundation year programmes. Authors such as Gillian-Daniel and Kraemer, (2015), Schmid et al. (2016) found the achievement gap between privileged students and disadvantaged students is reduced when lecturers engage in more inclusive and culturally relevant teaching practices.

> If higher education scholars want to study first-generation college students in ways that position them as having agency and power to contribute to their learning and remain connected to their communities, it would be helpful to rethink research designs, frameworks, and tools.

We have already noted that, similarly, to Global Majority students, many working-class students are commuter students, living at home and going to their local university. Their motivation is also less individually based and more about wanting to give back to their communities and families. Several authors (Allen et al., 2015, Harackiewicz et al., 2016, Tibbetts et al., 2016) find this extends to how they want to learn and what knowledge they value. Working-class students want to learn in community and want their learning to be connected to, and beneficial for, their families and communities. Similarly, working-class students often take an interdependent approach to academic learning, preferring to learn and benefit from learning with others (Eddy and Hogan, 2014, Pelco et al., 2014, Stephens et al., 2013, Tibbetts et al., 2016).

> Universities focused more on independent cultural norms than interdependent cultural norms ... overall, the American system of higher education reflects and promotes the middle-class cultural norms of independence.
>
> (Stephens et al., 2012, p1186)

Much research (Slate et al., 2009, Jehangir, 2010, Castillo-Montoya, 2018, Bass and Halverson, 2012) has shown that lecturers who recognize working-class students as already having valuable experiences that relate to subject-matter concepts are impactful. These authors suggest using multiple strategies, such as class discussion and writing reflections, to surface that knowledge and expand upon it to deepen knowledge of the academic concepts.

> When subject matter is connected to first-generation college students' lives, they are potentially positioned to help advance ways of knowing and doing in academia, and more specifically, their disciplines.
>
> (Ives and Castillo-Montoya, 2020, p159)

Working-class people also know their own skills and have agency. Smith and Lucena (2016) found that students developed ways to validate their class-specific backgrounds in engineering autonomously, and sought ways to incorporate their insights into their discipline. The students 'wished to change the way engineers consider ... the experiences and knowledges of people who work with their hands for a living' (Smith and Lucena, 2016, p23) for working-class students to display and integrate their cultural knowledge and lived experiences, some will identify ways to do autonomously.

Jenangir et al. (2011, 2012) emphasize the importance of self-authorship. If traditionally marginalized working-class students are enabled to integrate their cultures and lived experiences into the classroom it can lead to self-authorship – 'making decisions and navigating the world based on one's internal beliefs, values, and sense of self' (Jehangir et al., 2011, Jehangir et al., 2012). They found that this helps combat the marginalization and isolation they experience in higher education. Nuñez (2011) found that when working-class and BAME students learned more about their heritage through their studies, their confidence increased, and they were better able to handle racism and isolation on campus.

> Working with disenfranchised communities and learning about the systems that affect them ... was simultaneously liberatory and empowering, because it gave many of them the tools to critique the structural inequalities within that very same culture.
>
> (p59)

Castillo-Montoya and Reyes (2018) found working class-students' self-authorship 'enriched their understanding of sociocultural identities as well as their critical consciousness' (p13). Yeh (2010) recognized that this consciousness development enabled students to not only give back to their communities, but to relate these community issues to wider structural forces and tensions. Perhaps most importantly such approaches allow both students and the institution to grow rather than assimilate a new mutual way of learning can emerge.

> First-generation college students can learn the academy's and their disciplines' normative expectations while not sacrificing their own values. ... drawing on their unique knowledge to facilitate their success and to change the cultures they encountered in and outside the academy, including their disciplines and communities.
>
> (Ives and Castillo-Montoya, 2020, p163)

Going back to the idea of social capital (Putnam, 2000) and bridging capital in particular, such bridging social capital, as Ives and Castillo-Montoya (2020) described above has the potential to forge connections between heterogeneous groups, which promotes social connections and linkages with diverse groups, having the power to provide access to a broad range of 'new' opportunities. Through such capital, people from different backgrounds can connect and social mobility becomes possible. These networks and ties are outward looking and can comprise people from different social classes and identities. Bridging social capital may therefore provide an ideal mechanism to understand how individuals overcome the barriers associated with educational disadvantage. Access to bridging capital is crucial for facilitating progression to HE in low SES groups as it provides access to 'new' forms of capital, whereas bonding capital has the potential to close down opportunities within networks where progression to HE is not the norm (Vaughn, 2015, Hannon et al., 2017, Nicholson and Cleland, 2017).

Access

Perhaps unsurprisingly, people from socially advantaged areas are more likely to participate in higher education than those from socially disadvantaged areas (Blackburn et al., 2016, Harrison and Waller, 2017, Robinson et al., 2020). Richardson et al. (2020) found that there is increased competition for places, especially at the more selective universities, and this has had a disproportionately negative effect on students from socially disadvantaged areas (Blackburn et al., 2016). Official statistics show that despite increases since the mid-2000s of working-class students entering HE, there have been greater increases in middle-class participation, leaving working-class students still considerably less likely to participate (Rosado and David, 2006, Reay et al., 2017).

Crawford and Greaves (2015) found a consistent difference of around 38 percentage points in the participation rates of children in the top and bottom quintiles of the IMD (i.e. the least deprived and the most deprived neighbourhoods) and POLAR measures (pp31–2). According to HEFCE the 20 per cent most disadvantaged students are around six times less likely to participate in higher education than the 20 per cent most advantaged pupils. Recent research has consistently demonstrated a steep and persistent social-class gradient in overall rates of participation in higher education (Reay et al., 2017).

Outreach

Harvill et al. (2012) define five common components to successful outreach: counselling; mentoring; parental involvement; social enrichment (e.g. group field visits); and academic enrichment (e.g. supplementary after school academic tuition). Webb et al. (2017) stress the importance of human contact and not being too corporate, saying 'genuine' exchanges allow students to go 'beyond the curated and manicured portrayals of university that in a heavily marketised HE sector have become ubiquitous in official materials' (Webb et al., 2017, p45). Most authors agree interventions need to start early and engage young people at different stages of their educational career (Moore et al., 2013).

Undoing years of exposure to a gaslighting education system does not happen overnight, or more specifically with one off taster sessions. Evaluations of outreach and progression programmes with disadvantaged students highlight the importance of consistent and sustained interventions (Moore et al., 2013). Similarly, Bowes et al. (2019) found that engagement in multiple interventions is more likely to deliver positive outcomes than one-off interventions with a positive correlation between the number of outreach activities learners take part in and improvements in their self-reported knowledge, attitudes and intentions towards HE.

Financial

Growing up, it was instilled in me by my parents that university was important and that I would get a better job if I went. Quite why it was important, and how I would get better employment at the end of it was not quite clear, to my parents or me. Connor et al. (2001) and Stevenson and Lang (2010) note that potential university students from working-class backgrounds, and especially their parents, tend to emphasize the potential economic benefits of attending HE more than participants from other social classes, putting more emphasis on HE attendance as an effective way of increasing job prospects and future income.

Conversely, other authors (Archer, Hutchings and Ross, 2005, Callender and Jackson, 2008) say working-class students are more likely than their wealthier peers to perceive the costs of HE as a debt rather than an investment and, thus, to consider attending HE as an inherently risky endeavour that, despite requiring substantial investments of time, money and effort, affords uncertain benefits. We have also seen that, in real terms, while working-class graduates make more than their working-class peers who do not go to university, it is much less of a return on their investment than middle- and upper-class students.

Also, many middle-class students have suffered little financially during their degrees. Many parents have used the relatively cheap loans of their children to invest in property for them, who become student landlords with secure accommodation for three years, and a property to sell and set them up on the property ladder when they finish their studies. 'Buy for Uni' schemes are now promoted by mortgage companies for those that can have a deposit paid and guarantee assured by their parents of course. This is not accounting for the extra financial support that parents can give their children, including using their contacts to get them relatively lucrative work in the summer holidays.

Stevenson and Lang (2010) also note that fear of debt can affect the choice of universities to which working-class students apply. Students from low-income families are more likely to apply to universities with lower living costs and higher term-time employment opportunities or to enrol on shorter, less advanced courses so as to minimize debt and enter full-time work as early as possible. Forsyth and Furlong (2003) and Donnelly and Gamsu (2018) found that working-class students are three times more likely to be commuter students. As we note later, commuter universities tend to be new and new, new universities.

My upper working-class background instilled in me that one should live within your means and not be in debt. Memories of the workhouse and inescapable debt were still strong and only a couple of generations from being lived through. I went to university in the 1980s and had a full grant. I have no doubt that if I was university age now, I would never have gone. The 2019 Augar review (Post-18 review of education and funding: independent panel report) recommended bringing back a £3,000 maintenance grant for the disadvantaged. It also favoured capping fees to £7,500 with increased funding for 'subjects that align with the Industrial Strategy' and supporting disadvantaged students through increasing the Student Premium, which is a part of the teaching grant that goes to universities specifically for supporting disadvantaged students. However, two years later the government has only given an interim response to the report and not mentioned any of these aspects.

Foundation years

Foundation-year programmes are introductory years (occasionally shorter) aimed at students who, for a number of reasons, have not been identified as not being 'ready' for HE study. Webb et al. (2017) found that FY programmes can recognize that the challenges facing underrepresented groups in HE are complex and see the importance of supporting the development of peer relationships, academic skills and sense of belonging in the university. These activities aim to prevent students feeling under-qualified compared to their peers and aim to provide them with access to forms of bridging capital that support transitions and retention within HE. However, there are a number of philosophies of foundation years (Seal and Parkes, 2019, Hale, 2021), and they have different outcomes in relation to working-class students.

Talking to foundation year practitioners about how they perceive the role and purpose of foundation years in relation to social class, Hale (2021) found three discourses emerge. There is the radical discourse in which students are encouraged to challenge the whole system of HE and beyond, and staff do so openly. There is a second discourse where practitioners feel unable to challenge the system openly, but see the very existence of foundation years and their role in delivering them as subversive – changing the system from within by bringing working-class students into elite (and elitist) institutions. The final, and probably most common, discourse however is of assimilation in which the primary function of the foundation year is to prepare and equip (i.e. alter) students to fit into an alien environment through the provision of skills – as often social as academic – and giving them 'cultural capital'.

Hale (2021) goes on to note that the assimilation model most clearly represents a deficit model in which the student is mediated to fit an institution in which institutional change is seen as unnecessary, undesirable or impossible. In this, the student is an object to be acted upon. The discourse of subversion emerges from a more critical agenda but can use the working-class student as a political means to an end to subvert the system and end up damaging to them. Their years beyond the foundation year will often not have a culture of subversion, leaving them feeling alienated and being othered and blamed. Only the radical approach engendered in the discourse of challenge presents the student fully as subject, but this also brings its own problems and burdens. The more radical model confronts students with the fact that the odds are stacked against them. However, the ensuing anger and frustration can be channelled into a 'renewed sense of agency rather than a spiral into despair is the delicate path negotiated by foundation years' (Hale, 2021, p34). Exploring the radical model, Seal et al. (2019) suggest a set of aims for foundation years:

- to deconstruct and reconstruct students' previous educational experiences to resist internalized deficit thinking and negotiate the resources students will need to traverse higher education;
- to explore, deconstruct and reconstruct concepts encountered on the course including the language of higher education;
- to develop student confidence, self-belief and resilience to be able to traverse the landscape of higher education;

- to develop knowledge-generating spaces that are actively and mutually constituted to challenge those 'banking' models of education; and
- to discuss and co-construct student (and tutors) 'possible selves' that are drawn from and relate to past and future representations of 'self'.

The question then becomes what necessary pedagogic approaches are needed to achieve these aims. Elsewhere (Seal and Parkes, 2019) we identified the characteristics of these spaces in that they:

- are visceral, pedagogic and liminal, rather than safe, though certainly not dangerous;
- have an emphasis on deconstructing power both inside and outside of the space, and on the concept of knowledge and its creation;
- have a process framework of inter-subjectivity, encounter, recognition and working in the moment; and
- emphasize the cultivation of hope and a future orientation, recognizing an equivalence between reconstruction and deconstruction.

The pedagogic approach undertaken to date on Newman Foundation Years is underpinned by the aims outlined at the beginning of these concluding paragraphs above. Seal et al. (2019) acknowledge that this will not necessarily mirror the educational experiences students will then get on their degree. The moot question here is whether it should. We would argue that in order to promote the institutional transformation that Thomas and May (2011) assert is needed to support student transition for students with complex lives, it is in fact the pedagogies of subject areas that need to transform and change. Indeed, as a reflection of the complexity Foundation Years at Newman is working with, we include commentary below from our last two annual reports that identifies the characteristics of our students. These include:

- Highly complex lives that need sensitive processes such as mitigating circumstances, extensions, etc., that will be ongoing beyond the foundation year.
- The partial experiences of educational systems mean that while most students engage, this is often still fragile, fractured and needs nurturing. A lot of academic processes and conventions will not be natural to them. Many will not have the social and cultural capital of more traditional students.

- High levels of dyslexia and other learning needs that have impact on and are linked to their previous educational experience, often undiagnosed and unmediated.
- High levels of unresolved trauma and self-medication that have been a part of their previous non-engagement with education. Issues this year include bereavement, domestic violence, sex trafficking, sexual abuse, sexual assault, coming to terms with sexual orientation and others reaction to it, drug use, self-harm and suicidal ideation.
- High levels of diagnosed and undiagnosed mental health issues (around a third) as well as depression, anxiety, body dysmorphia, obsessive compulsive disorder, ADHD, etc.
- Other associated issues: approximately half of our students have had practical issues with finance, accommodation and other welfare issues, as they often live independently, but precariously.

Positively, Seal et al. (2019) found students after the course had high levels of self-awareness, resilience and ability to self-manage. The characteristics above remain a reality and thus do not reflect the 'ideal student': The university or the sector should not expect them to be. Many of these characteristics will prevail across the students' lives whilst at university: such dynamics cannot be undone within one academic year nor indeed, in some instances, at all. Nonetheless, as educators and institutions, we should strive to change our practices that take account of where the people in front of us are at. Here, we can build a students' confidence in their abilities and develop their responses to the demands of university study in the hope that this simultaneously fosters a sense of agency that sets them on a road to fulfilment and human flourishing. Seal et al. conclude about those who run these programmes:

> We consider ourselves Self Identifying Critical Pedagogues might have meaningful impact on our students through our pedagogy. Defending the rights of these students, prioritising their needs, and forcing wider the cracks in order to allow them to 'dance' in university spaces requires a determined, educated hope (Solnit, 2016) in those of us privileged enough to work on the programme.
>
> (Seal et al., 2019, p126)

Success

Several authors (Clarke and Beech, 2018, Office for Students (OfS), 2018a) note that disparities remain between different groups of students in the rates of continuation and final degree attainment. Some of these disparities are 'structural' (e.g. entry qualification, subject of study and age), while others are 'unexplained' once these structural factors are taken into account (OfS, 2019a). Students from low participation neighbourhoods are more likely to drop out (8.8 per cent) than students from other neighbourhoods (6 per cent). The number of UK-domiciled, young, first-degree qualifiers obtaining a first or upper second classification degree was 10 percentage points higher for students from POLAR4 (Participation of Local Areas) quintile 5 than for those from quintile.

In terms of attainment the OfS (2020) found the rate of achieving a first or upper-second-class degree reduces with socio-economic classification (not including mature students). Students from intermediate, manual and unemployed backgrounds all have lower attainment rates than students from higher backgrounds. For qualifiers in 2018–19, the attainment rate of students from an intermediate background was 5.2 percentage points lower than students from a higher background. The attainment rate of students from a manual background was 8.6 percentage points lower than students from a higher background. Students from an unemployed background had an attainment rate 21.5 percentage points lower than students from a higher background.

Interventions

First-year experience

Studies that focus on the experience of students during their first year are more plentiful, particularly in the states. McGrath and Burd (2012) found key elements of successful programmes included session on academic skills (such as note-taking), exploration of different subject possibilities, and engagement with teaching staff, advisors and student services. As many as 40 per cent of students who had attended the course continued through to the fourth year compared with just 6 per cent of students from previous years. While successful, all of these studies have highly individualized approaches. Huntly and Donovan (2009) see academic persistence and time spent on task as a precursor to individual retention. However, they also acknowledge cultural interaction and institutional change, recommending HEIs encourage contact between students and faculty; develop reciprocity and cooperation among students; use active learning techniques; give prompt feedback; emphasize time on task; communicate high expectations; and respect diverse talents and ways of learning. Alexander and Gardner (2009) developed a framework with nine 'Foundational Dimensions' for an effective first year and argue that meeting the needs of first-year students requires a cohesive strategic institutional approach.

Summer school after the first year

Webb et al. (2017) also found that the long summer break after the first year can be another trigger point for withdrawal. Adelman (2004) concurs that 'academic momentum' is needed for success of working-class students. Accredited summer schools can offer a 'boost' to the momentum of students at risk of withdrawal. The length of time taken to complete a degree programme is also a key factor as Jones, founder of the Complete College America programme, argues that, 'the longer it takes, the more life gets in the way and the less likely students are to graduate' (Austin and Jones, 2015, p26). The report, 'Time Is the Enemy' (Complete College America, 2011) argues that certain students' progress must be speeded up in the early years and shows that those who attended summer school at the end of their first year had between 7 per cent and 11 per cent point advantage upon graduation. Attewell and Jang (2013) note that although the summer schools have not historically been associated with attempts to increase retention and completion rates, students who attend summer schools at the end of their first year are 11 per cent more likely to continue their studies through to graduation.

Intersections with mental health

Many scholars have connected the concept of 'sense of belonging' and mental health-related factors; for example, Cohen and Wills (1985) found that social support, to an extent, promotes psychological health while others (e.g. Sargent et al., 2002) have found that sense of belonging, as a form of social support, contributes to overall well-being and is inversely related to depression Therefore, it is likely that working-class students' mental depression or stress may be attributed to their lower sense of belonging on campus. Hagerty, Williams, Boyne and Early (1996) identified linkages between the concepts of sense of belonging, social support and psychological and physical illness, noting the direct and indirect roles that sense of belonging plays in the 'management of stress and the prevention of amelioration of both physical and psychological illness' (p237).

Educators and administrators should consider the ways in which student development programmes and activities that aim to explore identity issues include a focus on social class identities of students. While some scholars such as Gos (1995) suggested that college professors work to help students 'overcome' their working-class 'markers' so that they can experience a 'border crossing that is less traumatic and carries with it no lifelong scars' (p33), Sofia et al. (2013) found value in helping working-class students to integrate their multiple identities instead of overcoming their working-class identity (Abes, Jones and McEwen, 2007).

We need an approach to pedagogy that recognizes working-class skills, knowledge, autonomy and ways of learning, and that such acknowledgement may give us a blueprint for a more liberatory view of the 'ideal' student. Stevenson and Lang (2010) writing ten years ago said academic staff 'need to develop pedagogies that engage socially, culturally and educationally diverse students more effectively, in both traditional and new subjects' (David et al., 2009, p25).

Furlong and Cartmel (2009) recommend that teaching need not penalize students who need to miss classes, who study part-time and who opt into, out of and back into higher education. Several authors (Smith, MacGregor, Matthews and Gabelnick, 2004, Jehangir, 2010, Soria, 2013) suggest educators might consider engaging working-class students through alternate strategies such as learning communities targeted towards working-class populations, allowing students who are employed or have other obligations and opportunity to interact with peers related to their academic work. Kuh et al. (2008) and Soria (2013) advocated that students have capstone experiences, common book experiences, writing intensive classes and other options that involve intentional academic engagement objectives (Kuh et al. 2005, Lardner and Malnarich, 2008). Study groups, peer mentorship and peer advising programmes can enhance working-class students' sense of belonging while at the same time helping them to feel less like 'outsiders' who need extra assistance from authoritative figures (Soria, 2013).

The need for working-class lecturers and working-class cultures and pedagogies

As Crew (2020) notes, the majority of lecturers, and particularly professors and senior management still pre-dominantly come from middle-class and professional backgrounds (Crew, 2020). Ultimately having well-meaning, but middle-class, lecturers attempt to accommodate working-class ways of knowing in an inherently colonial enterprise. Eventually we need a proportionate a number of working-class lecturers in university, who, as Crew (2020) says, have developed working-class solidarity and a counter-culture to the dominant cultural and pedagogic norms. Advance HE (2018) suggests that greater diversity of staff could address social-class disparities in student satisfaction. US sources found that diverse faculty (academic staff), namely global majority, women and working-class faculty, are more likely to integrate race, gender or class issues into their curricula (Zandy, 1990, Milem et al., 2001). A number also found that global majority, women and working-class faculty, employ a wider and more inclusive range of pedagogical techniques (Hurtado et al., 2012, Milem et al., 2001).

Several authors suggest diverse faculty create a comfortable environment and provide mentoring and encouragement for students from similar backgrounds to themselves (Stephens and Barber, 2003, Umbach, 2006, Griffith and Rask, 2014). Others discuss the potential downside of this, that is, diverse faculty can be overburdened with support for diverse students, and this can negatively affect research output and progression to senior levels (Baez, 2000, Social Sciences Feminist Network Research Interest Group, 2017).

Binns (2019) offers a pessimistic vision. She identifies three types of working-class academics. Those who had 'moved considerably away from the original working-class background [… and] saw themselves as middle-class nowadays'. A second group who 'comfortably straddled the two classes [… but] occasionally, were not sure which class group they belonged to' and a third group who 'found the process of social mobility to be painful' and generally 'considered themselves to be working-class despite their educational and professional achievements'. She talks about 'ghosts of habitus' that reappeared throughout their transition and progression through academia. Their habitus becomes split between their original working-class habitus and present middle-class habitus.

At the same time as experiencing several positive outcomes associated with entering a middle-class occupation – increased levels of economic and cultural capital, for instance – there was a simultaneous emotional ambivalence and consciousness of their social mobility. Crew (2020) notes how working-class lecturers who do not shed their background continue to suffer micro-aggressions, be passed over for promotions and their imposter syndromes persist. Positively, Crew (2020) offers a positive blueprint for working-class lecturer solidarity, which has the potential to change the dominant cultural and pedagogical hegemony.

Progression

Gaskell and Lingwood (2019) note how insufficient attention has been given to 'the equalisation of opportunity post graduation for students of a given ability' and level of achievement while at university, regardless of their social or financial background (Gaskell and Lingwood, 2019, p9). Gaskell and Lingwood (2019) also note that other measurements of disadvantage used here suggest that more disadvantaged students are less likely to enter further study six months after graduating (Gaskell and Lingwood, 2019, p10). Additionally, research from the Resolution Foundation outlines how 'very large educational advantages for those from higher socioeconomic backgrounds persist, and show few signs of abating' (Henehan, 2019, p23).

Working with employers

Aside from the problems of direct discrimination against potential working-class employees (Stevenson, 2019), Gaskell and Linwood talk about a tautology whereby working-class students are judged as having not shown communication, networking and resilience, the skills many employers talk about looking for, despite the fact that this was something that their middle-class counterparts came to university with these advantages. Such constructions do not look at context. Characterization of a perceived lack of these attributes as a personal social capital 'deficit' risks overlooking or undervaluing a richness in social capital associated with, say, membership of a close-knit and strongly connected community (Gaskell and Linwood, 2019).

Gaskell and Linwood (2019) recommend that employers consider both the individual and community aspects of social capital. They also recommend that universities help strengthen their students' recognition of the social capital and resilience they have drawn on, and have deepened and widened this. We also need to reconceptualize our relationships with our local area, for that is where working-class students will seek employment. In doing this we need to honour and incorporate working-class experiences and ways of knowing in such a way that we can liberate all and the teaching and learning experience. I will return to this in the conclusion, looking at the idea of regional mobility, as there are similar dimensions of localism for Global Majority and disabled students.

The class-based nature of the doctorate

Once when asked how I would sum up the experience of being a doctoral student, I responded 'class torture'. The doctoral viva was a classic example of this. To get through the viva you have to demonstrate the same level of social capital, confidence, self-assuredness and arrogance, which to the middle class may be 'natural', but which coming from a working-class background it was quite alien. Doctoral study is also meant to be 'independent study'. At best you have to identify what is your personal contribution, and preferably the study is undertaken just be the candidate. Constantly in my academic careers I have had to place less emphasis on 'we' and far more on 'I'. This is culturally laden – I have tried to operate collectively and collegially all my life, stemming from my class background which emphasizes collectivity. We will consider in further studies how doctoral study is also gendered, racialized, disablist and ageist.

Crew (2020) recognizes other classed dimensions of the doctoral student experience. In terms of finance, working-class students often have to work long hours to supplement their income, or suffer from an assumption that students will be supported by parents in the writing-up period. Crew (2020) also found that working-class students look for employment straight after gaining their doctorates, rather than waiting till their book comes out, and a few more articles, to then apply for more prestigious positions. Gaskell and Linwood (2019) recommend that further research is required to understand the decision making by individual graduates with respect to entering postgraduate study. The OfS survey on graduates' intentions after graduation identified course fees as the main factor students would take into account when deciding whether or not to progress to further study (OfS, 2019d). However, Strike and Toyne (2015) found countervailing factors may be for working-class students to overcome a competitive disadvantage associated with prior educational experience. Pennacchia, Jones and Aldridge (2018), in research commissioned by the DfE, identified barriers to learning such as cost, childcare, awareness of opportunities and employer support.

Conclusion

Working-class relative failure in going to, succeeding at, and progressing from university is endemic and not neutral. Middle-class constructions of what it is to be and succeed at university covertly dominate, both culturally and in exclusionary processes that do not really want to see working-class students' progress. We need to disrupt normative assumptions about learning and unearth the class-ridden nature of the assimilation model that much widening participation initiatives are underpinned by. Positively there is an alternative and more equitable view of who the working-class, and indeed all students are capable of being. We just need to 'support them holistically in their pursuit to learn by creating more equitable academic environments' (Ives and Castillo-Montoya, 2020, p163).

In terms of interventions we firstly need to look at practical and financial help, without collapsing into debunked 'hierarchy of needs' arguments – it needs to be practically viable for students to go to university. However, while this may enable working-class students to go to university, it by no means enables them to stay and thrive. For that we need to acknowledge and then deconstruct the classed idealized myth of a student norm around which universities and support services are constructed. Such deconstruction needs to happen throughout the lifecycle from outreach, through foundation years, and first-year experiences, through to leaving, enabling working-class students to recognize how education has gaslighted them with regard to their ability and cultural fit to date.

We also need to re-conceptualize progression, de-classing the graduate school experience and recognizing the class-bound nature of the doctorate. We will find in subsequent chapters that these dynamics are similar in terms of race and disability – an intersectional approach is needed. Finally, we need to acknowledge that changing things at the university level, which is what is in our power to do, does not impact on the significant structural issues focused on in the first section of this book.

I will leave the last word of this chapter to Bourdieu, who sums up the cultural construction of higher education at its worst and gives us something to aspire to not be.

> This privileged instrument of the bourgeois sociodicy which confers on the privileged the supreme privilege of not seeing themselves as privileged manages the more easily to convince disinherited that they owe their scholastic and social destiny to their lack of gifts or merits, because in matters of culture absolute dispossession excludes awareness of being dispossessed.
>
> (Bourdieu, Passeron and Nice, 1977, p210)

5

Global Majority Students: The Politics of Denial

Introduction

Historically there is a politics of denial around race in higher education (hooks, 2014). Singh (2011) suggests that racism has hitherto remained relatively unexplored. Citing Back (2004), he explains there is the possibility that white academics only ascribe attributes of tolerance and reason to themselves, and the university environment. This, Back (2004) maintains, leads to the belief that racism cannot exist within the atmosphere of higher education and that the problem must lay elsewhere. As hooks eloquently sums it up

> The goal of racial equality is, while comforting to many whites, more illusory than real for blacks. For too long, we have worked for substantive reform, then settled for weakly worded and poorly enforced legislation, indeterminate judicial decisions, token government positions, even holidays … If we are to seek new goals for our struggles, we must first reassess the worth of racial assumptions on which, without careful thought, we have presumed too much and relied on too long.
>
> (hooks, 2014, pp13–14)

Singh (2011) agrees that causal factors such as lack of family support, time in paid employment (Connor et al., 2004) and financial hardship (Dhanda, 2009 and 2010) are at play and need to be examined, but we should be permanently mindful of the wider structural context. Senior (2013) notes many of these attributes may be applicable to students from widening participation (WP) backgrounds generally rather than students from minority ethnic backgrounds specifically. However, there are some specific trends.

This chapter will begin by exploring the theoretical perspectives that seek to explain the relative disadvantage of Global Majority students, in particular anti-oppressive practice, critical race theory and intersectionality, within the context of the themes of the book. It will then consider the importance of taking a whole institutional approach, for without this we are simply tinkering and reinscribing deficit models of Global Majority staff and students. It will assess the empirical evidence exploring how, while Global Majority students are represented well compared to, say white working-class students, in higher education overall, they undertake certain courses and go to certain institutions. Once in higher education, Global Majority student attainment, continuation and progression rates are not positive. They drop out, achieve less and, even when their qualifications are comparable with white students, go onto less well-paying jobs and rarely further study, particularly doctoral study. Concurrently we will consider initiatives and approaches to outreach and access, retention and attainment and progression, evaluating peer approaches, developing senses of belonging and the importance of a representative staff force.

There will be a focus on staff and staff development as part of this, as we have already catalogued how Global Majority staff are marginalized with higher education, and have their labour exploited. The rest of the chapter will consider some of the debates and evolving knowledge base around decolonising and liberating the curriculum, assessment, epistemology and pedagogy. We will explore decolonising approaches, stemming from the campaign 'why is my curriculum white'. However, authors such as Gus John feel these campaigns have become too narrow in their focus, at a base level asking us to close the gaps in academic attainment and widen the selection of the reading list. However, this can become individualist and ignore the wider systemic issues as we have 'failed to dismantle the structural and cultural manifestations of discrimination and exclusion'. We need to go far beyond what gets onto reading lists, and contest the epistemological and pedagogical bases of the cannon, including who gets to create that cannon and unearth hidden, unfairly discredited and denied knowledge bases.

Theoretical positions

Until relatively recently the belief that black underachievement is biologically determined was the dominant discourse in the academy, most contemporaneously expressed through Murray and Herrnsteins 'Bell Curve' (1994). Higher education has a history of being actively racist. Threads of this argument are still at play. Stevenson and Whellan (2013) note:

> The notion of ethnic minority 'deficit', 'lack' or cultural deprivation has persisted, with the poor performance of minority students frequently considered the result of an impoverished home life, lacking parental support for education, and/or a language-poor environment. The deficiencies that appear to operate within many ethnic minority families (other than Asian) are perpetuated when white familial values are regarded as the norm.
> (Stevenson and Wheelan, 2013, p43)

One current manifestation of this is in the argument that increasing participation means that you get more students with less 'natural' ability. Amis (1960, p9) criticized proposals to expand UK higher education in the 1960s using the slogan 'More will mean worse'. Leslie (2005, p. 631) used the same argument to suggest that higher participation rates in Asian and Black students would lead to 'a diminution in average quality of applicant'. The 'More will mean worse' argument does not explain some of the disparities in attainment in higher education among different ethnic groups. For example, Leslie (2005) himself found that white students were still more likely to obtain good degrees than students from all ethnic minority groups, even when differences in their entry qualifications and subject choices had been taken into account. The HEFCE (2020, p22) data analysis also found that some but by no means all the variation in attainment across ethnic groups could be attributed to differences in their entry qualifications or other characteristics.

Anti-oppressive practice

Models such as anti-oppressive practice, anti-racism and cultural competence are well-documented (Thompson, 2012) and have been movements within higher education since the 1970s. They 'recognize the structural forces that create oppression at the same time as working with individuals in ways that mitigate its impact and promote social justice' (Hollinrake et al., 2019, p258). They have often been adopted within more radical versions of professional courses such as youth work and social work (Seal and Frost, 2014). However, its influence at a wider institutional level is more contested (Seal, 2021).

Kumashiro's (2002) work is closest to this book in its approach. He attempts to unite anti-oppressive practice with critical pedagogy and queer pedagogy (Seal, 2019). He critiques an activist anti-oppressive practice that reinforces binaries, essentializes and situates all oppression at the level of the structural. He similarly critiques a simple Freirean analysis with a rigid binary of oppressor and oppressed that 'merely replaces one (socially hegemonic) framework for seeing the world with another (academically hegemonic) one' (Kumshiro, 2002, p23) emphasizing instead articulations of critical pedagogy that emphasize developing critical capacities within students (Friere, 1996). I think he is accurate in his attack on the realities of much critical pedagogy, although this is more of a comment on lived practice than critical pedagogies foundations which foregrounds 'conscientization' (Seal, 2021b). I would also agree that critical pedagogues need to 'extend their analysis to their own lives, and critique it for what it overlooks or forecloses' (Kumashiro, 2002, p132).

Kumashiro (2002) then offers four approaches for educators to work with oppression which are illuminative. These are 'education for the other', 'education about the other', 'education that is critical of privileging and othering' and 'education that changes students and society'. It is the last approach that he favours. For him we have to explicitly examine how we individually and collectively create the 'other' within our pedagogic spaces. He outlines a variety of ways in which this can happen, through direct discussion, via an interweaving of critique of othering into specific subject matters, and/or through the implicit embedding of critique of othering into general classroom interactions and discussions.

Critical race theory

A more recent approach is critical race theory (CRT) (Gilbourn, 2015) which focuses on the structure of institutions and highlights the ways in which racism is manifested in higher education through the privileging of the (often male) white middle-class to the detriment of poor people of colour (Yosso 2005, Patton et al., 2007). CRT aims to question and challenge both the discourses and structures that produce and maintain racial injustices. Daniel Solórzano (1997, 1998) identified five tenets of CRT in education, as follows:

The intercentricity and permanence of race and racism. CRT starts from the premise that race and racism are central, endemic, permanent and a fundamental part of defining and explaining how United States and latterly UK societies function (Russell, 1992, Bell, 1995). CRT acknowledges the inextricable layers of racialized subordination based on gender, class, immigration status, surname, phenotype, accent and sexuality (Collins, 1986, Crenshaw et al., 1995).

Challenging white supremacy and whiteness as ideology. CRT challenges white privilege and refutes the claims that educational institutions make of objectivity, meritocracy, colour blindness, race neutrality and equal opportunity. CRT argues that traditional claims of 'objectivity' and 'neutrality' camouflage the self-interest, power and privilege of dominant groups in US society (Bell, 1987, Calmore, 1991, Solórzano, 1997). While contested as simplistic, D'Angelo (2018) coined the term 'White Fragility' to explain the defensiveness of white people when confronted with their complicitness in taking advantage of their white privilege afforded to them by their institutions. CRT implies that if a white person is afraid of saying the wrong thing, or of the results of challenging their own and others privilege, and consequently they do nothing, they are taking advantage of their own privilege.

Probably the most controversial aspect of CRT, Walmington sees naming 'white supremacy' as an attempt to distinguish white *people* from whiteness as ideology. In CRT white supremacy is 'a political system, a particular power structure of formal and informal rule, privilege, socio-economic advantages' (Taylor et al., 2009, p4). Nevertheless, Walmington also notes that whiteness can be used politically in that it can 'serve to unify both privileged and disadvantaged whites in ways that secure and stabilise the social order'. He notes that while advantages accrue principally to white elites, they can also be doled out strategically (and unevenly) to the white working classes such that they buffer white elites (the white working classes). This redistribution can also be a promise that is given, but remains unfulfilled.

The universal voting of white people in America across class divides for Trump, and the northern working-class voting for the conservatives in the 2019 UK general election is evidence of this. Recent parliamentary debates around the neglect of the white working class educationally, with a view that white privilege does not help seem to be a blatant example of this, with some very privileged white men trying to buy the support of the white working class once more, with probably empty promises. Trump never fulfilled his promises to the Rust Belt and Boris Johnson seems unlikely to do the same with the northern working class. While white working-class students may not feel their privilege or material gain from it relative to white elites, they are often relatively advantaged compared to Global Majority students, particularly from working-class backgrounds themselves. Perhaps more importantly, as we also do not want to fall into the regressive forces old trap of getting poor groups of people to compare their relative poverty, and playing them off against each other, the white working class need to be aware when they are being bought off with often false promises from white elites in exchange for buffering the status quo.

Commitment to social justice beyond 'interest convergence'. CRT's social and racial justice research agenda exposes the 'interest convergence' (Bell, 1987) whereby apparently progressive measures to address racial inequality are initiated only at moments when demands for reform converge with the self-interest of white elites. Resulting measures, steeped in 'liberal self-congratulation', tend to address only the most blatant kinds of discrimination which are then constructed as racism being resolved rendering further action unnecessary and excessive. Walmington (2020, p22) notes that 'it is only when racist practices threaten to destabilise rather than secure elite power that it is in the self-interest of elites to address racism through legislation and policy'. Instead, CRT argues for a more fundamental elimination of racism, sexism and poverty, as well as the empowerment of people of colour and other subordinated groups (Freire, 1996, Lawson, 1995, Solórzano and Delgado Bernal, 2001).

Centrality of experiential knowledge. CRT recognizes the experiential knowledge of people of colour as legitimate, appropriate and critical to understanding, analysing and teaching about racial subordination (Delgado Bernal, 2002). CRT draws explicitly on the lived experiences of people of colour by including such methods as storytelling, family histories, biographies, scenarios, parables, cuentos, testimonios, chronicles and narratives (Bell, 1987, Yosso, 2005). A particular emphasis is placed on the accumulation of everyday micro-aggressions, and their impact, as opposed to the white liberal emphasis on more evert extreme examples.

Transdisciplinary perspective. CRT extends beyond disciplinary boundaries to analyse race and racism within both historical and contemporary contexts (Olivas, 1990, Gotanda, 1991, Calmore, 1997, Delgado and Stefancic, 2000b, Gutiérrez-Jones, 2001).

CRT and the work of hooks certainly seem compatible with the book's first theme, and comes down firmly on the side that higher education re-inscribes elite privileged power bases, rather than HEIs being progressive forces for social good, justice and mobility.

Intersectionality, simultaneity and Kyriarchy

As outlined in the introduction, 'intersectionality' (Crenshaw, 1991, Davis, 2008, Collins, 2020), 'simultaneity' (Carastathis, 2016) and 'Kyriarchy' (Fiorenza, 1993) are approaches that have been foregrounded in the last forty years. To recap, they are all approaches which recognize that multiple oppressions can compound one another, that people can simultaneously have privilege and be oppressed, and that these processes interact. The importance of the approach for examining disadvantage in higher education has also come to the fore (Byrd and Adsit, 2019, Mitchell, Marie and Steele, 2019, Nichols and Stahl 2019). Byrd et al. (2019) give a comprehensive view on the state of play as experienced by student in the states. Mitchell, Marie and Steele (2019) give a particularly informative perspective, both theoretically and in terms of praxis for educators. However as Nichols and Stahl (2019) in their 2019 systematic review note, 'there is considerable work to be done to actively address the workings of intersecting systems of inequity impacting on participation and outcomes of students and faculty' (Nichols and Stahl 2019, p1255).

In 2021, in the UK, Anuj Kapilashrami produced the 'Intersectionality-informed Framework for Tackling Racism and Embedding Inclusion and Diversity in Teaching & Learning', explicitly aimed at higher education.

The framework has three core objectives. The first is situated learning and problem analysis, 'raising collective consciousness by reflecting on one's position and values, and challenging normative assumptions in the course content that "other" individuals and groups' (Kapilashrami, 2021, p4). The second is enhancing inclusivity by 'appraising accessibility and inclusivity of curriculum, content and pedagogy' (Kapilashrami, 2021, p4). The third is transformative practice, i.e 'taking broader actions to equip staff and students to appreciate diversity, tackle discrimination & transform learning through accountable, transparent and reflexive praxis' (Kapilashrami, 2021, p4). It has six guiding principles that are drawn from Hankivsky et al.'s IBPA framework (equity and social justice, intersecting identities or categories of justice, reflexivity, power analysis, multi-level analysis and respecting and unearthing diverse knowledges). She explicitly sees intersectionality as an analytical tool to avoid siloing, while recognizing that multiple oppressions compound one another. In this regards our approaches seem more than compatible. The framework is staged, but flexible and tries to 'embed the principles and objectives in teaching and learning cycle and environment' (Kapilashrami, 2021, p5).

Kapilashrami (2021) outlines practices at three levels that concur with my focus on the everyday experiences and interactions within higher education, which acknowledges and accounts for wider institutional and structural issues and forces. Firstly she foregrounds 'content design' where practitioners should 'ensure the imparted knowledge does not reinforce inequalities and prejudices against people of colour and other minorities and presents diverse perspectives' (Kapilashrami, 2021, p6). Secondly 'classroom delivery' where practitioners should 'ensure learning occurs in a reflective and interactive space, enabling respectful and meaningful participation from all' (Kapilashrami, 2021, p6). Finally there practitioners, and the institution, should engage in illuminating, analysing and changing 'Culture' pertaining to the 'wider institutional environment and system-wide changes necessary for an equal and fairer society' (Kapilashrami, 2021, p6). Kapilashrami (2021) provides reflexive questions and considerations for all of these dimensions, which we will return to when considering different Global Majority interventions.

The importance of and principles for taking a whole institutional approach

> The importance of embedding this agenda is also apparent, with both the pervading sense that this work has to occur at all levels of an institution, raising the awareness, skills and confidence of all staff, and ensuring that this agenda is included in strategic vision, strategic plans, and the work of various university boards and committees.
>
> (Miller, 2016, p32)

Writing back in 2016, Miller emphasized the importance of a whole institutional approach for Global Majority students. Even earlier, May and Bridger (2010) felt that change was required at both institutional and individual level to bring about inclusive policy and practice. As Arday (2020) notes, to truly counter some of the institutional denials around discrimination and the marginalization of Global Majority staff and students in higher education takes time, humility and commitment.

> Involvement in diversifying the existing canon requires a recognition of privilege, capital and essentially an unlearning or disrupting of knowledge saturated in historical amnesia and carefully curated colonial histories designed to subjugate and exploit 'the other'. The epistemological transformation of the Academy and the decolonisation of the curriculum requires targeted interventions such as PhD Studentships for aspiring ethnic minority scholars to diversify academic communities and pedagogical input within university institutions.
>
> (Arday, 2020, p232)

Kapilashrami (2021) advocates a number of approaches that strengthen institutional leadership and ensure that sufficient depth is achieved. She recommends steering bodies for institutional change have representational equity (e.g. race, gender, disability), allocate resources and provide support (including mentoring, shadowing, coaching). She also highlights a need for spaces for students, academic and professional staff to share experiences of discrimination. I have known institutions that resist such transparency, labelling it as unprofessional, undermining the confidence of students in the institution or somehow a burden to them. I have also seen Kapilashrami's (2021) recommendation to develop effective and anonymous reporting mechanisms and independent committees for grievance redressal, with a response that mechanisms already exist. There was a culture that when current mechanisms were not being used, it was seen as a sign that there was not an issue, rather than that processes were not working. I would also agree with Kapilashrami's (2021) call to institutionalize independent mechanisms to assess and monitor wider risks. However, this depends on how these mechanisms are framed and contracted. I have seen institutions undertake such reviews, and simply ignore or marginalize the subsequent recommendations.

Stevenson et al. (2019) also advocate some more interesting ways of holding institutions to account that pushes towards a more indepth approach, including making their Global Majority gap data public to all students and staff, both internally and externally and tying the performance-related pay of senior leaders to institutional progress made in addressing ethnic inequalities. They also suggest using a number of approaches that are again more radical. Firstly are positive action (PA) approaches, pioneered by Professor Chantal Davies at the University of Chester which built on the principles of affirmative action, saying the in-depth pro-active approaches are both necessary and legal. Kapilashrami (2021) concurs in terms of intersectionality, recommending that positive action measures are utilized to increase representation of intersectionally marginalized people among educators and professional staff in general, and in senior management.

Secondly Stevenson et al. (2019) and Kutscher and Truckwiller (2019) advocate developing participatory action research (PAR) interventions to research and evaluation, 'with people rather than for people driven by participants and based on their own concerns' (Stevenson et al., 2019). Of particular importance is that, as well as being a robust approach to research, participatory approaches impact on cultural change as they embed a culture of learning, co-production and of valuing research and each other within organizations, as well as creating mechanisms for developing evidence for, monitoring and evaluating other ideas and initiatives (Seal, 2018). Participatory research can help those who may have a naturally liberal disposition realize first hand that a more in-depth structural change is needed, and point towards ways of imagining and planning for such change.

Elsewhere I make a case for research to be a synthesis of participatory research, critical pedagogy, peer research and community organizing – a model I call Participatory Pedagogic Impact Research (PPIR) (Seal, 2018). Participatory research is not without its critics (Cooke and Kothari, 2001) and the book explores and hopefully ameliorates some of these concerns. In particular, participatory approaches are criticized for not having the impact they promise. PPIR ensures that the issues chosen, and the recommendations developed, serve the mutual self-interest of stakeholders, are realistic and realizable. At the same time this approach pushes the balance of power towards the oppressed using methods of dissemination that hold decision makers to account and create real change. PPIR also develops a robust method for creatively identifying issues, methods and analytic frameworks.

Thirdly Stevenson et al. (2019) advocate using a Community Cultural Wealth approach to designing interventions, based on the work of Tara Yosso. Yosso conceptualizes community cultural wealth as a critical race theory (CRT) challenge to traditional interpretations of cultural and social capital, designing interventions which challenge these traditional views and constructions of capital and honours the cultural practices that students bring from their communities and backgrounds. I agree with such an approach but would advocate retaining a critical eye, recognizing that the idea of cultural and social capital can all too often be a mask for raw privilege in that it is not something that disadvantaged students can attain, or more accurately a few are allowed to gain such capital to maintain the delusion that it can be attained, and that a meritocracy is achievable.

Training as a re-enforcer, not a strategy

As mentioned in the introduction, all too often, interventions come down to training, and training, in Kumashiro's terms, about the other, not for working with them towards emancipation. Even recent calls for unconscious bias training (Stephenson et al., 2019, OfS, 2020,), which is laudable in context, are in danger of individualizing racism unless such training is part of a wider strategy of deculturization with mechanisms for staff and students to reflect on wider institutional bias.

The emphasis should be on Kumashiro's (2002) 'education that is critical of privileging and othering', and 'education that changes students and society'. All too often inclusion training is one of many elements of corporate training to be ticked off. Additional courses and seminars are rarely compulsory, and often speak to the converted (or at least convertible). There is potential to build a more indepth consideration of Global Majority issues, and inclusivity in general, into PGCerts in Higher Education. However, these courses only meaningfully impact on new lecturers – arguably those with least power and cultural sway within the institution.

Access

Interestingly, in the UK children from all ethnic minority groups are more likely than white children to proceed from secondary education to higher education (DOE, 2015, OfS, 2020). Interestingly, these patterns remained very similar even when variations in the children's social class (as measured by parental occupation) had been taken into account (Crawford and Greaves, 2015). Aspirations for higher education show similar patterns (Berrington et al., 2016). Positive aspirations to participate in higher education were highest in Black Caribbean children (86 per cent), Indian children (82 per cent), Black African children (81 per cent) and Bangladeshi children (78 per cent).

However, patterns of which institutions and courses Global Majority students go to are very different from those of white students. MIller (2016) found that Global Majority students are less likely to take science or maths, more likely to study arts. Engineering, architecture and science subjects attract a greater proportion of young Pakistani and Bangladeshi, Chinese and Indian and other Asian students compared to students from other groups. Global Majority students are also more likely to come from and study in urban areas, be commuter students (Thomas and Jones, 2017), to study at low entry profile HEIs (majoritively post-1992 universities) and to study where there are other Global Majority students and Global Majority culture/history on the syllabus.

Boliver (2013) found that Black and Asian students were less likely to receive offers from Russell Group institutions than white students with similar qualifications. Essentially elite universities have not recruited Global Majority students, while post-1992 universities have. There is nuance and studying with other Global Majority students seems to be a dominant factor. Post-1992 low-tariff commuter universities from areas with low Global Majority populations, such as Gloucester and Suffolk, still recruit below the average for the local areas Global Majority population.

Debt

'Social debt' plays a part in considering HE study – Global Majority students are more likely to be funded by parental contributions, which can foster a feeling of needing to pay them back in kind (Miller, 2016). Global Majority students are the least likely to take out loans, more likely to live at home, and are more debt-averse. Students from low socio-economic backgrounds are more likely to take on part-time work. The more hours a student works in term time, the lower their attainment is likely to be. Expected course costs and debts influence the choices made about where and whether to study. While this is not unique to Global Majority students, these factors may have a larger impact on them due to their increased likelihood of coming from low socio-economic backgrounds, and the higher rates of debt aversion.

Family

The impact of family is contested. Several authors (Bernhardt, 2013, Gonzalez, 2013, Webb et al., 2017a) found family support integral in motivating students' HE applications. A survey of access programmes in Virginia found that 27 per cent had parents as a major influence, and a further 53 per cent listed them as a secondary influence (Alleman et al., 2009). However, this depends on the target group and we will explore family and community impacts in more depth in subsequent chapters.

Research in the UK (Strand, 2011, 2012, Vincent et al., 2012) has consistently found that Black-British parents tend to value education highly and strongly encourage their children to attend university. However, Jacobs et al. (2005) reported that parents of some Global Majority students exerted pressure on their children to undertake degrees such as Law, Accounting or Medicine rather than 'non-vocational' choices such as subjects in the humanities. Cotton et al. (2016) suggest that strong family influence when choosing a degree may result in students being on courses with in which they have little interest, ultimately limiting the extent to which they engage with the content, tutors and other students. Regarding the use of peers (including family and community leaders), Webb et al. (2017) found that it is a major challenge to ensure that influencers working with under-represented groups are well informed about HE. However, this view can play into the 'information fallacy' that Global Majority students are not informed about the positives of university, and if they know them they would come.

A live debate is whether interventions should be targeted at Global Majority communities or students, or whether existing provision should be more culturally sensitive and inclusive. Singh (2011) details literature that discourages institutions from targeting interventions directly at Global Majority students in order to prevent the reinforcement of negative 'racial and cultural stereotypes' (see Law et al., 2004, Jacobs et al., 2007). Singh (2011) asserts that in compulsory education the evidence advocates clearly a strong student support framework complemented with 'an unequivocal strategy to tackling racism maintains high expectations of Global Majority students, while acknowledging their cultural experiences' (p40).

However, Hockings et al. (2008) and (Senior, 2012) urge avoiding isolating Global Majority students by not treating them as 'non-traditional' and needing dedicated provision. In doing so, they can circumvent the potential for stereotypical bias to affect the way in which they regard Global Majority students' academic potential. Singh (2011, p46), in summarizing, agrees with this and urges caution in implementing strategies targeted at Global Majority students. Institutions should where possible embed assertive support activities for the benefit of all students rather than explicitly and openly targeting Global Majority students as a 'special needs' category.

Initiatives

Generally, the evidence on successful access and outreach interventions with regard to Global Majority students is partial. In reviewing interventions targeting HE access for ethnic minority students from disadvantaged backgrounds, Doyle and Griffin (2012) located only fourteen qualifying studies as many initiatives, especially from the UK, were not robustly evaluated. More learning is available in the United States, and Stevenson and Wheelan (2013) produced a useful guide. These studies, similarly to Wheelan (2013), typically detail more liberal approaches that emphasize changing the student rather than the institution such as partnering with local schools to improve students' college-preparedness; targeting resources on first-year transition programmes; enhancing teaching on introductory courses; establishing early warning systems; providing student support services such as tutoring and advice centres, study skills and counselling. Some initiatives that recognize structural inequalities are detailed, such as providing full institutional grant funding for low-income students and financial aid advice; providing training for faculty academic advisors, but are again individualized (Engle and Theokas, 2010, ACT, 2010a, 2010b, 2010d) similar to UK approach such as Aim Higher (Whitty et al., 2018).

In the UK, Stevenson et al. (2019) recognize more of the structural issues and make a number of interesting recommendations regarding outreach with Global Majority students, particularly building long-term, sustainable relationships with community groups and other community-based stakeholders (schools, families, etc.) and prioritizing the funding that this necessitates. They also say HE provider activity should be led by staff from diverse ethnic backgrounds, whilst remaining mindful of the need to not position diversity work as the responsibility of those from 'diversity' backgrounds or overburdening them – such activity needs to be recognized, rewarded, and linked to career development and progression. Maylor (2010) and Morgan (2016) similarly suggest that greater representation of Global Majority people amongst HEI staff could increase recruitment of Global Majority students, where they are underrepresented, although the recent Advance HE (2018) study found no empirical evidence to support this hypothesis. However, there is evidence in terms of success and progression.

Success (retention, continuation and attainment)

Keohane and Petrie (2017) found that the proportion of Global Majority students at university drop-out rate were statistically significant. They cite Teaching Excellence Framework data that suggest that 10.3 per cent of Black students drop out, compared with 6.9 per cent of the general student population. In a separate analysis, the Office for Fair Access found that Black students were 1.5 times more likely to drop out than either white or Asian students. Neves and Hillman (2016) found that Global Majority students tend to rate their overall satisfaction with university as lower than white students at the same universities.

Parkes (2014) notes that success, particularly retention has historically been seen as attributable to entry characteristics such as family, class, race, academic aptitude and economic status alongside the level of student involvement in social and academic activities (Goodenow and Grady, 1993, p60, Walker et al., 2004b, p53, Berger and Lyon, 2005, p20). However, more recently, it has been seen as part of a much more complex social and cultural picture (Quinn, 2004, pp59–63, Walker, 2004, p45) and 'though many of the aforementioned student characteristics play a part, student persistence is further influenced by the interaction between individuals, institutions and "wider society"' (Parkes, 2014, p4).

Student motivations

Guiffrida et al. (2018a) found that HEIs operate to the aforementioned assimilation model that expects these students to abandon their culture and communities, despite students wanting to give back to these communities being a major extrinsic motivation, and embrace a culture that will rarely embrace them. They found HEI's largely based interventions on self-determination theory (SDT), theorizing that students motivated largely by intrinsic motivation tend to be more successful and enjoy their learning experiences more than students who are motivated by extrinsic motivation. Within this approach, controlling approaches, from tutors or families, such as strictly monitoring them, imposing their own goals on students and punishing them for not meeting these imposed goals, can undermine students' intrinsic motivation towards learning. Conversely, educators and parents can increase student intrinsic motivation towards learning by providing autonomy-supportive conditions, which include encouraging students to study areas of interest to them, allowing them the autonomy to make their own decisions, providing rationales for the advice they provide and freedom to decide whether to follow their advice.

However, this can be a classed racialized view on motivation. Guiffrida et al. (2012) found that Black students in the United States had stronger intentions to persist, and were more motivated to attend college than white students, when the extrinsic motivation to give back to their home communities was acknowledged. Guiffrida et al. (2018a) hypothesize that this was because Black students came from more collectivist cultures (Triandis, 1989, Guiffrida et al., 2018b) which tend to value interdependence and familial and societal goals over individual goals. These results indicate the need for university counsellors and support staff to recognize student cultural orientation when designing intervention and support strategies with Black students. Issues include:

Guiffrida et al. (2018) counter Tinto's (1993) theory of integration. Tinto (2006) theorized that university students need to break away from family members so that they can become fully integrated into the academic and social realms of the university. Failure to do this leads to a lack of academic and social integration and results in student attrition. They say this ignores the Global Majority experience and has Eurocentric assumptions about family norms and identity development. Guiffrida et al. (2018), looking at the states, found high-achieving students' families supportive. Conversely, low-achieving students said their families made them feel guilty for being at university because it was costly to the family and distracted students from serving head of household duties at home. They also described their parents as being critical of the university environment and sensitive to changes they noticed in their children as a result of their transitions to university. However, these many again apply to other widening participation groups, particularly social class.

Miller (2016) identifies common tactics for reducing the attainment gap and improving success as being within the liberal tinkering position. She talks about a sector-wide lack of staff awareness of Global Majority issues, which amongst other things includes a tendency to frame the issue within the 'deficit model', rather than having structural concerns. She also agrees that there is a 'hidden curricula' 'that needs to be brought out into the open, discussed and critiqued' (Miller, 2016, p21). She also notes other approaches that have potential leverage to become more radical including raising staff knowledge and awareness; working with students as collaborative partners; the provision of safe spaces for discussion; and the use of language that revolves around success, empowerment and aspiration.

Building a sense of belonging

Building on our work on this in Chapter 1, Cureton and Gravestock (2019) found that while a sense of belonging was the same for white and Global Majority students at the beginning of their undergraduate studies, it rose significantly for white students and declined for Global Majority students throughout their time at university. What builds a sense of belonging is multifaceted. Miller et al. (2016) found that Global Majority students highlight a lack of role models available to them and a lack of Global Majority perspectives in course material. However, they also warn against the promotion of role models in a tokenistic fashion. Global Majority students stressed the importance of having their perspectives included and being allowed to help shape the content of their courses. The NUS survey showed that Global Majority students did not feel they could bring their perspectives to their education and had experienced feelings of alienation and exclusion at their institutions.

Peer support

Many studies (Singh, 2011, Miller et al., 2016, Universities UK, 2019) have found peer support aids retention across the board with students. Conversely, Guiffrida (2006) suggests that Black students are much less likely than white students to express satisfaction with peer relationships at university or to feel part of university life. Singh (2011) found that Black students often experience barriers when attempting to form relationships with white peers. Several studies (Stevenson, 2012, Gover et al., 2017) found that Global Majority students generally socialize primarily with other Black students, which can be troubling to Black students who attend universities that promote marketing materials with images of students having diverse social relationships at university (Stevenson, 2012).

Sims (2007) suggests that involvement in student unions provides one important means of connecting students with peers. However, research also indicates that student unions are often not inclusive of Black students. For example, a study by the National Union of Students (NUS) found that Black students comprise only 20 per cent of NUS membership and only 4 per cent of the elected officers nationally (NUS, 2019). According to Sims (2007), one way in which some universities have sought to increase Black student participation in student unions is to initiate special 'black officer posts' in each union that can only be held by Black students. Such positions show potential not only to increase Black student participation in student unions, but also to increase the attention that these associations pay to issues of inclusiveness and fighting racism on campus.

Other authors (Sims, 2007, Singh, 2011) suggest encouraging membership in Black student organizations such as African and Caribbean student societies. While there is potential for such groups to isolate Black students from the larger campus community (Stevenson, 2012), these authors indicate that participation in these groups can assist in retention by allowing students opportunities to socialize in ways that are comfortable and by connecting them with successful Global Majority mentors from the university and the wider community.

Supportive staff?

Most research (Togerston et al., 2014, Singh, 2011) says that having supportive relationships with academic staff is vital because of the unique psychosocial and academic challenges Global Majority students often encounter. Unfortunately, research also indicates that many Black students do not feel they receive adequate mentoring and support at UK universities (Guiffrida et al., 2018). Research indicates that one reason for feeling unsupported is racial stereotyping (Guiffrida et al., 2018, Singh, 2011) such as increased surveillance of Black students, measuring Black students against white norms, making stereotypical comments about them and demonstrating lowered expectations of their academic abilities. This decreases Global Majority student's academic self-efficacy and sense of belonging (Senior, 2013).

Examining community cultures, Miller (2016) notes Global Majority concerns about lack of academic support and, similarly to working class students, they are less likely to come forward for help and want lecturers to reach out to them instead. Anticipating Stephenson et al.'s call for a participatory approach to research, Miller (2016) recommends shared ownership of this work with Global Majority students, and recognition of the Global Majority student voice. She lauded examples where Global Majority students were 'used as a source of knowledge about the institution, as a support network for other students, as research subjects, and as conference participants'. Many authors (Singh, 2011, Iverson and Jaggers, 2015, Guiffrida, 2018) make the point that racial stereotyping will only change by overtly acknowledging and challenging it. However, educators may frequently find it psychologically hard to accept the presence of racial stereotyping in their institutions, and themselves associating it more with other sectors like the criminal justice system than with education (Guiffrida, 2018).

Role models and the presence, recruitment and development of Global Majority staff

Research (Singh, 2011, Griffida, 2018) suggests that Global Majority students find Global Majority academic staff generally more holistic and culturally sensitive in their support and teaching than white academic staff. Qualitative research conducted by Guiffrida in the United States (2013) found that African-American college students described Black academic staff as more likely than white staff to provide them with comprehensive academic, social and personal support; to demonstrate high expectations for Black student academic achievement; and to integrate culturally diverse perspectives into their lessons, and there are parallels in the UK (Stevenson, 2012). Other US sources found that Global Majority faculty are more likely to integrate race, gender or class issues into their curricula (Zandy, 1990, Milem and Astin, 1993, Tate, 1998, Hurtado, 2001, Milm, 2001). A number also found that Global Majority faculty employ a wider and more inclusive range of pedagogical techniques (Hurtado, 2001, Milem, 2001, Umbach, 2006).

However, there is also the danger that Global Majority staff are expected to take responsibility for issues of race (Singh, 2011), and the blame when progress is not made. US research revealed that diverse faculty can be overburdened with support for diverse students, and this can negatively affect research output and progression to senior levels (Baez, 2000, Social Sciences Feminist Network Research Interest Group, 2017). Kapilashrami (2021) similarly recommends that adequate support and recognition of the additional burden of these roles, particularly with regard to intersectionality, is enacted. Several authors found that Global Majority students may hold high expectations in terms of the diversity competence of Black faculty, which did not always hold true (Guiffrida, 2005, Tuitt, 2012). Advance HE (2018) found that, while showing an impact of staff diversity on learning and teaching, the US literature generally does not link this to impacts on student outcomes, with the exception of Hurtado (2001), who shows student growth on a number of educational outcomes.

Bhopal (2020) makes a number of recommendations regarding the recruitment and development of Global Majority staff and leaders in HEI's that are worth building from.

1. *Mentoring (formal and informal), by senior Global Majority academics.* The mentor role was seen as particularly important and was a key source of support in the progression of successful career trajectories for Global Majority academics.
2. *Diversity in interview panels, such as the inclusion of Global Majority staff.* Greater understanding of the factors related to Global Majority academic success was needed through both inclusive practice and representation with greater diversity on interview panels, particularly in relation to promotion and recruitment.
3. *The setting up of Global Majority networks within individual HEIs to provide specific support to address issues that affect Global Majority academics (such as racism and prejudice).* Global Majority networks are useful in sharing experiences and finding mutual support as a strategy for career progression. Note that any support networks for Global Majority staff need proper resourcing, authoritative support and links to decision making.

4. *Access to relevant training and events which would enable career progression.* Greater support in the form of training would benefit their career progression and emphasized the need for HEIs to invest in these (for example, the recent Diversifying Academic Leadership programme specifically designed for Global Majority leaders). Bhopal (2020) says we should ensure 'safe' mechanisms are available for Global Majority staff to report dissatisfaction with their progress and experiences, for example, concerning access to training, assignment of responsibilities and duties, feedback on performance or promotion opportunities. Take appropriate action where there is dissatisfaction.
5. *A formal requirement for HEIs to ensure Global Majority representation at managerial and senior academic levels (this could take the form of a quota system).*
6. *Interviews for promotion for Global Majority groups if essential criteria are met (such as positive discrimination).* Respondents emphasized that due to the underrepresentation of Global Majority academics in senior levels in HEIs, there was a need for senior managers to recognize and implement specific policy changes to address this. This included the possibility of a form of positive discrimination in which Global Majority academics were represented at senior levels, as well as a guaranteed interview for promotion (if all selection criteria were met).
7. *Recognition that Continued Professional Development (CPD) training must include diversity awareness for all staff and the impact of this on career progression* (Bhopal, 2020).

Decolonizing approaches

Universities have reached a critical juncture in relation to the decolonising movement, in that there is an opportunity to actively involve and integrate students of colour in the process of curriculum transformation, teaching and learning. An agency that has previously and historically not been afforded to students of colour.

(Arday, 2020b, p312)

In recent years, student campaigns such as 'Rhodes must fall, 'why is my curriculum white' and the 'decolonisation campaign' have highlighted how the university experience continues to be largely framed through a Eurocentric gaze and call for this to be countered.

Decolonizing the curriculum

Arday and Mizra (2018) highlight debates about how to decolonize the curricula with some emphasizing the need to decolonize, indigenize and interculturalize it and others to tackle specific inequities more actively through anti-racist pedagogy or a 'transformative' approach, such as Global Majority inclusion and associated addressing specific intersectional issues. Several authors say we should scrutinize the 'hidden curriculum' for knowledge that privileges some while claiming neutrality (Johnson-Bailey and Cervero 2004). Thomas, Arday and Adewumi (2018) suggest ten considerations in conducting a reading list review that are a good starting point.

Apple (2011, p3) questions the very nature of knowledge as well as addressing what is included in the curriculum 'what counts as legitimate knowledge is the result of complex power struggles among identifiable class, race, gender and religious groups'. Similarly, Smith (1999) has talked about the marginalization and undermining of indigenous knowledge and ways of knowing in academia for over twenty years. To embrace intersectionality, Kapilashrami (2021) raises similar epistemological concerns about what constitutes knowledge. Kapilashrami (2021) says we should acknowledge and utilize wider 'expertise' including 'embodied expertise' derived from lived experiences of oppressions via co-production with students and other communities.

Decolonizing pedagogic approaches

Singh (2011) advocates the integration of components on social justice and global citizenship into all courses, implemented in such a way so that a focus on social problems or victimization does not dominate and perpetuate negative stereotypes. Senior (2013) felt that teaching should 'transcend an academic purpose and encourage an inclusive relationship between students and staff' (2013, p9). Nixon and McDermott (2010) maintain that dialogues that challenge students on both a personal and academic level can contribute to their understanding of a critical theory of race. It also opens up an understanding of organizations and agencies that are, potentially, part of the problem. More recently Stevenson et al. (2019) have the following ideas for lecturers to reflect upon in their teaching. Specifically, experiential learning, transformative learning and culturally situated pedagogy all have their place and can be combined. My own work (Seal, 2019, 2020) has called on foundation years to start from an anti-deficit model of students whereby the starting point is that they have been failed and demonized in their previous experience of education.

Focusing on intersectionality and the classroom itself, Kapilashrami (2021) advocates exploring the composition of the class; its diversity (or its absence) is assessed and acknowledged within the classroom for its impact and significance. Elsewhere others talked about the importance of acknowledging 'what is happening in the room' (Seal and Smith, 2021). Kapilashrami (2021) also asks practitioners to consider what factors constrain participation in class such as seating arrangement, and whether activity design allows interaction and learning across groups. Kapilashrami (2021) also advocates creating space and informal mechanisms as well as formal ones to elicit student voice and concerns and communicate actions taken.

Decolonizing assessment

Moody (2020) describes how assessment practices can be seen as processes through and in which specific values and constructions – such as rationality, individuality, objectivity and written linguistic capabilities – are reflected and enshrined. Such practices are normalized and, in so doing, can marginalize and exclude certain students and cohorts for whom such practices are unfamiliar and inaccessible. Moody (2020) also discusses how assessment can also hierarchize knowledge: in our inevitable selection of content for assessments, we subconsciously communicate to learners what disciplinary knowledge is important/valuable, and what is not. It is no accident that we are often asked whether what is taught is required for the assessment. She calls for inclusive approaches, involving students from the outset, and social justice approaches where social justice is envisaged as both an intrinsic quality of and a core learning outcome of assessment. She draws upon a cross-pollination of the two pedagogic frameworks of universal design for learning (UDL) and culturally sustaining pedagogy (CSP).

Progression

The OfS in May 2020 found that progression rates (a distinction is not made between progression to further study or employment) have decreased for all Global Majority students. The Equality Challenge Unit (2017) found that 7.8 per cent of Global Majority leavers were unemployed six months after qualifying compared with 4.3 per cent of white leavers and six months after qualifying, 61.2 per cent white leavers were in both full-time work, compared with 54.8 per cent of Global Majority ex-students. Stevenson et al. (2019) recommend a number of initiatives regarding progression of Global Majority students. They firstly suggest monitoring work-based learning and progression into employment and work with employers to build up links and relationships; they should also invest in ensuring their careers' support services understand and challenge discrimination. They also suggest mentoring programmes for underrepresented and under-attaining groups with community partners and employers that avoid using deficit discourses about students. Finally they say we should develop employers, seeing them as potential partners, 'not only in employing graduates, but also in informing universities and colleges about future economic opportunities and partnering with those employers challenging inequalities in the labour market'.

The last point seems particularly important, because many of the issues of progression are structural and institutional, in terms of both the HEI and the employer. Unless research into the Global Majority graduate experience in employment is prioritized by both sides, tinkering will be the dominant driver.

The Global Majority doctoral experience

The situation is similarly stark for Global Majority postgraduate and doctoral study. Arday (2020) notes that in September 2019, Leading Routes revealed that of 15,560 full-time UK first-year PhD students, just 3 per cent of those students were Black (Higher Education Statistics Agency (HESA), 2019). Similarly, over the last three academic years (2016/17–2018/19) of the 19,868 PhD-funded studentships awarded by UKRI research councils collectively, 245 (1.2 per cent) were awarded to Black or Black Mixed students, with just thirty of those being from Black Caribbean backgrounds (Leading Routes, 2019). In the States attrition rates for Global Majority graduate students are up to 70 per cent, 20 per cent higher than for their white counterparts. In the UK Global Majority students are 50 per cent more likely to drop out than their white peers (Clegg et al., 2016).

The graduate school experience is well documented as culturally white (Bhopal, 2020, Boliver, 2016, Rollock, 2016, Leading Routes, 2019, Aday, 2020) with many students experiencing covert, covert and cultural racism, and being perceived as very quickly, and unfairly, 'playing the race card' if they complain (Arday, 2020a). Advance HE (2018) found a range of research that suggests a lack of Global Majority role models amongst academics is one reason why Global Majority students are less likely to progress into postgraduate study, and ultimately academic careers (Maseti, 2018, Maylor, 2010). Truong (2010) identifies themes including loneliness and isolation; differential support and investment; low expectations and disproportionately high standards; exploitation of students; neglect; devaluing of research on race; the cumulative effects of racial micro-aggressions; and violations of institutional and governmental policies.

Several authors have found that Black students feel unsupported in British universities through the lack of Black role models in the staff, particularly at a higher level (Singh, 2011, Senior, 2013, Griffrida, 2018a). These authors see them as important to embody how to survive, traverse and challenge the racism Global Majority students will encounter. As the Leading Routes Report (2019) notes,

For Global Majority Doctoral students the dearth of academics of colour within the Academy, only serves to remind that entry into the Academy for ethnic minorities remains problematic with regards to access and opportunities, as targeted diversification and representation of BAME academic staff continues to remain an after-thought.

(Leading Routes, 2019)

Global Majority staff remain a minority in terms of staff representation, with many authors (Bhopal et al., 2016, Boliver, 2016, Rollock, 2016, Leading Routes, 2019, Arday, 2020) cataloguing how they are often passed over for promotion, are much more likely to be on part time and temporary contracts and have disproportionately high pastoral roles with students. In the 2018–19 academic year, only 0.7 per cent of UK professors were Black, compared with around 7 per cent of the total student population (HESA, 2020). Furthermore, there were no Black academic leaders, defined as 'managers, directors, or senior officials', across the entire UK higher education sector for the eighth consecutive year.

Conclusion

As described in the introduction, we are at a crossroads in getting a fair deal for Global Majority students in higher education. We either continue to think that it is a process of tinkering with our approaches to make the playing field a little more level, or to recognize that higher education needs to rethink itself fundamentally as we are a part of maintaining white elite power structures. This means embracing some the critiques of frameworks such as critical race theory, as Walmington says,

In academia, we have seen deepening feelings of marginalisation among students and faculty of colour, whose efforts to decolonise the curriculum have been widely caricatured… the emergence of Critical Race Theory has been a significant departure from the script. That departure has helped shape many of the current youthful movements to dismantle racism in higher education, such as 'Decolonising the University' and 'Why is my Curriculum White?'

(Walmington, 2020, p22)

This critical stance sees universities not being neutral knowledge creators – we need to seriously challenge who gets to create the knowledge and the nature of the knowledge created as at the moment we are maintaining white supremacy, and at best challenge only most overt discrimination, and only when it converges with our own interests, but not asking the fundamental questions.

> A reconceptualization of social justice is required in attempting to establish a collective and targeted focus towards social justice and racial equality in the Academy and the education sector more generally. The ever-changing nature of the inequitable racialised terrain remains problematic. Major theoretical and intellectual insights reflect the true potential for an equitable and egalitarian education system by decentring whiteness and the strands of power, privilege and oppression that accompany this phenomena.
>
> (Arday, 2021, p231)

As Ardays (2021) indicates, to meaningfully challenge the disadvantage of Global Majority students in higher education entails some serious soul searching within institutions. Institutions need to commit to decolonizing the institution and seriously challenging its power structure, and the strategic commitment that this entails. If instead they remain content to simply tinkering with 'extra support' for Global Majority students this will reinscribe the existing hegemony and white supremacist constructions, and, ultimately, fail on its own terms. This is not to say that support mechanisms should not be developed, only that if they are done in isolation without institutional change, they will not succeed. Once institutional change is achieved the nature of this support may change radically, seeing Global Majority students for the resource they are. Deep thinking is also required on how we can de-colonize and liberate the curriculum, assessment and pedagogy, challenging who gets to create knowledge, what knowledge is valued, and how it is created, transmitted and transferred. This may mean that new knowledge needs to be created, and older hidden and buried knowledge unearthed and honoured.

6

Student with Disabilities: The Politics of Marginalization

Introduction

A simple reading of disability discourse in higher education and a consequent call for recognizing disabled people's rights and fighting discrimination are not enough. Instead, Shildrick (2012) advocates adopting a more radical critical approach to disabilities *'would shake up not just law, policy and socio-cultural relations, but would contest the very nature of the standards that underpin their normative operation'* (Shildrick, 2012, p32). Shildrick goes on to say that in-depth soul searching and empirical research are needed into underlying dynamics and ableist constructions that continue to dominate. This chapter will try and unearth these dynamics and constructions, and explore how they could be engaged with.

One of the critical concerns with the term disabilities is what concepts or disabilities it covers, and what are the common issues and differences between them. As with analyses of sexuality, with its ever-growing label of LGBTQAI+, both are in danger of becoming deficit labels, negatively defined against an ideologically constructed 'normal'. In reality the groups or constituencies contained within it may have little in common aside from being oppressed by a constructed hegemony. Disability is also a very broad term and of its variations could warrant its own chapter, or indeed book. It would therefore have been impossible to consider all disabilities in this chapter. I apologize for any omissions the reader considers pertinent. I have tried to cover aspects relating, at different times, to physical disabilities such as hearing and sight, cognitive disabilities such as dyslexia, dyspraxia and ADHD, and non-neuro typical disabilities such as Autism. Mental health is covered by other chapters. The examples are therefore intended to be illustrative rather than definitive.

This chapter will consider barriers such as finance and the politics of disclosure, linked to theoretical debates around stigma, self-determination, self-advocacy and identity. It will then explore theoretical models, noting that they are underdeveloped in higher education. It will start with a brief overview of the overall medical, social and critical models of disability, making a case to adopting the latter. It then explores specific models of disability that may be applicable to the higher education context including Weidman's (1989) Conceptual Model of Undergraduate Socialization, Perna's (2006) Conceptual Model of College Choice, Hurtado et al.'s (2012) Multi-contextual Model for Diverse Learning Environments, and Hewett et al.'s (2017) Bioecological Model.

Concurrently the chapter will consider issues and interventions focusing on access, success and progression for these different groups. The chapter will also focus, again, on the importance of taking a whole institutional approach, the need for training, nuanced support, changing our approach to teaching, assessment and pedagogic approach, including personal tutoring. We will focus in particular on Universal Design for Learning, which recognizes that many of the issues may equally apply to non-disabled students, and we should focus on learning, assessment and curriculum design that works for all.

Theoretical models and concepts

Models of disability

A broad distinction is often made between medical and social models. Medical models link a disability diagnosis to an individual's physical body. The model supposes that this disability may reduce the individual's quality of life and the aim is, with medical intervention, this disability will be diminished or corrected. The medical model focuses on curing or managing illness or disability (Fisher and Goodley, 2007). Social models see people as disabled by barriers in society, not by their impairment or difference. Barriers can be physical, like buildings not having accessible toilets, or they can be caused by people's attitudes to difference, like being afraid of people with mental health. The OfS explicitly adheres to the social model of disability. In its insight briefing 'Beyond the Bare Minimum: Are Universities Doing Enough for Disabled Students' (2019c), it says:

> The social model of disability is widely accepted as the most effective way that universities can respond to the needs of disabled students (Barnes, 2007). The social model developed out of an understanding that disability is not something medical to be treated, but rather a failing on the part of society. Understood this way, a response to disability is not about 'fixing' the individual, but rather about restructuring the environments and attitudes around them (Oliver et al., 2012). By building inclusive practices into an institution's structure and operations, fewer reasonable adjustments will be needed over time. Where such adjustments are needed, the institution can be much more responsive to individual needs.
>
> (OfS, 2019c, pp1–2)

The social model as espoused by the OfS adheres to the universal principle that we should try and make services more accessible to all, rather than singling out disabled people. 'In a university setting, an example of inclusive practice would be to reform a service or practice so that all students have an equal opportunity to thrive. This more flexible approach can also help students who are not disabled, such as those with caring responsibilities, and those who choose not to disclose a disability' (OfS, 2019b, online). However, while this model is commonly espoused by universities, the empirical evidence shows reality can be somewhat different (Kimball et al., 2016). Manuel et al. (2010, p647) found that 'despite verbal adherence to the "social model of disability", many institutions still saw a disabled person as a "problem" to be solved'. Brown and Leigh (2020) found that ableism persists in academia with disabled academics viewed as being suspect, particularly those with specific learning disabilities.

Critical disability theory (CDT) is a framework for the analysis of disability which de-centres disability and challenges the ableist assumptions which shape society (Hoskins, 2008). Meekosha and Shuttleworth (2009) see CDT as a logical extension of the Social Model. CDT's central theme is that disability is a social construct, as is the artificial 'normal' against which it is measured. Disability is not the inevitable result of impairment. As Hoskins says,

> Disability is a 'complex inter-relationship between impairment, an individual's response to that impairment and the physical, institutional and attitudinal (together, the 'social') environment. The social disadvantage experienced by disabled people is the result of the failure of the social environment to respond adequately to the diversity presented by disability.'
>
> (Hoskins, 2008, p2)

Important questions within CDT are how 'normal' is constructed and who does constructing normal in this way benefit. This seems particularly important and speaks to this book's theme that behind the predominant assimilation model in higher education is an unacknowledged archetypical ideal student around which structures and services within higher education are designed – this student is able bodied.

More generally, Kimball et al. (2016) note the lack of theorization in the literature on disability in higher education.

> Much of the literature on students with disabilities does not identify an explicit theoretical framework or even provide a theory-informed definition of disability, instead utilizing a general theory of action that might be summarized as 'disability plus intervention equals improved outcome'. Ultimately, this disconnect from theory produces a situation whereby higher education journals show little connection to the disability studies field, and disability-focused journals, even those explicitly focused on college students, show little engagement with higher education's theory base.
>
> (Kimbal et al., 2016, p123)

However, they identify some orientations. Social justice orientations focus on deconstructing ableism and engaging in anti-oppressive education (e.g. Abberley, 1987, McCune, 2001, Hackman and Rauscher, 2004, Hutcheon and Wolbring, 2012a). Social approaches emphasize the importance of institutional allies for under-represented groups such as students with disabilities (Giri et al., 2021). Psychological approaches tend to emphasize concepts like stigma, self-advocacy, self-determination, self-regulation, self-efficacy, metacognition and meaning-making processes as a form of student development (Baxter-Magolda, 2009). It would seem prudent to have a combination of all of these, perhaps an overall social justice orientation, the only one that seriously engages with CDT, which also sees developing allies and being mindful of some of the psychological dimensions of student meaning making in the face of oppressive forces.

Kimball et al. (2016) also identify other commonly used conceptual constructs in higher education research such as campus climate (e.g. Beilke and Yssel, 1999, Cress and Ikeda, 2003, Junco and Salter, 2004), student persistence (Hedrick et al. 2010, Mamiseishvili and Koch, 2012, Dong and Lucas, 2014), social and cultural capital (Bourdieu, 2006), social integration (DaDeppo, 2009, Wessel et al., 2009, Mamiseishvili and Koch, 2011, 2012) and social identity (Henry et al., 2010). We have covered these before and will come back to them again when assessing initiatives.

Common issues and concepts

Social identity

Social identity-based approaches seem worth considering in some details as they dominate the US literature (Kimball et al., 2016). Dole (2001) sees social identity models, as opposed to more individual models, are preferable as they affirm the importance of family members, peers, teachers and mentors. He also defines social identity as processes of self-knowledge, self-acceptance, self-advocacy and self-determination. Other authors (Troiano, 2003, Olney and Brockelman, 2005, Hutcheon and Wolbring, 2012a) feel disability as a social identity is context dependent with salient features including gender, diagnosis, and the extent to which societal messages regarding disability are internalized. There are also intersectional dimensions to identity. Lombardi, Murray and Gerdes's (2012) examination of the academic performance of first-generation students with disabilities revealed lower grades, social support, and greater financial stress, but increased use of disability support services.

Some authors emphasize the role that other students play in the development of identity for students with disabilities seems to be connected to prevailing social stigma towards those with disability (Tinklin et al., 2004, Trammell, 2009, Dunn and Burcaw, 2013). Myers and Bastian (2010) and Evans, Assadi and Herriott (2005) found that students with disabilities are often required to place students without disabilities at ease in social situations. Trammell (2009) found many students with disabilities 'may worry that accommodations will give them an unfair advantage, or that it will appear to others that they are not competitive' (Trammell, 2009, p107).

Several authors (May and Stone, 2010, Markoulakis and Kirsh, 2013) found that in addition to worrying about the perceptions of others, disability stigma engenders students with disabilities to doubt themselves more relative to their peers. Depending on how students with disabilities experience, accept and conceive of their identity, they may report different experiences of isolation, shame and differentness (Fleischer and Zames, 2001, Dunn and Burcaw, 2013). Kimball et al. (2016) note that stigma affects all people with disabilities, but the effects will be influenced by how disability manifests.

Disclosure

Fabri et al. (2016) note that some students that know they are autistic choose not to declare it (Huws and Jones, 2008, Davidson and Henderson, 2010, Baines, 2012). This can be for a variety of reasons including not identifying as disabled, believing they are not entitled to support or wanting to fit in with their peers. Further, a large number of students with an autism spectrum condition have not been diagnosed by the time they start university, especially female and gender non-conforming students. The OfS (2019c) notes that many applicants and students with impairments do not disclose them because of a continuing social stigma or fears of being discriminated against, or because they do not identify themselves as disabled.

We will come back to the impact of stigma more generally later. There are a number of ways in which the disclosure process could be made less laborious. They give the example that students with multiple disabilities can only choose the 'multiple disabilities' category on their UCAS form. They are then asked which is their 'primary' disability. They also call for students who have been diagnosed with learning differences while at school to be able to carry this diagnosis over into higher education without having to pay for a new assessment.

Self-determination and self-advocacy

Primarily looking at the states, Kimball et al. (2016) found research suggests that self-determination and self-advocacy play key roles in higher education access and outcomes for students with disabilities (Bae, 2007, Chambers et al., 2007, Fowler et al., 2007, Cobb et al., 2009). Self-determined behaviours encapsulate 'volitional actions that enable one to act as the primary causal agent in one's life and to maintain or improve one's quality of life' (Wehmeyer, 2005, p117). However, Wehmeyer (2004) also recognize it is contested and colonized as a term. Test et al. (2005) say self-advocacy refers to a student's ability to recognize and pursue her or his own needs based on knowledge of their rights and effective engagement with others. Kimball et al. (2016) and Janiga and Costenbader (2002) found widespread dissatisfaction among higher education-based disability service coordinators with the way that students with disabilities are prepared to succeed in the higher education learning environment, with ineffective development of self-advocacy skills prior to university being identified as a particular weakness.

KImball et al. (2016) found that the impact of significant others of influence, such as parents and teachers, in the development of self-determination and self-advocacy, is mixed. Family participation in educational planning can play a critical role in the cultivation of self-determination (Wehmeyer, Morningstar, and Husted, 1999) and is also related to better self-advocacy and improved higher education outcomes (Morningstar et al., 2010). Zhang and Katsiyannis (2002) conversely found fewer than half of parents fostered self-determination in their disabled children. They also found that some teachers and parents have lower expectations for students identified as having a learning disability than for similarly achieving and behaving students who are not labelled in such a way (Shifrer, 2013). Morningstar et al. (2010) found high levels of self-determination and self-advocacy underpin the philosophy of university services, in contrast to schools and are thus particularly important to be developed when moving from school to university. KImball et al. (2016) also suggest this problem is compounded if students with disabilities take time off before enrolling.

Institutional climate

Lombardi and Murray (2011) noted that existing models and interventions pay only scant attention to the relationship between disability and institutional climate. Kimball et al. (2016), looking at predominantly literature from the states, found the overall climate of universities for disabled students to be historically 'chilly' (Olney and Brockelman, 2005) or 'hostile' (Cress and Ikeda, 2003). However, they also found there is significant variation from institution to institution based on differences in the access mission, available academic support services, and curricula (Collins and Mowbray, 2005).

Kimball et al. (2016) also found that stigma was sometimes internalized by students with disabilities, with some students having reported that they have made modifications to their classroom behaviour to avoid attracting attention due to their disability (Stage and Milne, 1996). Marshak et al. (2010) found negative perceptions of students with disabilities extend beyond the attitudes held by their peers and appear to be pervasive on campus. Dowrick, Anderson, Heyer and Acosta (2005) found attitudes by higher education personnel presented as a difficulty faced by students with disabilities.

Stigma expanded

Many authors (Crocker and Major, 1989, Goldstein and Johnson, 1997, Weiner, 1999, Loewen and Pollard, 2010, May and Stone, 2010, Markoulakis and Kirsh, 2013, Kimball et al. 2016) view people with disabilities as a stigmatized group, and that disability stigma has a negative impact on students with disabilities in higher education settings. Students experiencing disability stigma fear discrimination, exclusion from academic opportunities, social isolation and diminished prospects for employment upon graduation (Trammell, 2009, Markoulakis and Kirsh, 2013). One aforementioned effect is reluctance to disclose one's disability and not to ask for help (Weiner, 1999, Markoulakis and Kirsh, 2013) and not to use available services (e.g. Denhart, 2008, Hartman-Hall and Haaga, 2002). Several authors (Tinklin, Riddell and Wilson, 2004, May and Stone, 2010, Markoulakis and Kirsh, 2013) found students with learning disabilities frequently have to spend more time on academic tasks than the typical student, leaving less time for co-curricular activities and socializing and leading to fear of judgement by faculty and peers.

Kimball et al. (2016) also note that students with hidden disabilities are often perceived as outsiders (May and Stone, 2010). However, due to the less apparent nature of their impairments, students with hidden disabilities may attempt to pass as not having a disability, rejecting disability group identity (Doosje, Ellemers and Spears, 1995, Dovidio et al., 2001, Tinklin et al., 2004, Riddell and Weedon, 2014). Those with hidden disabilities may also choose to selectively identify themselves in some environments in order to receive services while not claiming this identity in other contexts (Tinklin et al., 2004).

Kimball et al. (2016, p100) think, 'This tactic of leveraging disability identity might be viewed as exploitative, but it is also indicative of the strength of stigma and resulting undesirability of disability identity.'

Models of HE and disability

A whole institutional approach

As with all groups considered in this book, a whole institutional approach is recommended. Kutscher and Tuckwiller (2019) recommend universities focus their attention on practices and policies at the institution level (i.e. academic and social engagement, accommodations). Williams et al. (2019) say that positive change for disabled student in higher education needs strong leadership; a holistic approach covering all students and involving shared responsibility across the institution; collaboration within institutions between core disability services and across all staff groups; balancing inclusive approaches with tailored support for individuals; encouraging disclosure across the student life-cycle; improving accessibility to services, digital resources and estates; giving students a voice and involving them in the creation of services; focusing on mental health and well-being; ensuring adequate resources; and harnessing technology. Furthermore, senior management need to commit to inclusive practice and culture and involve all university staff in encouraging students to disclose an impairment, build considerations of inclusivity and accessibility into curriculum design and programme review including offering alternative formats of lectures and course materials as standard practice, purchase appropriate services and equipment; and provide guidance and training on digital accessibility for staff.

Williams et al. (2019) note that the approaches and experiences of HE providers appear to be influenced by their size and structure. The attitudes of senior staff are also a key factor. Senior leadership is pivotal, particularly where there are multiple agendas and competing demands. Where senior leaders prioritize support for disabled students, signal their commitment to a wider culture of inclusivity and are actively working to integrate it across their institution, there is likely to be a better chance of success in bringing about the shifts required. The implication is that HEIs should work to establish environments where the disclosure of disability is welcomed. For example, Pino and Martari (2016) suggest adopting an institutional cultural view of dyslexia not as a deficit, but as neurological or cognitive diversity, and that students with it have strengths and weaknesses similar to any other form of neurological or cognitive functioning (Griffin and Pollak, 2009). However, the question arises of which institutional models could be adopted. Kimball et al. (2016) conducted a particularly useful review of institutional models.

Weidman's (1989) Conceptual Model of Undergraduate Socialization

This model addresses the many factors that shape socialization processes including the influence of others, organizational impacts, social interaction and social integration as they apply to undergraduate students. The university experience is the primary focus of the model. It consists of 'normative contexts' – such as academic programmes, student organizations and peer groups – that interact to produce socialization processes which include interpersonal relationships, intrapersonal reflection and feelings of integration. Weidman's model also accounts for both 'pre-college normative pressure' and 'in-college normative pressure' that shape a student's response to the college environment and are influenced by a student's pre-college characteristics, parents, non-college peers and understanding of employer preferences.

It acknowledges the critical role that parents play in shaping both the initial and ongoing reactions to the university's environment, the powerful role of normative trends in society and the related concept of affinity group membership. The model resonates with the need for studies of students with disabilities that address inclusion and exclusion in the higher education space. However, the model does not account for several important issues such as access to, and the quality of, disability support services (Kimball et al., 2016). The model also only addresses issues of class and not race/ ethnicity, class or gender. However it does have the potential for these to be incorporated.

Perna's (2006) Conceptual Model of College Choice

Combining perspectives from both economics and sociology, Perna's (2006) conceptual model of college choice is 'an attempt to organize the influences on university going from most-to-least proximate' (Perna, 2006, p32). It consists of four layers: habitus (layer 1), the school and community context (layer 2), the higher education context (layer 3) and the social, economic and policy context (layer 4). Within the habitus layer, demographic characteristics, cultural capital, social capital and a student's cost–benefit analysis of both present and future options shape individual preferences for college. At the university level, major influences include a wide variety of institutional characteristics as well as marketing activities.

Perna (2006) also contextualizes these factors within a broader societal context comprised of trends in social mobility, the economy and public policy. Finally, the model suggests that by modelling the interrelated effects of these four contexts, college choice decisions can be understood and predicted. Perna's model acknowledges the importance of intersectional identity via its attention to gender and race/ethnicity. However its confluence of context, circumstance and individual needs does not allow for socio-economic analysis, and consequently the identification of appropriate initiatives (Kimball et al., 2016). Kimball et al. (2016) also feel that it gives insufficient attention to stigma as a mediating influence on all layers.

Hurtado et al.'s (2012) Multicontextual Model for Diverse Learning Environments

This model brings together consideration of campus climate with an explicit focus on curricular and co-curricular practices in order to better understand college outcomes. It positively gives attention to the historical construction of higher education, particularly around race. It incorporates the five features of the campus racial climate model upon which it is based: (a) the historical legacy of inclusion or exclusion, which includes factors such as past discriminatory acts and institutional mission; (b) the organizational and structural dimension, which includes the policies and practices that help form the campus environment; (c) compositional diversity, which includes the relative representativeness of the student body and campus workforce; (d) the psychological dimension, which includes attitudes towards difference and perceptions of racial tension or discrimination; and (e) the behavioural dimension, which includes social interaction across difference and the inclusiveness of curricular and co-curricular experiences.

Curricular processes explore student identity, instructor identity, course content and pedagogical strategies. Likewise, student identity is seen as structuring a student's interaction with the co-curriculum through its relationship to staff identity, administrative practices and campus programming. According to Hurtado et al. (2012), these institutional processes – along with the elements of the campus climate outlined above – comprise the institutional climate for diversity and are part of the broader institutional context. The institutional climate for diversity and the institutional context further interact with a variety of influences external to the institution, including community, policy and socio-historical factors. Kimball et al. (2016) suggest that to better account for the needs of students with disabilities, the model might be adapted to take into account the way in which varied access to disability services alters a student's experiences.

Hewett et al.'s (2017) Bioecological Model

This model was originally developed and refined by Bronfenbrenner (1979, 2005) over his career and specifically considers visual impairment (VI), but has transferability to other disabilities. The later version of the theory (Bronfenbrenner, 2005) consists of four key interrelated elements: 'process' (human development through interactions with the environment around them); 'person' (personal characteristics that impact on development, e.g. age, skills and temperament); 'context' (the environments in which the person sits); and 'time' (the time in which this process occurs) (Tudge et al., 2009). The context in which the individual sits is described by Bronfenbrenner with reference to five systems: microsystems (factors in the environment immediately around the individual); mesosystems (interactions between factors within the microsystems); exosystems (factors outside the individual's immediate environment that impact upon their development); macrosystems (factors and culture outside the physical environment); and chronosystems (human development over time).

There are, of course, many other models of disability in higher education. Advance HE advocates for John Swain and Sally French's 'affirmative model' which asserts that 'even if the social model was successful and all barriers were removed, it would still be possible for impairments to be seen as a personal tragedy and in turn for disabled people to be seen and treated as victims' (Advance HE, 2018, p4). Swain and French think the affirmative model helps develop a positive view of disabled people, recognizing impairments as part of what makes the individual themselves, not as a tragedy. However, it seems to lack the critical edge of CRT, which explores who benefits from constructions of disability being as they are, as well as who suffers. All the models seem to have some merit. Socialization processes are important, as are factors that influence students' decisions. Looking at the impact of the wider context on the forming of campus climate also seems vital, although the campus climate narrative may well be redundant in the light of the pandemic. Whatever new normal emerges, the campus as the primary site for higher education looks to shift significantly. The level of the bioecological model seems to also have traction; all its identified levels contribute to the culture of the universities with regard to disability.

What seems important to me, and something curiously absent from these models, is the interaction between individual agency and structural forces. A balance needs to be struck, as it is all too easy to individualize the issues and ignore structural forces, and conversely to over-emphasize structure, leaving little account of how the individual and groups exercise their agency and make sense of the competing narratives they are subject to.

Rights and policy of student with disabilities in higher education

Supporting students with disabilities has a statutory footing in most countries. In the UK, since 2001, universities and colleges have had a legal requirement to make 'reasonable adjustments' for disabled students. Under the Equality Act 2010, universities and colleges have a duty to ensure equality of opportunity for disabled students for changing rules or practices, altering or removing physical barriers and providing support services or devices.

There are a number of avenues for recourse when a disabled student feels a provider has not done enough. They can raise the issue with their provider, make a complaint to the Office of the Independent Adjudicator after they have exhausted the provider's internal complaints procedure, and take their provider to court. In 2018, the largest amount of compensation recommended by the Office of the Independent Adjudicator was to a disabled student who complained about the non-medical support they received from their provider. This type of action does, however, place the onus on the student to challenge their university or college, which takes time and can be stressful.

Kimball et al. (2016) and Heyward (2011) detect a tension between efforts to promote paths to access for students with disabilities in higher education, and the perception among some academics that the provision of accommodations and programmatic modifications can compromise pedagogic standards and academic freedoms (Scott, 1997, Bourke et al., 2000, Jensen et al., 2004). Kimball et al. (2016) further this tension leads to some disability services providers developing, and then disregarding, rigorous documentation requirements (e.g. Sparks and Lovett, 2009) and other policy-practice discontinuities and inconsistencies (Kurth and Mellard, 2006). Positively other authors (Bourke et al., 2000, Jensen et al., 2004) found most academics to be generally agreeable, and that disability services offices can mitigate many academic concerns by providing accurate information and reliable support.

The Disabled Students' Commission (DSC) was announced by the government in June 2019 to take forward the work of the Disabled Students' Sector Leadership Group (DSSLG). The task for the commission is to both challenge and support the sector to make further and faster progress on this journey, avoiding delays and removing obstacles to inclusion. It will 'advise, inform and challenge the English higher education sector (including providers, sector agencies, regulators and government) to improve models of support for disabled students in higher education' and 'identify and promote effective practice that helps those with disabilities have a positive and successful experience at university'.

The position of student with disabilities in higher education

Access

Current position

According to the OfS (2019c) they cannot measure whether disabled young people are entering higher education at a lower rate than their non-disabled peers. There are small-scale studies which suggest this might be the case. The National Deaf Society (2018) found that deaf children are 50 per cent less likely to go to Russell Group universities. The number of new entrants with a disability (i.e. first-year disabled students) has grown from 68,000 in 2013/14 to over 94,000 in 2017/18 – an increase of 38 per cent. In 2017, 13.2 per cent of students attending an English university or college reported having at least one disability (OfS, 2019c). The most commonly reported disability is a specific learning difficulty (SpLD), followed by a mental health condition (Williams et al., 2019).

Williams et al. (2019) note that the increase in the numbers of disabled students is likely to be driven by a number of factors: improved special educational needs and disability (SEND) support for children in the compulsory education system; students' increasing willingness to disclose a disability, especially a mental health condition; sustained efforts in the sector to widen participation to traditionally underrepresented groups, including disabled students and changes in legislation related to the requirements HE providers, are expected to meet in providing support for disabled students.

Finance is a significant factor. According to the Department of the Environment (DOE) (2019) only 40 per cent of disabled students knew about Disabled Students' Allowances (DSA) before starting their course. The proportion of those reporting a social or communication impairment has more than trebled from 0.1 per cent to 0.5 per cent of all undergraduate students over the same period (OfS, 2019d). The increase in reporting may be down to a number of factors, including; availability of funding, greater social acceptance of disabilities, reforms at school level, greater efforts by colleges and universities to understand the makeup of their students, and changes in the law (Vickerman and Blundell, 2010).

Looking now to specific disabilities, Toor et al. (2016) found autistic people experienced challenges in terms of their school environment, lack of support, expectations of self, modes of assessment and transitions. At the same time, Toor et al. (2016) found many autistic students had unrealistic expectations in terms of the demands of university study and their chosen subject, the need to 'up their game' for university and their and other students' motivation and dedication. Transitions were problematic with difficulties moving away from home for the first time, time management and establishing routines and an unfamiliarity with advocating effectively for oneself. Assessment seemed a particular problem, with the norm expected, not matching their abilities. Specifically, they found difficulty interpreting ambiguous and open assignment briefs correctly, difficulty planning studies and revision and uncertainty how much time to spend on a given task.

Pino and Mortari (2014) found that, while students can initially react negatively when informed of their dyslexia diagnosis, the diagnosis brings awareness of one's own condition and thus an opportunity to improve the learning experience. While previous school experiences may have produced the feeling of being 'stupid', the diagnosis provides an explanation for the difficulties with literacy. Norwich (2009) states, 'Positive self-conception arises from a key aspect of the historic meaning of dyslexia, which excludes low intellectual abilities as a cause of the literacy difficulties' (p186). Pino and Moartari (2016) found that, in time, students can acquire a more balanced view of their strengths and weaknesses and develop cognitive and affective strategies that enhance their learning experience.

Saunders (2013) found that although most deaf students felt they were supported in their transition to university, the type and amount of support varied. In general students from specialist colleges for deaf students or at places where there were greater numbers of deaf students applying took part in programmes of support. At institutions with smaller numbers of deaf students the transition programme on offer seemed to be less formal and more influenced by parents', teachers' or advisors' personal knowledge of the transition process. Saunders (2013) also found that within the Deaf World once a reputation is formed about an institution or its support services, it will take time for that opinion to be revised. O'Neill and Jones (2007) concluded that the more preparation done before university, the happier deaf students were when they got there.

Multiple authors (Owen-Hutchinson et al., 1998, Simkiss et al., 1998, Cole-Hamilton and Vale, 2000, Bishop and Rhind, 2011) have written about visually impaired students barriers to going to university; Owen-Hutchinson et al. (1998) suggested that these barriers may be encapsulated by four broad categories: attitudinal, institutional, environmental and physical. Bishop and Rhind (2011) expanded this to include the student's attitude (i.e. self-identity, positive aspects of being visually impaired, engagement with support), institutional provision (i.e. campus navigability, central services support, school-level support), external support (i.e. travelling to and from campus, external financial support) and others' attitudes (i.e. parental attitudes, staff attitudes).

Most recently, Simui et al. (2018), looking internationally, found that disablers include (1) negative attitudes, (2) absence of inclusive education policy, (3) inaccessible learning environment and learning materials, (4) exclusive pedagogy and (5) limited orientation and mobility. They also found that amidst the disabling environment, a positive attitude, self-advocacy, and innovativeness stood out as key enablers to academic success. Exclusive practices were manifested through inflexible time limits for assessment, lack of adaptive technologies, technical difficulties using e-learning and connecting to websites and Course Management Systems and poor use of e-learning by lecturers. Attitudinal barriers refer to the attitudes of key individuals with whom a visually impaired student will interact. Parental influence is very significant (Levinson, 1998). They can be gatekeepers to the child accessing support services and the acquisition of the skills and knowledge required to be independent (Bishop and Rhind, 2011b). Attitudes of teaching and support staff in schools and in universities during transition can significantly impact the experiences of visually impaired students (Machell, 1996, Kinnell and Creaser, 2001).

Interventions around access

Noble (2010) found that little is known about the potential solutions to widening access to deaf students, and there is a dearth of research on the effectiveness of support services available, including interpreting, note-taking, real-time captioning (a written rendering of the dialogue spoken, in the same language) and tutoring, particularly when attempting to take into account the impact of such support on academic achievement (Lang, 2002). Bishop and Rhind (2011) similarly highlight the importance of institutional support for visually impaired students. They also thought accessibility should be broadly conceptualized to go beyond resources (see Waterfield and West, 2002) to include the campus and accommodation. Amendments to campus design that are not only visually impaired student-friendly, but also environmentally friendly (e.g. PIR lighting) are warranted.

Regarding Autistic Spectrum Condition (ASC) Toor et al. (2016) recommend, in response to a lack of understanding amongst staff, that universities need to educate both staff and students about the nature of ASC, its increased prevalence, and the issues that people with ASC commonly face (Nevill and White, 2011). Fabri et a.l (2016) also advocate looking at the positive attributes of autism, including that they have: expertise and passion for their subject; desire and commitment to be accurate; a drive to seek knowledge; adherence to rules and instructions; ability to maintain intense focus, rational and logical thinking, adopting unconventional angles in problem-solving and spotting errors that others may overlook.

Fabri et al. (2016) also recommend active involvement of those with ASC in the co-production of training. Such an approach would not only increase understanding and awareness, but also have the potential to reduce the social isolation of students and support their transition to higher education (Nevill and White, 2011, Griffith, Totsika, Nash and Hastings, 2012; Matthews, Ly and Goldberg, 2015). Outside educational establishments, many individuals with ASC also require ongoing support from their families and others to ensure success (Hewitt, 2011). Indeed, some individuals with ASC report remaining highly dependent on their families or support services while studying (Howlin, Goode, Hutton and Rutter, 2004, Jennes-Coussens, Magill-Evans and Koning, 2006).

Success

According to the OfS, students who report a disability have lower degree results overall (OfS, 2019b). The OfS (2019c) found that undergraduate disabled students are doing less well than non-disabled students in terms of continuation (0.9 per cent), degree attainment (2.8 per cent) and progression onto highly skilled employment or postgraduate study (1.8 per cent). The pattern is also uneven: 54 per cent of universities and colleges had a gap of less than 2.5 per cent (either positive or negative) between the continuation rate for their non-disabled and disabled students. There are also intersectional issues. Waterfield and Whelan (2017) described differences in the everyday experience of disabled students from working-class backgrounds who do not have the financial or social means to address barriers at university.

There is a marked difference between different disabilities. Those with cognitive or learning difficulties had higher continuation rates (91.4 per cent) than non-disabled students (90.3 per cent). The biggest difference is for those with mental health issues (see separate literature review. Between 2009 and 2013, students with a declared disability had a consistently lower than average overall satisfaction rate. This result persists even when other factors (such as choice of subject, gender and ethnicity) were taken into account (HEFCE, 2018). Disabled students are less satisfied with their professional placements and report more difficulties with them than non-disabled students (Hill and Roger, 2016). Many authors (Yorke and Longden, 2008, Rydberg et al., 2009, Noble, 2010) found that policy changes have not been sufficient to reduce the unequal level of educational attainment between deaf and hearing people. Brennan et al. (2005) found that many deaf students reported a need to work harder than their peers to achieve similar goals, with group tutorials and seminars identified as the most challenging. Karchmer and Mitchell (2003) suggest that students with significant hearing losses continue to have substantial problems lagging behind hearing peers in a variety of academic settings.

Ultimately, speaking to the book's themes, disabled students do not feel they belong and do not feel they are supported. Recent studies and government reports (Hewett et al., 2017, Johnson et al., 2019) detail incidences of disabled students not receiving support until well into their first term, often meaning they fall behind in their course and, in extreme cases, have to repeat a year. Other students raised concerns about the lack of clarity around returning to their course after an interruption in their studies (Weale, 2019). Vickerman and Blundell (2010) outline key areas that need to be addressed (e.g. pre-course support, institutional commitment to developing support services). Goode (2007) talks about extra-visibility (drawing attention to their disability) where disabled students have to be proactive. Madriaga (2007) found lack of support at university to be linked to negative attitudes from professional. Disablist attitudes have still been prominent within some areas of education.

Reports reveal disabled students continuing to experience microaggressions (Osbourne and Osbourne, 2018) that accessible student halls tend to be more expensive, and many teaching spaces are not fully accessible (Hewett et al., 2017). Williams et al. (2019) found that providers still face challenges in making their teaching and learning spaces, and particularly their student accommodation, fully accessible. Positively they also found providers' engagement with students in relation to disability issues – for example, in the co-design of student support services – has increased substantially.

Several authors (Norman, Caseau and Stefanich, 1998, Rao and Gartin, 2003, Baker, Boland and Nowik, 2012, Kimball et al., 2016) pick up on other negative experiences from academics for their departure from being 'normal' students. They explore how academics are less likely than students to believe that students with disabilities are capable of meeting programme expectations and are more likely to believe that students with disabilities do not require or already receive appropriate accommodations. Other authors (Baker et al., 2012) found such opinions are also rarely based on experience as, many of whom are unwilling to disclose their status to peers or faculty due to stigma.

Looking at individual disabilities, although some deaf students report a positive social experience at their HE institution, many find social participation difficult (Foster et al., 1999, Papastiriou and Windle, 2012). Saunders (2013) found that deaf students experience higher levels of social isolation than hearing students; they have fewer social networks and do not feel part of the university community, and stand out as 'the deaf one' (Simcock, 2010). Several authors (Foster et al., 1999, Vasek, 2005, Rydberg et al., 2009) found that some staff in HE make few, if any, modifications for deaf students, identifying the support service faculty as responsible for the success or failure of deaf students and Lang (2002) found deaf students in HE face many barriers as they attempt to gain access to information in the classroom. Noble (2010) and Burgstahler and Doe (2006) found many deaf students decide not to disclose their disability to the university in order to avoid being labelled.

Regarding dyslexia, Pino and Martari's (2014) systematic review showed that disclosing one's own dyslexia is sometimes costly in psychological terms and that many students may prefer to give up the opportunity to receive support to avoid embarrassment or stigmatization, especially when they have suffered these effects in previous school experiences. The implication is that HEIs should work to establish environments where the disclosure of dyslexia is welcomed.

Regarding ASC, Toor et al. (2016) found that many academically able young people with ASC face challenges with student life (Shattuck et al., 2012) including loneliness, isolation, social interactions and self-advocacy (White et al., 2011) and through finding themselves in an environment which is less structured than they have been used to at school and thus have trouble with practicalities such as time management and scheduling (White et al., 2011). Toor et al. (2016) also found ASD student found their social and physical environment made them experience difficulties in terms of picking up unwritten social rules when interacting with tutors and fellow students, tolerating background noise, lighting, crowding or other sensory aspects of the university environment, and handling the social isolation that often comes with living in a new environment. Lack of appropriate support was experienced right from the start with support workers focusing on the deficits of autism over its strengths. Students also experienced a lack of consistency in reasonable adjustments, autism-specific services and personal support.

In accounting for such difficulties, it comes as no surprise that increases in mental health issues are noted among students with ASC in universities (e.g. anxiety and depression) and that these may affect academic attainment (VanBergeijk, Klin and Volkmar, 2008). Fabri et al. (2016) identify the following worries from autistic students: communicating and working in groups; ambiguous questions in interviews; assignments and exams; not knowing who to ask for support; getting lost; being stressed or distracted by certain sensory aspects; concern about their level of disability being misunderstood or belittled and fear of public speaking tendency to go off on tangents or talk too long about their special interests.

Interventions around success

Kimball et al. (2016) and Burchard and Swerdzewski (2009) found that students with disabilities may benefit from classes specifically targeted towards improving metacognitive awareness and learning strategies, as well as from interventions providing course-specific content (Allsopp, Minskoff and Bolt 2005), demonstrating that both general and course-specific assistance can improve performance for some students with disabilities. Intervention strategies can also address common instructional issues like writing quality, such as by having students with developmental disabilities learn a specific writing strategy to improve their essay writing (Hua et al., 2013). Additionally, students with specific disabilities such as autism spectrum disorders can be assisted through targeted academic interventions such as learning explicit reading comprehension strategies (Hua et al., 2012).

Fabri et al. (2016) found that personal tutors can be key to the success of autistic students, as many of them find it difficult to initiate communication or find appropriate services without help when they are in distress. Especially when there is no consistent disability support provision within HE, the personal tutor may be the first or only person who is aware of emerging challenges affecting the student's progress, and a natural point of contact between the HEI and external organizations that provide specialist autism support. They have a series of useful recommendations to tutors including being strength based, building strong personal relationships and being open to exploring new, perhaps unorthodox, ways of working; encourage students to study in their own way, with flexible approaches to deadlines, coursework and modes of study if that helps them to focus on the teaching material better.

Pino and Martari (2016) found that students positively evaluated teaching approaches that went beyond traditional formats such as straight lecturing. They favoured teaching styles that allowed them to employ the full range of their communication and expression abilities to exhibit their knowledge and competence. This became possible in learning environments that provided ample opportunities to access study materials in multiple formats and to autonomously regulate the speed of information processing. The possibility of gaining control of the medium was, hence, a key component of successful learning experiences and was enhanced by the use of ICTs. The students also favoured interactive and student-centred teaching approaches.

They suggest that academic staff should work at different levels to (1) design courses in flexible and multi-layered ways, for example by incorporating multiple formats of content delivery to meet the needs of diverse students and (2) provide individualized adjustments to students who display further difficulties and special needs (in collaboration with university disability services). They cite Norwich and Lewis' (2001) notion of continua of teaching approaches, implying that 'the various strategies and procedures which make up teaching can be considered in terms of whether they are used more or less in practice' (p325). Pino and Martari (2016) found that students positively experience flexible course designs that offer the following: (1) opportunities to access contents in multiple formats; (2) use of media to enhance student control and self-pacing (as evidenced in studies focusing on the use of ICTs); and (3) additional forms of support to meet individual needs. Research is needed to ascertain how a multi-tiered, multi-faceted course design can be implemented in HE and how it might be received by students with and without dyslexia.

Interventions around support

Kutscher and Tuckwiller (2019) in their systematic review and Madaus et al. (2018) found that there has been very limited research on interventions to support the success of students with disabilities in postsecondary education (Madaus et al., 2018). Williams et al. (2019) note that there is no one perfect model of inclusive support, and what works in one institution may not directly translate into another. Kutscher and Tuckwiller (2019) also found personal characteristics of a student 'encompass a complex space at the intersection of individual emotion, cognition, and behavior' (p152), e.g. identification as empowered being resulted in behaviours and actions re-inscribed perseverance, and resulted in positive emotional states. As they say,

> Students who feel empowered believe that they have control over the outcomes of their studies and are likely to take steps to continue their studies, even in the face of challenges. In turn, discovering that they are capable of persevering through difficult times can further support students' sense of empowerment and result in positive emotional experiences.
> (Kutscher and Tuckwiller, 2019, p152)

Peer support

Kimball et al. (2016) and Ness (2013) found peer mentoring grounded in a self-regulated learning model helped students with Asperger syndrome.

Similarly, Jones and Goble (2012) suggest that such mentoring programmes may present a promising practice for future investigation. Additionally, students with learning disabilities may be educated in test-taking strategies or techniques such as progressive muscle relaxation to positive effect (Wachelka and Katz, 1999, Holzer, Madaus, Bray and Kehle, 2009). Since learning disabilities represent a large group of students with disabilities, such studies present promising practices.

Other issues of teaching and learning

Kimball et al. (2016) felt that the impact of disability on the learning and development processes of college students is poorly understood – in part due to a paucity of high-quality empirical research (McCune, 2001). The OfS (2019c) says that 'teaching and learning in higher education is becoming more inclusive, but these positive developments are uneven. Universities and colleges could go further by, for example, offering alternative formats of course materials as standard, and ensuring more buildings are accessible.' Williams et al. (2019) found that the use and coverage of assistive technology (AT) is increasing. In particular, the vast majority of providers use 'lecture capture' (audio or video recording of lectures), with two in five HE providers using it to capture more than half of all lectures. They found 'this not only benefits disabled students but is an example of an inclusive strategy that benefits any student unable to attend or get all they might from a live lecture experience' (Williams et al., 2019, p3).

Universal design for learning

Fabri et al. (2016) say we should move away from the terminology of reasonable adjustments say 'trying to find "reasonable adjustments" for autistic students can separate them from their peers, increase social anxiety and exacerbate their sense of difference (Madriaga, 2010). A more socially-just approach that understands the desires as well as problems of disabled students would not require students to disclose their differences or seek extra support and would benefit all students by default' (Fabri et al., 2016, p15). They talk about adopting Universal Design for Learning (UDL) approaches. Kutscher and Truckwiller (2019) also support approaches which aim to make education accessible and inclusive to any student, regardless of disability diagnosis, so do others (Roberts et al., 2011).

Pino and Martari (2016) similarly supported UDL approaches for dyslexic students. They additionally thought that HEIs should also provide individualized support and adjustments because learning needs vary among students and across different territories of their learning experience. They found that not all students used adjustments, and students did not use adjustments in all courses. Individualized adaptation and lenience helped the students to navigate HE Helped. This was especially true regarding assessment domain as students can be unaware of their right to require adjustments and modifications. Some students felt that standard adjustments (such as the use of a laptop and extended time) were sufficient. Others felt discriminated against by the dominance of written assessment because it does not enable them to fully express their actual level of knowledge and competence.

As Hanafin, Shevlin, Kenny and Mc Neela (2007) stated, 'the over-reliance on written techniques of assessment can exclude many learners from successful assessment experiences as can the practice of requiring learners to communicate all they know about a topic within a limited and rigidly imposed time frame' (p438). Sometimes, students prefer not to use adjustments because they want to prove to themselves or to others that they can succeed without external help. At the same time, this preference might reflect students' adaptation to teaching environments that are unreceptive to diverse student needs.

Progression

Government research shows that disabled people with a degree have employment rates of 74 per cent, compared with 49 per cent for those disabled people whose highest qualifications are at GCSE level. While there is still a substantial employment rate gap between disabled and non-disabled graduates, it is smaller than for other qualification levels, but is still 15 per cent (OfS, 2019b). There are again differences between different disabilities. For full-time undergraduates who graduated in 2016–17, only 61.8 per cent of those with a social or communication impairment had progressed into highly skilled work or postgraduate study after six months compared with 73.3 per cent of their non-disabled peers (HEFCE, 2018).

Many authors (Roessler et al., 2007a, Kimball et al., 2016, Madaus et al., 2018) found that disabled student did not feel they got adequate career advice at university, such as information about technology or accommodations in the workplace. Hitchings et al. (2001, 2010) found (a) the nature of the disability produced differential outcomes; (b) students with disabilities receive many other services and interventions that may take time away from career development; (c) parents and instructors may have low expectations for or be over-protective of students with disabilities; or (d) some students with disabilities may fear failure, have poor goal orientation, or may hold other attitudes that hamper career development.

Interventions around progression

Some studies investigate what colleges can do to better prepare students with disabilities for a successful transition to employment. Results suggest that providing mentoring, internships and informational interventions on relevant topics such as the ADA, health insurance or Social Security are some possible avenues to pursue (Madaus, 2006, Hennessey et al., 2006a, Roessler et al., 2007b).

Studies generally vary as to the type of disability they focus on with some taking a broad focus and some focusing on a specific disability. Factors that contribute to successful transitions are work experience/previous vocational experience and self-determination although vary across stages with some (e.g. disability effects, low educational expectations) being strongest in the earlier stages. Various intervention strategies are mentioned including: mentoring, job coaching, general transition programmes (which can vary in focus) and group-based exercises. Some research papers focus on careers within a specific industry (e.g. STEM or the arts).

Graduate students

In the States only 5–10 per cent of doctoral students are disabled (Lizotte and Simplican, 2017). Lizotte and Simplican (2017) found that doctoral students face discrimination and disadvantage from application to graduation. Doctoral students encounter inaccessible university websites, are missed in terms of outreach, and have inaccessible student handbooks. Other authors find disabled students are not mentioned or represented in these materials (Holt and McKay, 2000, Thompson, Burgstahler and Moore, 2010). Doctoral students with physical disabilities report difficulties getting to an adviser's office, classrooms, and departmental social events (Farrar and Young, 2007).

Graduate students with visual impairments report difficulty acquiring accessible texts in a timely manner (Farrar and Young, 2007, Orellana et al., 2016) and accessing transportation (Galdi, 2007). Hannam-Swain (2017) similarly talks about the 'extra labour' of being a graduate student. She talks of a lack of representation, support services which are geared for undergraduate students, and procedures that do not take account of disabilities and lack of appreciation of 'the complexities of juggling the additional time-consuming events which occur when you are disabled'. Many authors (Hannam-Swain, 2017, Lizotte and Simplican, 2017) talk about an ableism in higher education that is particularly prevalent at graduate level, with students choosing not to disclose for fear of being discriminated against, with a fine line between being barely tolerated and being seen as too disabled for graduate level study.

This is replicated at the level of staff representation. Several authors (Daughtry, 2009, Sahlin, 2009) found that the proportion of successful doctoral students who go onto academic positions is below that of student without disabilities. Even for faculty in departments in which diversity are foregrounded, disability is often ignored and faculty with disabilities are perceived as getting 'special treatment' when they receive accommodations. I have myself encountered disbelief that a professor can have a disability, and resistance from the institution when I ask for reasonable adjustments, one person expressing surprise that this would be needed at professorial level.

Perhaps unsurprisingly, I could find no literature focused on interventions for students with disabilities at doctoral level. The NUS in the UK wrote an open letter to research councils in 2020 urging for automatic funding extensions for all PhD students who are registered as disabled, neurodivergent or chronically ill. However, as with class race and mental health issues, academics and institutions need to reflect on their model they have constructed, and reinscribe, of a graduate student, and an academic. Of 2,100 professors in the UK, only two openly identify as being dyslexic.

Conclusion

Higher education is ableist in that university structures have in mind a particular mythical student, who is culturally and materially male, comes from an elite background, white and, in this case, 'able' bodied. It is also full of staff who are similarly encultured and, as described in the conclusion to the last chapter, subject to society's prejudices and constructions about disability. To undo and counter both of these forces will take training reflection and a whole institutional commitment and approach – we have a lot to undo.

> Discussing issues of social justice and accessibility in higher education on the grounds of disability necessitates a nuanced analysis of the myriad of hidden dynamics that create power inequities and exclusionary regimes for disabled students. Such an attempt requires analytical openness as well as convergence in the unpacking of exclusionary matrices and discriminatory practices that have a cumulative and overlapping effect on the lives and educational trajectories of disabled students.
>
> (Liasidou, 2014, p131)

As Liasidou (2014) expands upon above, we need to have a critical view of disability in universities and build a detailed theoretical model of its dynamics in higher education. This model should reveal and ameliorate hidden constructions and operations of power to truly enable us to engage with the phenomena. Institutions need to develop models, both theoretical and practical, that explain the dynamics of disability and norm construction in higher education and move away from a reductionist, pseudo-practical, but eminently ideological, 'what works' approach. 'What works' approaches inevitably focus on small-scale individualized initiatives, ignore structural factors and try to make universalist claims from them. This approach has systematically failed for the last twenty years and I cannot see why, if pursued, it would not equally fail for the next twenty years. A combination of the approaches of the four models outlined, with scope to incorporate new thinking as it evolves, would be a good starting point.

As with mental health, there is a politics of disclosure. Ownership of disabilities can lead to better self-efficacy and determination, but whether we should own a potentially stigmatizing label created in opposition to a constructed and contested norm is debatable. Utilizing a CDT approach, higher education institutions need to turn to the question of what ideal student is constructed by and through our services, structures and assumptions, and whose interests this is serving. Then, if we are to change this contested ideal student, we need to understand how it was constructed and can therefore be deconstructed.

Drawing on the positives, Weidman's (1989) model seems good in exploring the normative contexts of higher education, exploring the factors that shape socialization processes including the influence of others, organizational impacts, social interaction and social integration. Perna's (2006) model is good at looking at the wider context, and considers factors such as social capital and social mobility. Hurado's (2012) model looks at issues such as institutional racism, identity, both institutional and individual, and how this is embedded in approaches to learning and curriculum design. Hewett et al. (2017) develop these ideas and take a systems approach, looking at the interface between the institutional and the individual, or collective, and start to address issues of agency and structure (Seal, 2020).

7

Students with Mental Health Issues: The Politics of Complicity

Introduction

As noted in the introduction, there seem to be four dimensions to mental health issues to consider in higher education: the experiences of those who come to university with a diagnosed mental health issue, the experiences of those who develop mental health issues while at university, the impact that university has on a persons' mental health and the wider issues of student and staff well-being, i.e. positive mental health. These issues, obviously, intertwine and interact with each other. The chapter argues that higher education providers are often guilty of not facing up to the extent of poor mental health in their institutions, and particularly of not recognizing their own culpability and how they exacerbate it. To recognize it they need to undertake a number of approaches that this chapter will consider. This includes, again, taking a whole institutional approach.

The chapter will critically explore statistics around the access, success and progression of students with mental health issues and explores models of mental health including social, medical and critical disability perspectives. It will explore other theoretical themes and concepts including the politics of disclosure, transitions to universities, staff, student and employers view of mental health and their impacts on the university experience of those with mental health conditions. As with other issues, Hugues and Spanner emphasize the necessity of taking a whole institutional approach to mental health issues.

In terms of interventions, we will consider ways of developing social capital for those who have, or are developing conditions, as well as managing transitions, into, during and out of higher education. We will also consider the nature of support that people may need, and who is best placed to deliver it. Universities are generally accepted to have a duty of care towards their students and this includes a duty to ensure the health and welfare of their students. We have statutory duties in this regard. HEIs have duties under the Equality Act 2010 to provide 'reasonable adjustments' for students with disabilities, which includes people with mental illnesses. The Act also protects individuals from discrimination based on their disability.

The chapter will also consider the key debates within providing mental health services, particularly how we should interact with statutory mental health services. Should HEIs be merely a signposting service, or should we have more comprehensive mental health services? The chapter argues for somewhere in between, that thinking a signposting service is enough neglects the politics of mental health services. Conversely, trying to provide a comprehensive service has the potential to blur boundaries and duplicate services. The chapter will also consider the degree to which we should embed issues around mental health within the curriculum: learning, teaching and assessment including psychoeducational approaches. Finally, the chapter will look at issues of progression, in particular the importance of working with employers and of recognizing and ameliorating mental health issues within doctoral study.

Theoretical perspectives

Definitions and conceptual models

It is not my intent to debate the nature of mental health here. As with disability in general, I would position myself somewhere between the social and critical disability model. There are many models of mental health relevant to higher education. The University Mental Health Charter in the UK (Hugues and Spanner, 2019) recommends Byrom and Murphy's (2018) psychosocial conceptual model of mental health. This model holds that mental health is an interplay of genes and the environment, with learning should be seen as a third mediating factor, i.e. 'that it is the learned responses of individuals to their genes and environment that determines mental health'. Byrom and Murphy (2017, p32) suggest that a whole university approach needs to be adopted, and they elaborate on dimensions of genetic, environmental and learning factors.

Byrom and Murphy (2017) found that genetic factors can necessitate proactive specialist support and/or adjustments for students and staff with particular genetic characteristics that may make them more vulnerable to poor mental health. Environmental factors are predicated on the universal principle that all members of the university community must encounter an environment that is conducive to good mental health that has considered the environments from which students are coming to university and the impacts these may already have had. Learning as a factor means students and staff may need to develop 'insights, understanding, skills and strategies' drawing on previous learning to better manage their well-being.

Taking a whole institutional approach

> Along the decades, different groups have campaigned and struggled for respect and rights; some have been successful at achieving symbolic and cultural reparation, others less so ... Yet, Mad individuals, and madness more broadly, are yet to feature in the conversation on respect and identity, a conversation still dominated by framings that emphasize the medical idiom and the notions of distress and disability.
>
> (Rashed, 2019, p170)

Thorney (2017) considers 'buy-in and direction from senior leadership' by universities to be the most important factor in helping to improve student mental health and well-being, recommending. Bolton and Hubble (2020) note that most HEIs have a mental health policy which sets out the institution's approach to mental health services and provision for students. Mental health policy documents generally show a commitment to providing a supportive environment for students with mental health difficulties. Universities UK's 'Stepchange Mental health in higher education' framework provides guidance for higher education institutions on mental health strategies.

The Framework states that universities should adopt mental health as a strategic priority, and that HEIs should implement a whole university approach with students and staff involved at all stages. The Framework gives guidance on leadership, data, staff, prevention, early intervention, support, transition and partnerships. However, less than one-third (29 per cent) of universities have designed an explicit mental health and well-being strategy, less than half (43 per cent) design course content and delivery so as to help improve student mental health and well-being, two-thirds (67 per cent) do not provide students access to NHS mental health specialists who can deliver interventions onsite and 23 per cent do not work closely with NHS secondary mental health services (Hugues and Spanner, 2019). There are a number of models that might be useful for understanding disabled student journeys through HE and how to take a whole institutional approach. Kimball et al. (2016) evaluated them.

Access

First looking at prevalence, the OfS (2019a) found full-time students aged twenty-one and over were more likely to have reported having a mental health condition than full-time students under twenty-one for all years from 2013–14 to 2017–18. For both full-time and part-time students, those of mixed ethnicity were most likely to report having a mental health condition for all academic years since 2013–14. Duffy et al. (2020) conducted comparable work in Canada that looks at mental health predictors. They found that at entry to university, almost one-third of students screened positive for depressive (28 per cent) and anxiety (33 per cent) symptoms, which were associated with significant impairment in 45 per cent and 47 per cent of students respectively. As many as 29 per cent of students endorsed lifetime suicidal thoughts, 6 per cent suicide attempts and 18 per cent self-harm.

They also found that approximately one-fifth of students met screening thresholds for sleep problems (21 per cent), with more females compared with males. Close to half the students they surveyed (48 per cent) endorsed substance misuse, largely attributable to binge drinking – higher in males compared with females (52 per cent vs 42 per cent). As many as 18 per cent reported low self-esteem, especially females compared with males. Hesa found that in 2018/19, 59,200 female students (5.3 per cent of all female students) said they had a mental health condition. This rate was almost double the rate for male students of 2.8 per cent. Thorney (2017) found female first-year students are more likely than male first-year students to disclose a mental health condition (2.5 per cent compared to 1.4 per cent) (2015/16).

Thorney (2017) also found that students experience lower well-being than young adults as a whole, and experience lower well-being than was the case in previous years. In 2017, less than one in five students reported high levels of each of these four key well-being indicators. The University Student Mental Health Survey 2018 found that 34 per cent reported having a serious personal, emotional, behavioural or mental health problem for which they felt needed professional help. The most common diagnoses were depression (10 per cent) and anxiety disorders (8 per cent). They also found that 9 per cent think about self-harming often or all the time, 43 per cent are worried often or all the time, 33 per cent reported suffering from loneliness often or all the time and 45 per cent use alcohol or recreational drugs to cope with problems in their life.

Issues of non-disclosure

Hubble and Bolton (2020) note that the proportion of students who disclosed a mental health condition to their university have increased rapidly in recent years. OfS (2019) reported a broad trend of increased reporting across the whole sector. Thorney (2017) found that mental health conditions account for an increasing proportion of all disability disclosed by first-year students (17 per cent in 2015/16 compared to 5 per cent in 2006/7).

Despite the aforementioned increase, there is serious under-reporting with regard to mental health (OfS, 2019). Hubble and Bolton (2020) note that NUS surveys have found much higher rates of mental ill health than those disclosed to universities and 21.5 per cent had a current mental health diagnosis and 33.9 per cent had experienced a serious psychological issue for which they felt they needed professional help. Hubble and Bolton (2020) felt that survey responses are confidential and are likely to give a better idea of the full extent of mental ill health. Hartrey et al. (2017) found that just under half of students who report experiencing a mental health condition choose not to disclose it to their HEI. Hartrey et al. (2017) found students fear disclosure will negatively affect their relationships with others, their relationship with faculty and future career prospects. Other authors drew similar conclusions (Dougherty et al., 1996, Knis-Matthews et al., 2007).

Students fear disclosure will precipitate stigma, discrimination and the perception by others that they are telling lies and seeking privileges (Weiner and Weiner, 1996, Stanley and Manthorpe, 2001, Knis-Matthews et al., 2007, Salzer et al., 2008, Martin, 2010). Students weigh the decision to disclose, with a perception that disclosure may bring perceived negative consequences such as stigma, and an awareness non-disclosure will result in an inability to attain support. This creates a sense of dilemma and anxiety (Dougherty et al., 1996, Knis-Matthews et al., 2007). Non-disclosure was also found to be a protective mechanism against stigma (KnisMatthews et al., 2007).

Thorley (2017) found that higher education providers have – over the past five years – experienced significant increases in demand for counselling and disability services. As many as 94 per cent report an increase in demand for counselling services, while 61 per cent report an increase of over 25 per cent. In some HEIs, up to one in four students is using, or waiting to use, counselling services. As many as 86 per cent report an increase in demand for disability services, while 31 per cent report an increase of over 25 per cent. In some HEIs, up to one in four students is using, or waiting to use, disability services. HESA (2021) found higher rates of mental health conditions were reported among women, undergraduates, full-time students and those in their second or later years.

Acquiring social capital – pre-entry and induction

Hugues and Spanner (2019) note that students who have had the opportunity to acquire the necessary social and navigational capital are more likely to settle quickly into their new environment (Yorke and Longden, 2004, Pennington et al., 2018a). This has implications for most widening participation groups who do not have such university capital (Harvey et al., 2007). Citing Zepke et al. (2005), Hugues and Spanner (2019) say that universities need to ensure that practice, pedagogy and culture are adapted for the whole population.

Hugues and Spanner (2019) and Pennington et al. (2018) show how pre-entry interventions can have positive impacts for a range of students. Examples in the literature demonstrate benefits in helping to build belonging, academic self-efficacy, familiarization and well-being. Hugues and Spanner also feel universities need to consider that their pre-arrival interactions with students may have negative impacts on their well-being such as marketing material that sets unrealistic expectations about the university experience (e.g. that it is always fun) may set false expectations. Mayhew et al. (2010) talk about early poor experiences of the new university environment that can reduce student persistence, self-belief and sense of belonging. Similarly, Hill et al. (2018) discuss how students are supported during the first days and weeks of term, and the strategies, tools and assistance which the university provides to enable success and belonging can have significant impacts. Well-planned and structured induction programmes have been shown to improve integration, well-being and confidence (Hugues and Spanner, 2019, Mayhew et al., 2010).

In several studies Kift (2008, 2010, 2015) suggests that induction needs to be embedded into an inclusive and scaffolded curriculum and that academic programmes utilize curriculum design that has a focus on transition pedagogy. Hugues and Spanner (2019) and Kift (2008) both talk about the need to 'move away from the concept of induction being an information–providing process and focus on the felt experience and social and academic integration' (Hugues and Spanner, 2019, p12). Furthermore, induction works best when embedded beyond the first few weeks and managed as a process over the entire first-year experience (Hugues and Spanner, 2019, p25).

Transition to university

As many authors (Fisher and Hood, 1987, Harris, 2019, Hugues and Spanner, 2019) note, going to university is a significant transition (TInto, 2003, Kahu and Nelson, 2018) that can be a very stressful process. Good transition experiences, where students feel supported, help them develop a sense of belonging, confidence and motivation that can lead to increased persistence, achievement and well-being (Palmer et al., 2009). Transition experiences appear to have long-term effects on student socialization, health behaviours and self-efficacy (Kleiber et al., 2018). Hugues and Spanner (2019) and Richardson et al. (2012) note that for a large proportion of the student population, the beginning of university can be a mix of positive, neutral and negative experiences, but is manageable. Research has identified that, during this period of transition, many students experience psychological distress, anxiety, depression, sleep disturbance, a reduction in self-esteem and isolation (Fisher and Hood, 1987, Gall et al., 2000, Stanley et al., 2009, Harris, 2019).

Many students who withdraw from university in the first year do so in the first weeks of term because of these negative experiences (Palmer et al., 2009). Even where they persist, student well-being does not reset to their original, pre-university, baseline for many months (Gall et al., 2000, Bewick et al., 2010). Withdrawals often related back to experiences in this time period (Palmer et al., 2009) can have long-term effects both on academic persistence and success and on student well-being (Tinto, 2005). Some research has also identified links between transition experience and student suicide and suicidal ideation (Stanley et al., 2009).

Several authors (Lizzio, 2010, Morgan, 2010, Tett et al., 2016) see the transition to university as one stage of an ongoing process of transition throughout their university career and beyond – one of becoming a student, which is in itself never ending (Thomas, 2012, Parkes, 2014, Seal and Parkes, 2019). Several authors (Stallman, 2010, Macaskill, 2013, Lieberman and Remedios, 2007) found that for many students, mental health, well-being and positive engagement with their programme may dip in the years after first year. Hugues and Spanner (2019) found that progression from year to year, placements, study abroad and the transition beyond university as areas which they believed impacted on the mental health of some students and therefore required attention from universities.

Several US studies (Morgan, 2011, Whittle, 2018, Webb and Cotton, 2019) and two UK ones (McBurnie et al., 2012, Thompson et al., 2013) talk about the second-year slump, with a reduction in motivation, engagement and enjoyment of their course in the second year. Some students appear to experience increased academic anxiety and less self-efficacy (Scott and Cashmore, 2012). Yorke (2015) highlights that second-year students face a range of additional challenges, including an expectation to undertake increased independent learning and the fact that, for many, the second year counts towards final degree classification. Morgan (2011b) and Zaitseva et al.

(2015) found that students are stressed and distanced physically from support if they move into private accommodation, away from the supported living arrangements provided by halls of residence.

Mental health at university

Duffy et al. (2020) found that, at the end of the first year, the proportion of students with clinically significant depressive and anxiety symptoms increased to 36 per cent and 39 per cent, respectively, with rates of associated impairment at 54 per cent and 48 per cent, respectively. They found that 17 per cent of students screened positive for both anxiety and depressive symptoms at entry and 23 per cent had clinically significant anxiety and depressive symptoms and suicidal ideation/attempts. Similarly, at the end of first year 39 per cent had clinically significant anxiety and depressive symptoms, and 18 per cent screened positive for all three mental health outcomes.

The effect of mental health issues on students can lead to consequences such as: academic failure, dropping out of education, poorer career prospects and in the worst cases suicide. (Hubble and Bolton, 2020). Data on students in England from the Office for Students (2019) shows that students with a declared mental health condition were less likely than average to continue in higher education after their first year, achieve a first or upper second degree, secure higher-level employment or go on to study as a postgraduate. Thorney (2017) found that in 2014/15, a record number of students (1,180) who experienced mental health problems dropped out of university, an increase of 210 per cent compared to 2009/10.

Hartrey et al. (2017) found that students who experience their first episode of mental illness in college often do not recognize they are unwell, require help or know how to access help (Becker et al., 2002, Collins and Mowbray, 2005, Quinn et al., 2009). Hartrey et al. (2017) found that students who experience a first episode of mental illness are unlike many other disability groups in higher education because they do not have a lived experience of disability since birth or childhood, nor do they have past experience of utilizing and navigating supports systems in education to act as points of reference. They (Hartrey et al., 2017) found that this adds to the importance of imparting mental health literacy to students together with knowledge of supports and access routes should they become unwell.

Duffy et al. (2020), comparing reporting of mental health at entry and end of first year, found that 51 per cent were persistent and 49 per cent were new onset. Similarly, for anxiety symptoms 56 per cent were persistent; for suicidal ideation/attempts 79 per cent were persistent. Furthermore, 27 per cent of students with a negative screen for anxiety, depression or suicidal thoughts or attempts at entry to university screened positive at time 2, whereas 29 per cent of students who screened positive on entry no longer reported clinically significant mental health symptoms at the end of the first year. They also found that all psychosocial and lifestyle risk factors, anxiety and suicidal ideation at entry to university such as exercise frequency or social support, with the exception of substance use, were significantly associated with a positive depressive screen at completion of first year. Specifically, lower self-esteem, poorer sleep quality and higher perceived stress were associated with an increased risk of clinically significant depressive symptoms. Duffy et al. (2020) found that anxiety and depressive symptoms at the start of university were associated with lower grades over the year, whereas anxiety and depressive symptoms along with a number of psychosocial and lifestyle risk factors at entry to university were associated with lower levels of school connectedness at the end of the academic year.

Bolton and Hubble (2020) note that many factors have been suggested as contributing to the rise in cases of mental ill health among higher education students – work pressures, moving away from home, financial worries or more generally higher education institutions are said to be feeling the impact of the rise in metal health conditions among the sixteen to twenty-five age population. They report that some of the increase is due to students with mental health conditions being more likely to report this. This increase in disclosure may be because of greater public awareness and reduced stigma associated with mental ill health. UCAS reported an increase in home applicants who 'declared' they had a mental health condition on their application between 2014 and 2018. This was up by nearly 10,000 to around 17,000.

Several authors note that when universities address transition effectively, it is possible to ensure that the balance of experience is positive for all students (Hill et al., 2018, Pennington et al., 2018b, Hugues and Spanner, 2019,

Thomas, 2012). I have talked in other chapters about transition models, and the idea of transition as becoming (Parkes, 2014, Seal and Parkes, 2020) in which emotion, social connection, efficacy and well-being are key elements (Hugues and Spanner, 2019). Hugues and Spanner (2019) go on to say that to ensure that transition is positive for all students, it must be structurally embedded into every aspect of university planning and activity. As Kift (2015, 2010) has argued, transition must be 'integrated and implemented through an intentionally designed curriculum by seamless partnerships of academic and professional staff in a whole-of-institution transformation' (Kift, 2015, p65).

Researchers have found that students with mental health problems receive lower grades and experience higher rates of educational attrition than their peers (Kessler, Foster, Saunders, and Stang, 1998, Hysenbegasi, Hass and Rowland, 2005). OfS (2019) found that for all full-time undergraduate students starting in 2015–16, the continuation rate was 90.3 per cent. For part-time students, it was 63.4 per cent. Continuation rates were significantly lower for both full-time and part-time students who had reported having a mental health condition, when compared with the continuation rate across the whole sector, though the gap has narrowed slightly since 2012–13. In 2015–16, full-time students who reported having a mental health condition had a continuation rate of 86.6 per cent.

In the UK, OfS (2020) found that once they arrive, students face many new pressures. According to a recent poll, over 87 per cent of students said they struggle with feelings of anxiety, and one in three experienced a serious psychological issue which required professional help. Thorney (2017) found that between 2007 and 2015, the number of student suicides increased by 79 per cent (from 75 to 134). Just 25 per cent of people to die by suicide in the UK were in contact with mental health services during the year prior to their death. OfS (2020) found that part-time students who reported having a mental health condition had a continuation rate of 52.1 per cent. Across all ethnic groups, full-time students were less likely to receive a first or 2:1 if they reported having a mental health condition. Black full-time students had the largest attainment gap of any ethnicity group; Black full-time students with a reported mental health condition had an attainment rate 5.8 percentage points below that of all Black full-time students.

Supporting transitions during and after higher education

Hugues and Spanner (2019) suggest that students encounter multiple, ongoing transitions during their university career, including access, between years/levels of study and exiting university. Universities should ensure that support for these transitions is structurally embedded into curriculum and university practice. Morgan (2011a, 2011b) and Stewart and Milson (2015) found that effective and relevant scaffolding within the curriculum, and between year to year, can provide students with the opportunity to develop the skills, resources and understanding needed for the next phase of study and student life and suggest using structured re-inductions at each level. Hugues and Spanner (2019) note that there is significantly less evidence in relation to the mental health and well-being of final-year students. Their research highlighted the negative impact of workload and the perceived pressure many students experience to get good degree classifications.

Hugues and Spanner (2019) also suggest universities provide targeted support for students on placement and professional programmes. Giar and Baglow (2018) and Hugues and Byrom (2019) concur. Professional placements can place pressure on student mental health due to the nature of the issues to which they are exposed (such as safeguarding issues or patient death), as well as isolation, reduced access to support, financial difficulties, workload and burn-out. Hugues and Spanner (2019) also suggest adequate support for students taking breaks in study and proactively support their transition back into education. Story et al. (2019) found that student would benefit from transitional support when they have taken unplanned breaks such as breaks of study due to illness, or having to take time out because of caring responsibilities and other domestic issues. Maintaining contact with the university and receiving ongoing support during such a break can better support students to make a successful return to university

Support during university

Markoulakis and Kirsh (2013), in their systematic review, found students with mental health problems perceived a lack of awareness and understanding of their difficulties among university faculty, staff and students (Weiner,

1999, Megivern, Pellerito and Mowbray, 2003, Tinklin, Riddell and Wilson, 2005, Martin, 2010). They also found that students struggled with a fear of stigmatization and would avoid disclosing their difficulties on campus to protect their privacy and prevent undue discrimination (Weiner and Wiener, 1996, Weiner, 1999, Tinklin, Riddell and Wilson, 2005, Martin, 2010). Students also indicated feelings that they did not deserve special consideration and avoided disclosing their concerns to prevent being perceived as deceptive or as seeking unmerited privileges (Weiner and Wiener, 1996, Weiner, 1999, Megivern, Pellerito and Mowbray, 2003, Martin, 2010).

In some cases, students were not aware that their disability qualified them for special academic consideration, mainly because they did not see themselves as having a disability (Weiner and Wiener, 1996, Weiner, 1999, Megivern, Pellerito and Mowbray, 2003). Authors did not acknowledge, Markoulakis and Kirsh/Students with Mental Health Problems 91 however, that this reticence might also be an internal manifestation of the stigma students were subjected to. Constant fear of and exposure to stigma may affect students' identities, so that they begin to see themselves as undeserving of special consideration as a result of their perceptions of how university faculty, staff and peers view them. Hugues and Spanner (2019) outline three characteristics of effective services.

First, effective services are those that understand the context of student life and of the relationship between academic learning and well-being (Postareff et al., 2016). Second, services should understand their local community and establish mechanisms for the student and staff voice to influence service development (Piper and Emmanueal, 2019). Finally, services should be responsive to changes in need among their population. Several other authors (Student Minds, 2017, Thorley, 2017, Smithies and Brysom, 2018) have also developed principles for services, common denominators being that services must be safe, effective, accessible to all, appropriately resourced, relevant to local context and well governed.

Staff and other students' attitudes

Looking at the UK, Canada and the States, Hartrey et al. (2017) found staff attitudes to be a barrier. Some academics are afraid of students with mental illnesses and believe students with mental illness are dangerous. Others do not feel comfortable engaging with students with mental illness (Becker et al., 2002). Teaching staff report a perceived lack of skill in relation to engaging with students with mental illness (Stanley and Manthorpe, 2001). Academics hold more positive attitudes towards inclusion of students with physical and sensory disabilities in comparison to students with psychiatric disabilities (Hindes and Mather, 2007, Sniatecki, Perry and Snell, 2015).

Attitudes held by non-disabled students towards inclusion based upon disability type are also less positive towards students with psychiatric disabilities than towards students with physical and sensory disabilities (Hindes and Mather, 2007). A Priory study in 2019 found that almost seven out of ten respondents said they found it hard to believe that their peers were suffering from a mental health condition. Factors included a general lack of awareness regarding mental health issues amongst students and that conditions are not always obvious and may fluctuate depending on how the student is feeling and the treatment they receive.

Older students in the age bracket thirty-five to forty-four were found to be the least likely to believe their student peers, with 93 per cent of them admitting to having doubts about the truthfulness of their statements. This age bracket also seemed to be the most judgemental, with 89 per cent of them believing that mental health issues carry a stigma. The tendency to stigmatize those with mental health issues echoes the trends revealed in the Priory Group's 2014 UMHD survey, which found that 25 per cent of students felt uncomfortable talking to their peers about mental health issues, and half of the respondents experienced negative backlash. Worryingly, the recent 2019 survey also found that six in ten students have actually witnessed a fellow student with a mental health condition be stigmatized.

Looking at student view of schizophrenia specifically, Cadge et al. (2019) found lack of knowledge about the condition, particularly the negative symptoms. There were mixed ideas on the causes and sources of available help for schizophrenia. While there was a general misconception among the students that schizophrenia caused multiple personalities and was a dangerous illness, there were some differences in perceptions and understanding between ethnic groups, with more Indian students perceiving upbringing as a causal factor in the development of the illness and more Pakistani students perceiving possession by a spirit as a cause.

The structure of services

In most HEIs support for students with mental health issues is delivered through the Student Services department (Hugues and Spanner, 2019). They found that support may be provided through a specific Wellbeing Service. HEIs may provide counselling, student advice services, support networks, mental health workshops or other resources. Student unions may also provide student-led services such as peer support groups and advice lines (Hugues and Spanner, 2019). AMOSSHE (2019) found that services vary according to size and type of provider, but often include some combination of mental health teams, counselling, inclusivity teams, disability teams, well-being teams, nursing teams, chaplaincy, residential life teams and financial advice services. Many universities are therefore devoting considerable resources and effort into supporting student well-being. However, this does not necessarily mean they are effective.

Hugues and Spanner (2019) firmly recommend having gp's on campus.

> Where GPs are based on a university campus, this can result in much better relationships and closer working between universities and GPs to support individual students, although this is not guaranteed. Building effective relationships between universities and GPs off campus appears to be much more difficult and variable. This becomes more problematic when GPs are based out of the area, are not used to working with universities and are less likely to understand the nature of the support universities provide. University staff identified that it has become increasingly difficult for students to access secondary care, even when in crisis or seriously mentally ill. This increases risk and places additional strain on university support systems. Gaps in care between universities and statutory services means that the responses and support an individual receives may become fragmented and even contradictory, leading to harm.

Connell et al. (2018) and Conley et al. (2017) found that evidence shows that traditional services, such as counselling and therapy, can be effective responses to poor student mental health. However, other authors (Wampol and Brown, 2005, NHS, 2019) have found that there can be significant variations in outcomes between counsellors/therapists and between services, to the point where some are damaging (Berk and Parker, 2009). Other interventions, such as mental health teams, are more contested (Barkham et al., 2019) especially in how success should be measured (Grant and Schwartz, 2011). Hugues and Spanner (2019) found that mental health teams are supporting increasing levels of risk and complexity and conclude it is vital that staff in these roles are properly equipped, qualified, registered and supervised.

Arising issues

Hugues and Spanner (2019) found that access is crucial and consideration should also be given to how mode of study or the geographical spread of a campus may affect accessibility, as well as opening hours and mode of provision of services (online, digital applications and by telephone). Recent reports have raised concerns that some services may not understand the experiences and needs of particular student groups, e.g. Global Majority students (Akel, 2019, Reza, 2019), LGBTQ+ students (Smithies and Byrom, 2018), international students and postgraduate students (Hugues and Spanner, 2019). Baker (2018) and Mecer et al. (2018) indicated that a lack of informed cultural understanding, from support staff, can result in students not accessing support or not returning after a first appointment.

Hugues and Spanner found that if students in need have to wait several months or if service lists are closed down all together, then a service is no longer genuinely accessible. Thorney (2017) and Mercer et al. (2018) raised concerns about the length and ubiquity of long waiting times for support services and the impact on students and other staff. Hugues and Spanner (2019) say it should be recognized that there are a number of reasons waiting lists can grow, including unpredictable rises in demand, management and triage practices. However, appropriate resourcing can be a factor. They conclude 'It is therefore incumbent upon universities to ensure that they are providing sufficient resources, recruiting the right staff and managing services effectively and efficiently' (Hugues and Spanner, 2019, p30).

Hugues and Spanner (2019) talk about the difficulties of universities being dumped on. They describe multiple accounts of students being discharged to 'University support services' without consultation with the university. Others reported instances of ill and distressed students being returned to halls of residence late at night, as a place of safety, when no staff are available. Many of the staff interviewed were or had been NHS clinicians and said such decisions were not about mis-communication but desperation given the current availability of resources and demand. They call for accountable partnerships.

For this reason, many government report and studies (Raddi, 2019, Royal College of Psychiatrists, 2011, Universities UK, 2018) have called for universities and local NHS/Social Care providers to form collaborative partnerships Collaboration across organizations is generally recognized as being necessary to ensure that individuals receive consistent, safe, effective, integrated and cohesive care and support (British Medical Association, 2017, South East Clinical Senate, 2017). Hugues and Spanner (2019) found a myriad of models of partnership with local voluntary agencies, across institutions and with the local NHS. Typically they focus on developing either a hands off approach or an integrated one.

Hugues and Spanner (2019) challenge the 'hands off' approach, where once notified, universities let the mental health services take over. It is unclear when and where hands are taken off and this approach does not have the flexibility that a sensitive response to mental health issues needs. They feel the individual ends up being passed around with such a model. As they say, 'mental health is subject to fluctuation, sometimes rapidly, which may mean an individual passing back and forth between university and NHS as their health fluctuates, fragmenting care' (Hugues and Spanner, 2019, p38). They call instead for 'thresholds of responsibility and collaboration between services and the student', that recognize that once a student becomes a patient, they do not stop being a student, and vice versa. Duffy et al. (2019) attempt to bring some definition to these principles and there are significant echoes between this paper and the views of participants in the consultations.

> Central to the model is a student friendly and engaging first contact interface, which would trigger an expert triage assessment accessible through a variety of means including on-campus health services walk-in, online through the health services website and via direct phone line. The model aligns with a stepped care approach in which students would be assessed by experienced mental health professionals (i.e. psychiatric nurse supported by a psychiatrist)

and matched to evidence-informed levels of support or care ranging from low to high intensity. Low intensity or entry-level mental health resources might include online supported psychoeducational resources and short-term supportive counseling (individual or group). Students manifesting clinically significant symptoms and uncomplicated psychiatric syndromes would be triaged directly to a campus-based multidisciplinary integrated mental health care team providing students with appropriate targeted interventions including psychotherapy (individual or group), and when appropriate medication. Students assessed to be at high-risk and/or manifesting serious or urgent psychiatric presentations would be immediately triaged or have a facilitated transfer to the appropriate community-based specialty or urgent care service. In some settings, it may be possible to organize partial integration with community specialty.

(Duffy et al., 2020, pp9–10)

Hugues and Snapper (2019) also unearthed potential risks in arrangements between universities and private providers of DSA-funded support to students who experience mental illness. Providers may be supporting students who are seriously ill and potentially at risk but may be unaware of what support is available within the university and how to contact or access this support. They found that confidentiality arrangements or understanding may also act as a barrier to this information being passed to the university. As a result, support services may be unaware that a student is significantly ill, despite them receiving support for their illness on university premises.

Tutors' roles with students with mental health conditions

Hugues et al. (2018) and Houghton and Anderson (2017) note the importance of learning and teaching in addressing mental health as 'the only guaranteed points of contact between a student and their university are their academic staff and the curriculum. Therefore, any genuine whole university response has to consider the role of academics and the curriculum in supporting good mental health and wellbeing' (Hugues and Spanner, 2019, p26). Earlier research (Hugues et al., 2018) revealed that academics have become the frontline of student support. However, most academics are unprepared for the inevitable demands of their role in relation to student mental health and, in the absence of training, support or supervision, draw from personal experience. This creates substantial variability in the skills that academics bring to the role and means that students cannot be sure of the response they will receive if they turn to an academic for support.

They found that many academics lack clarity about their role and boundaries, feel they lack the skills to appropriately respond and that gaps between academics and support services negatively impact on student and staff well-being. This lack of clarity creates risk for students, staff and universities. They conclude that the role of academics must be clarified. Staff must be guided to maintain supportive boundaries and to understand how they can support student mental health and well-being through good pedagogic practice. NUS suggests that personal tutors are needed to enhance the student experience and many institutions have them as part of their 'student charters'. However, the role they play is often ambiguous or underestimated, at least with the time and skills it takes to support a student effectively. Often naïve 'signposting' models are applied, as if the role is as simple as identifying the student needs, and if they are beyond academic, signposting them to an 'appropriate service' that will 'deal' with that issue, and not interfere with academic progress. It is never this simple. Personal tutors are needed to build relationships with students and act as a conduit to the institution and beyond.

Important here is a 'holding role' that recognizes that there is gap between the manifestation and identification of support needs in students, the acceptance of the need for support by the student, the identification of appropriate support services, which the student may have either stigmatized views of or genuine bad experiences of. Even when a referral is made, services normally have a waiting list and we often hold them till they can access them – often for months, sometimes for years. We then need to support them through the process of engaging with support.

Where services do not exist, or do not help, we have a role to act as a human face who cares and support the student until they build the right resilience to engage, or not, with services and most importantly sees them as a person beyond their 'condition'. Student support services rarely have a case worker, instead having workers dedicated to certain roles – the central role to a student is often a tutor, or a professional services worker who takes on this role beyond their remit. To do this effectively tutors also need to be supervised and supported properly. The hopelessly vague vision of giving pastoral support needs to be defined and refined.

Curriculum, learning, teaching and assessment

Hugues and Spanner (2019) recommend that learning, teaching and assessment enable all students to develop skills, confidence, academic self-efficacy and improve performance, at an appropriate pace foregrounding deep learning, meaning, mastery and development. Citing Haggis (2003) they define deep learning as where students engage deeply with their subject, 'motivated by their passion or interest, reading widely, connecting what they have learned to previous learning and seeking understanding' (Hugues and Spanner, 2019, p27) as opposed to surface learning, where students are more likely to skip over the surface of the subject, focusing only on what they need to know, to get the grade they want regurgitating material rather than understanding it and learning subjects in isolation from each other, with the minimum amount of effort (Hugues and Spanner, 2019, p27).

Postareff et al. (2016) found that students who engage in deep learning appear to have better well-being than those who primarily surface-learn. Hugues and Spanner (2019) also say surface learning focuses on extrinsic motivators in higher education such as grades, which, as I talked about in other chapters, does not make for retention. Deep learning allows students to gain meaning and fulfilment from their academic study, focuses their motivation intrinsically and develops their analytical ability, which is directly linked to retention.

More generally, Hugues and Spanner (2019) recommend that pedagogic practice and academic processes consider and seek to impact positively on the mental health and well-being of all students. A common response from academics is that they need to make their teaching challenging (Thomas and Asselin, 2018). However, Thomas and Asselin (2018) say there is a difference between positive challenging and pedagogy that causes mental health issues. They make the distinction between academic work being challenging because it is unclear, the students are unprepared and/or they lack necessary resources, and when it being academically stretching (Thomas and Asselin, 2018). Workload, classroom practice, teaching and learning methods, assessments and approaches to feedback and grading can have both beneficial and detrimental effects (Houghton and Anderson, 2017, Hofmann and Mühlenweg, 2018, Thomas and Asselin, 2018). Consultation with Global Majority and disabled students specifically identified that a lack of inclusive practice in curriculum and teaching can have negative consequences for their well-being (Hugues and Spanner, 2019, p26).

Cultures in and out of the classroom: Safe space reconsidered

Hugues and Spanner (2019) talk about the importance of academics setting classroom culture and discussing expectations in and outside of the classroom as well as naming and deconstructing social capital itself. Other authors talk about how about academic students' mental state can impact on their learning, and how phenomena such as imposter syndrome (Cusak et al., 2013), perfectionism (Sotardi and Dubien, 2019, Starley, 2019) and academic anxiety (Postareff, 2016) can reduce learning and performance.

However, the concept of safe space, as opposed to pedagogic space, is heavily contested (Baber and Murray, 2001, Allen et al., 2020, Seal, 2021), and there can be conflation between pedagogic and therapeutic notions of 'safe' (Seal, 2021), particularly pertinent with issues of mental health. I talk elsewhere about how notions of safety are culturally bound, and this has implications for disadvantaged students. Crucially the desire for safety is often a call from the privileged (Seal, 2018, 2019). The oppressed are quite used to functioning in unsafe, unstructured, emotionally driven and fractious circumstances. The questions must be asked who is this place of safety for.

This is not to deny that they should not be unsafe or damaging spaces, but interpretations of what constitutes these terms need to be de-constructed and negotiated (Seal, 2020, p245). Hugues and Spanner (2019) recommend collaborative classrooms and pedagogic spaces in which students are encouraged to support each other's learning, finding that they improve the learning and well-being of all students, as opposed to competitive classrooms reduce performance and well-being. There is a lot of literature written on what constitutes a collaborative or democratic learning environment, particularly for widening participation students.

Psychoeducation and the role of the academic

Interestingly, Hugues and Spanner (2019) citing a number of psychotherapy pedagogues (Hattie, 2008, De Bruyckere, 2018, Pakenham and Visovich, 2019) say students would benefit from 'good quality psychoeducation and meta-learning' being included in the curriculum, to support them to develop their ability to manage their own well-being and learning. They recognize that this should be delivered by appropriate staff and that untrained academics cannot automatically provide this safely and effectively (Hugues et al., 2018). However, they do not define what psychoeducation could look like, and who should be delivering it.

Higgenbotham (2012) explores combining proven psychoeducational approaches into a semester class under the umbrella of effective stress management. This class integrates physiological and psychological understandings of stress and stress management with evidence-based skills including relaxation techniques, problem solving, mindfulness, cognitive restructuring and assertiveness shown to be effective not only in the treatment of stress but also in the treatment of common mental illnesses such as anxiety and depression. Further, this course encompasses a set of skills consistent with the positive psychology literature on the development of resilience. However, it seems that more research is needed in this area. Barrable (2018) investigates online mechanisms for this.

Issues of progression

The OfS (2019) reports that progression rates were lower throughout the period 2012–13 to 2016–17 among students who had reported having a mental health condition for both full and part-time students.

Graduate students

There is less data on the incidence of mental health issues amongst the postgraduate researcher (PGR) population and how these needs are met. There was an HRCE Catalyst programme ending in 2018 that looked at this, the final report being 'exploring wellbeing and mental health and associated support services for postgraduate researchers' (Metcalfe et al., 2018). Metcalfe et al. found that only 0.9 per cent of graduate students declared a mental health condition to their HEI in 2013–14 in marked contrast to the results of the most recent Postgraduate Research Experience Survey (PRES, 2017) where 3.3 per cent of respondents reported that they had a mental health condition.

A recent literature review commissioned by the Royal Society and Wellcome Trust into the understanding of mental health of researchers (Gutherie, 2017) found limited evidence of the prevalence of specific mental health conditions among researchers and only a small number of studies that focused on PGRs. The majority of literature relates to work-related stress, which can lead to depression and anxiety. This is reported to be higher amongst academic staff than across the general population and is at a similar level to that for healthcare professionals.

However, there is similar under reporting as with undergraduates. The General Health Questionnaire (2019) identified that 32 per cent of the PGR population 'is at risk of having or developing a common psychiatric disorder, especially depression'. A similar study in Leiden University in the Netherlands identified that two in five PGRs are at risk of having or developing a psychiatric disorder (http://nos.nl/op3/artikel/2180638-ook-leidse-promovendus-heeft-grotere-kans-op-depressie.html). Stubb et al. (2018) found doctoral degrees to be stressful for students and arguably that PGRs are potentially at higher risk of developing a mental health condition than undergraduates. The 2017 PRES found that more than 60 per cent of PGRs were satisfied with their work–life balance, and 85 per cent felt their degree programme was worthwhile. However, 26 per cent of respondents had considered leaving or suspending their degree programme.

Levecque et al. (2017) conducted an online survey with 4,069 participants (response rate of 33 per cent). Selective non-response analyses showed a slightly higher proportion of females, respondents in the youngest age categories, social scientists and Belgians compared to the total population They found that some communities within the PGR population are likely to be more susceptible to developing a mental health condition, such as women (who are more susceptible than men in the general population), part-time researchers, distance learners, self-funded PGRs and those working in isolation. PGRs with physical health problems or learning difficulties are also more likely to experience a higher percentage of mental health. The 2017 PRES results show that PGRs who consider they have a disability, and particularly a mental health impairment, are more likely to have considered leaving or suspending their doctoral studies at 48 per cent and 60 per cent, respectively. The Flanders study identified work–family balance, job demands, job control, supervisor leadership style, and team decision-making culture, all to be linked to mental health problems in PGRs.

Metcalfe et al. (2018, p3) recommend that more should be done to collect, analyse and act upon existing data on PGR use of well-being and mental health services to measure the level of engagement, and where this data is not effectively created, mechanisms should be developed for doing so. They further recommend 'providing a safe working environment for PGRs that supports their wellbeing and mental health requires systemic culture change and top-down commitment to promoting mental health'. They recognize that the prevailing academic culture of competition, high achievement and high workloads creates a stressful environment and because of power differential with supervisors, particularly on university-funded doctorates, doctoral students may feel less able to talk about their well-being and mental health. They recommend contextualizing the Universities UK Framework for Mental Health, investing in doctoral student specific services to 'provide increased mental health literacy and prevention activities targeted specifically at PGRs and supervisors'.

Further transition issues

Reino and Byrom (2017) highlight the impact of the end of university, when students may effectively be changing occupation, or becoming unemployed, moving accommodation, losing their friendship network and experiencing long-term financial uncertainty. This was seen to contribute to an existential uncertainty and loss of identity and structure. They found graduate well-being is adversely affected by poor preparation for the workplace and life outside university. Layer (2005) and Perry (2011) call for universities to have Outduction, to support students to be ready for this change and to be able to enter the next phase of their life positively.

Employment and employers

Biggs et al. (2010) in their systematic review found that employers had a high level of concern around employing people with mental health issues. They found that employers reported issues of trust, needing supervision, inability to use initiative and inability to deal with the public for individuals with either existing or previous mental health needs. More recently, research by Pettersen and Fugletveit (2015) concluded more attention must be focused on changing business leaders' attitudes and changing unhealthy corporate cultures that create and sustain the idea that people with mental health problems are disabled. In order to reverse the trend of increasing numbers of people with mental health problems being excluded from the labour market, it seems imperative that business leaders develop their understanding of how the workplace can accommodate employees who have a history of mental health problems.

Brohan et al. (2012) in their systematic review found that applicants with a mental health problem were rated as significantly lower in suitability than an applicant with no known disability and were significantly less likely to be appointed. There was a significant difference in employers' attitudes to employing people with mental disabilities compared with physical disabilities. Biggs et al. (2010) also found that awareness among employers of what constitutes a mental health problem and of the prevalence of mental health problems had significantly improved between 2006 and 2009. However, this increase did not translate into an increased use of formal mental health policies in the workplace or an increase in employers' knowledge about the law regarding mental health in the workplace.

They emphasize the need for employers' concerns to be discussed frankly with appropriate mechanisms to develop their confidence in their abilities to manage individuals with mental health problems and that occupational health professional have a key role to play in this task. They felt that by considering evidence on the workplace beliefs and behaviours of employers, occupational health advisors can dispel myths and address concerns regarding hiring, managing and working with individuals with a mental health problem. 'Recovery-oriented' and 'see the person messages' may be particularly suitable for use in public health campaigns. Similarly, targeting interventions around these messages may be useful for employers. Interventions that focus on workplace and non-workplace social contact with individuals with a mental health problem, as well as a focus on clarifying current legislations are also recommended.

Brohan et al. (2012) found that those with mental health issues perceived, that is, they disclosed their mental health (1) they wouldn't be hired (2) they would be subject to unfair treatment in the workplace; (3) they would lose credibility in eyes of others; (4) legislation would not provide protection; (5) they would be subject to gossip and rejection. The sub-theme 'wouldn't be hired if disclosed' represents the belief that a person would be treated unfavourably in finding work, if their mental health problem was known about'. Pettersen and Fugletveit (2015) concur, finding that there was a large amount of self-censorship going on. Brohan et al. (2012) found positive reason for disclosure included (1) role model for others; (2) to gain adjustments; (3) positive experience of disclosure; (4) to obtain support; (5) to be honest; (6) to explain behaviour; and (7) concealing as stressful. Being honest is interesting in that Pettersen and Fugletveit (2015) found that some employer expressed greater concern about someone lying about their mental health than them having mental health issues. It seems that a programme of confidence building in those who are debating whether to disclose and mediation with employers might be positive interventions.

Conclusion

Poor mental health amongst students is beginning to be recognized, with the publication of the student mental health charter. However, there is a concurrent rise in mental health incidents in Higher education amongst staff. Moorish (2019) in her Higher Education Policy Institute report *Pressure Vessels: The Epidemic of Poor Mental Health among Higher Education Staff* and her follow-up in 2020 found that at one institution, occupational health referrals rose by 170 per cent. The largest occupational health referral increases were at Kent (500 per cent), De Montfort (392 per cent) and Bristol (334 per cent). There was a rise in referrals to counselling of up to 300 per cent in the same period. The report argues three factors are behind the increases: new workload models, more directive approaches to performance management, and short-term contracts, which provide less security. Recognition of the impact of university and working conditions for academics needs to be recognized and acted upon. Only a whole institutional approach can make a discernible impact in this regard.

Hugues and Spanner in their university mental health charter recommend the following principles of good practice (2019, p25):

- Universities take a whole university approach to transition, embedding measures to support the positive transition of all students across their provision and into the curriculum. (It would seem sensible to extend this recommendation to staff.)
- Measures to support transition begin from pre-application and continue through application, pre-entry, arrival, induction and through the first year.
- Measures to support transition aim to promote well-being, efficacy, academic integration and social connectedness.
- Universities provide additional or specific interventions for students who face additional barriers.

Prejudice against and false assumptions about those with mental health conditions is not unique to higher education and our starting point is to recognize that many academics, professional staff and potential employers will be subject to dominant hegenonomies of discrimination. This needs to be actively challenged through education and reflection, with time, space and support to do this. We also need to support the transitions of people in, through and out of higher education, recognizing that many of our structures have certain student norms built into them. For examples, we need to see interruptions, deferrals and suspensions not as signs of deficit, but as valid ways of managing fluctuating mental health conditions and personal circumstances.

It is not enough to have a signposting approach to both support services and personal tutoring. If services do not exist, or there is a time delay in accessing them, the person will turn to the person in the university closest to them for support – this 'holding' role needs to be anticipated, articulated and supported. Our pedagogic approaches, assessment regimes and curriculum design should be audited for their ableist and neurotypical assumptions, and recognize the lifecycles of all students, including those with mental health conditions or potential conditions, diagnosed, undiagnosed and not always recognized by the student, or member of staff themselves.

The doctoral experience needs particular attention as dropout rates are terrible, and particularly for disadvantaged groups. All of this is new territory so as Duffey et al. (2020) suggest, ongoing research and evaluation should be built into initiatives 'to inform the development of resources and services moving forward which also takes into account the local context'. In the UK, this is one of the more positive requirements of the OfS, although, as discussed before, they look at research and evaluation in a particular positivist way that needs to be challenged.

Duffy et al. (2020, p43) also make some recommendations for further research. We need to explore the effectiveness of universal mental illness prevention initiatives targeting university students and/or university organization at a system level requires more rigorous study in order to ensure the designs are robust and the intervention is having the desired effect. We need to research the identity of high-risk student populations in a non-discriminatory asset-based way, and assess the effectiveness of targeted early intervention and prevention efforts. Finally, we need to understand the determinants of emotional well-being and academic success at an individual and institutional level. Honouring this aforementioned importance of student voice, I suggest that, similarly to research into the Global Majority experience, any research conducted should be participatory, involving those with lived experience from the outset and based on their indigenous knowledge and ways of knowing.

Perhaps to finish, and as a critique of this chapter, the next step would be to recognize that there are different perspectives on mental health, and normative and neurotypical assumptions in higher education discourse, and we need to recognize the contested nature of mental health discourse and the rights of some individuals who might identify differently in how they relate to their mental health. As Rashed remarks, 'along the decades, different groups have campaigned and struggled for respect and rights; some have been successful at achieving symbolic and cultural reparation, others less so … Yet, Mad individuals, and madness more broadly, are yet to feature in the conversation on respect and identity, a conversation still dominated by framings that emphasize the medical idiom and the notions of distress and disability' (Rashed, 2019, p170).

Conclusion: Setting a Realistic Goal for the Access, Success and Progression of Disadvantaged Students in Higher Education

In 1963, the Robbins Report on the future of HE argued for the immediate expansion and democratisation of the university system in the UK as essential to the development of 'a learning society'. The gravitas of such a proclamation hinged on the idealistic, utopian view of what HE should resemble without acknowledgement of the intersectional challenges that continually undermine aspects of inclusion while simultaneously marginalising minority groups, who still consistently remain on the periphery of the academy. In attempting to challenge and dismantle inequitable structures which have their roots firmly embedded within divisive rhetoric; custodians of the Academy must continue to question the purpose of the university, who it serves within our society; and whether it mirrors the multi-cultural hybridity reflected within modern society.

(Arday, 2020, p32)

As I have stated elsewhere, 'commitment to social mobility in the guise of widening participation is espoused by most universities and governments, though increasingly not in the form of giving it resources' (Seal, 2021). However, it goes far deeper than this. As a project widening participation has largely, and systematically, failed for twenty-five years, in reality widening participation initiatives have resulted in the expansion of post-1992 universities, where the majority of disadvantaged students have gone. Even in these institutions, while more disadvantaged students go to university, they have consistently higher drop-out rates, get lesser degrees and go into less high-paying and professional jobs (even when they gain the same degrees or better than less disadvantaged students).

These patterns are repeated at postgraduate and doctoral level, although far less disadvantaged students even start doctorates. The pattern is again repeated in terms of the workforce. Disadvantaged students with doctorates go into academia in far less proportions than non-disadvantaged students. Aside from blatant discrimination, which seems more and more evident the higher up you go in higher education, the sector has fundamentally failed to look at the issue seriously, and its own culpability in perpetuating disadvantage. This book has identified a number of factors in this failure.

1. Most WP initiatives have tinkered around the edges and avoided more fundamental questions about higher education, such as whose interests it serves, who it privileges and what cultures are dominant and operant.
2. Higher education institutions often work to naive outreach models that assume that disadvantaged students just need to see the benefits of higher education and are ignorant of its advantages, rather than they have made a realistic cost–benefit analysis that it will not advantage them.
3. There is a covert 'ideal' student archetype around which higher education structures and cultures are built, which informs other concepts such as 'engagement' and 'participation'. The archetype is young, white, male, middle or upper class, able bodied and living away from home with no caring responsibilities.
4. Those traditionally disadvantaged are treated as in deficit and expected to assimilate into the idealized student archetype, while their indigenous knowledge and ways of knowing marginalized and unacknowledged.
5. In doing so higher education expects those already disadvantaged to abandon their cultures and communities, despite students wanting to give back to them being a major extrinsic motivation, and embrace a culture that will not embrace them. Disadvantaged students, even those who do try and assimilate, continue to be treated as' other'.
6. Overt discrimination is rampant with regard to race, class disability and mental health and continues to be ignored within higher education. This is partly because higher education continues to regard itself as a force for social good, including social mobility, rather than its reality of re-inscribing elite power, discrimination, and being a force for social stratification and division.

Given these factors, the question is where should higher education start. Thomas's (2012) research identifies seven areas as significant for supporting retention: (1) academic preparedness, (2) the academic experience (including assessment), (3) institutional expectations and commitment, (4) academic and social match, (5) finance and employment, (6) family support and commitments and (7) university support services. Thomas (2012) outlines the following general principles for interventions and approaches to improve student retention and success. Activities should, as far as possible, be embedded into mainstream academic provision and should proactively seek to engage students and develop their capacity to do so.

Initiatives should be informative, useful and relevant to students' current academic interests and future aspirations. Early engagement should be viewed as essential, and be through a variety of mediums. Activities should encourage collaboration and engagement with fellow students and members of staff to develop meaningful relationships. Finally, the extent and quality of students' engagement should be monitored and followed up where necessary. Building on these principles, and going deeper, HEIs have a number of steps and priorities it needs to attend to.

Institutional commitment

Senior management needs to take responsibility for action, and be accountable for continued failure. In the UK the APPs are meant to be this accountable mechanism, with a threat that if the targets are not met institutions will have to charge lower fees. However, this initiative has fallen into the old 'tinkering' trap and ignores wider structural issues – just saying that institutions 'have to get better' and meet their targets, without giving sufficient direction or a realistic roadmap and ignore wider structural forces at play. If all institutions just game their figures the exercise will be meaningless. If they are honest, and all institutions miss their targets, will the government really hold all institutions, and not themselves to account? I suspect there will be a re-invention, and a new initiative which will again ignore structural factors and be yet another version of 'what works', focusing on the minutiae because the wider issues are too unwieldly and too fundamental.

Re-balancing the cost–benefit analysis

We have to acknowledge that some disadvantaged students are making an accurate cost–benefit analysis of university, and concluding it is not worth it – for them. This can be both financial and personal, as we are asking them to often give up their communities and values to embrace a culture that will never properly accept them. If we do not like this analysis, for it exposes the lie or at best un-evenness of trying to achieve social mobility through higher education, then we have to ask how this has been allowed to happen. Governments need to look at finances, but we also need to look at and prioritize our relationships with employers. Local universities need to acknowledge that they are that, and celebrate it. I will talk in the next publication about how we can become an anchor institution, a central driver in the local economy. Social mobility is more than a moral imperative for a modern university; it is what is needed for our economy to thrive. Universities need to redefine their civic purpose and engage communities proactively. It needs to explore how higher education needs to change to meet communities and the economy's needs. This will entail a different kind of partnership, pedagogic approach and notion of what constitutes legitimate knowledge creation.

Taking a look at ourselves

Regardless of government initiatives, if universities are serious about better serving disadvantaged students, they need to recognize they are not neutral. Their structures privilege certain students and serve vested interests that need to be acknowledged. They need to look from root to branch at what they teach, how they teach, how they assess and even what they consider constitutes legitimate knowledge. The curriculum, learning and teaching, assessment, epistemology and the institution need to be thoroughly de-colonized and liberated. This includes de-coding loaded terms such as engagement and participation, which are structured in certain ways with an ideal student in mind that is not reflected in most disadvantaged students. The need for de-colonization and liberation equally applies to the structures of higher education, from induction, to enrolment, to student records, to mitigating circumstances, to reasonable adjustments, to exam boards and especially graduation. These are antiquated mechanisms that do not need to be this way, and all re-inscribe certain privileges. In particular we need to look at support structures, how they are accessed, how and who delivers them and how they are planned for.

Activist challenging themselves

Activists also need to challenge themselves and look for new allies. I would also call on Marxists, of which I would count myself, to not demonize and accuse critical race theorists of ignoring class – they do not and such accusations play into the wrong hands. We need to look at how class manifests contemporarily, and intersects with race, including whiteness. There is a desperate need to articulate a progressive white working-class identity and a progressive inclusive nationalism, and not let these ideas be colonized by the forces of the right. Classic Marxist analytical and organizing tools like the workplace as a site to build working-class identity and solidarity rarely hold in our diffuse modern society with the rise of the precariat, the zero hours and gig economy and, with the pandemic, increasing social isolation and narrowing. We need to think differently.

Developing a new relationship with our students and the local community: All this calls for a new relationship with our students and the communities we are meant to serve. If we are to conduct research into the pertinent issues, and properly evaluate initiatives that are meant to serve disadvantaged students, we need to involve them in this, and beyond just asking them to do some data gathering for us. We need to make our research and evaluation properly participatory. There is a reason for this beyond it being ethical. I have catalogued elsewhere how conducting research and evaluation in a participatory way starts to achieve, and create momentum for, that most elusive, but vital, change needed – cultural change.

Participatory research embeds a culture of learning, co-production and of valuing research and each other, within organizations, as well as creating mechanisms for developing evidence for monitoring and evaluating other ideas and initiatives. However, to embrace this needs a cultural shift in itself.

I have had senior managers deny to me that participatory research is even an approach, or that 'we are talking to people so that is kind of participatory' or talk of it as one tool in your toolbag – sorry, but this is not good enough – you have to undertake participatory research properly and not bring it out when it is convenient. As I say elsewhere, this takes effort and commitment.

> We need nothing less than a paradigm shift. Our epistemological stance on what constitutes knowledge and how it is to be created needs to shift, particularly within the academy. The co-production of research needs to move from being seen as exotic, radical or added value, to being the only meaningful way to conduct an investigation. We need to move from asking when and if we should involve community partners in a piece of research to asking how. We need to stop seeing the difficulties and barriers to involving community members in a particular research context as reasons for non-involvement, but as obstacles to be overcome.
>
> (Seal, 2018, p241)

We should also engage with communities and students on a day-to-day basis starting with those communities where universities are situated. We must challenge the common position where universities celebrate and congratulate themselves as being demographically representative of the world, but do not attract students, or engage the communities from the square mile where they are located. As I have said elsewhere, this takes time and commitment.

> Local relationships built over time and through mutual self-interest lead to more meaningful integrated research, where long terms impacts can be accounted for and articulated. Such relationships also develop impact and have resonance beyond the local, with national and international reach, as our often diasporic community partners have such reach themselves.
>
> (Seal, 2018, p242)

Hopefully such co-production will lead to other changes in our relationships with each other. Learning from our students, peer work and peer learning all need to be embraced if disadvantaged students are to truly feel that they belong. Longer term we need to look at the workforce and particularly who becomes academics. Working-class and Global Majority academics and those with disabilities including mental health conditions have all said that they often still feel outsiders – torn between their community values and those in academia. Structural discrimination is still endemic and while a simple mirroring of communities of disadvantage will not make disadvantage go away, unless people from these communities are present in academia, their absence will service as a continual reminder of the glass ceiling in higher education and that, as a person from a disadvantaged community, you will never truly belong.

Recognizing and celebrating local universities

More widely we have to look at the disadvantaged student differences in mobility after university. In some of my recent writing (Seal, 2020) I talked about three types of UK universities: international, national and local. This distinction is made regarding student demographics rather than reputation, although there are overlaps. International universities have a large contingent of international students, much higher levels of middle- and upper-class students and are more prestigious. They are largely the Russell Group and many of the old universities, perhaps one or two of the new ones. National universities predominantly draw students from the UK and have a more state school demographic, although often 'good' state schools, with a smattering of international and private school students. They constitute some old universities and most of the new ones. Local universities draw students majoritively from the local area and almost exclusively from state schools and colleges. It is no surprise that those universities with the highest percentage of working-class students are local universities.

Moving regions has been shown to increase social mobility (Gaskell and Linwood, 2019). However, the Social Mobility Commission (2019) found that those from working-class backgrounds are less likely to move regions and less likely to move to London where there are proportionally more jobs. This equally allies to Global Majority and disabled students. This has a distinct impact in areas where graduate employment opportunities are less and are less well paid, which is also where many of the local universities are based (Birmingham, Leeds, Ipswich, Plymouth, etc.). Gaskell and Linwood (2019) also note that graduates remaining in the area where they studied are of significant benefit to the economy where an institution is based. To encourage more graduates to move to the cities with higher wages could have a potentially damaging effect on some local economies (Swinney and Williams, 2016).

However, graduate employment and pay levels are one of the key measures being used by the OfS in terms of progression. In recognition of this tension, the OfS launched the 'No Place like Home' initiative for universities to develop and implement projects that improve the outcomes for graduates seeking employment in their home region (OfS, 20120b). Many of the Pilot initiatives fall into the raising aspirations trap. However, there are a number that have more interesting initiatives challenging employers' perspectives and even trying to stimulate the local economy.

References

Abberley, P. (1987). The concept of oppression and the development of a social theory of disability. *Disability, Handicap & Society*, 2(1), 5–19.

Abes, E. S., Jones, S. R. & McEwen, M. K. (2007). Reconceptualizing the model of multiple dimensions of identity: The role of meaning-making capacity in the construction of multiple identities. *Journal of College Student Development*, 48(1), 1–22.

ACT (2010a). *What Works in Student Retention? Fourth National Survey. Community Colleges with Twenty Percent or More Black Students Enrolled.* Available from: http://www.act.org/research/policymakers/pdf/droptables/Community_BlackEnroll.pdf

ACT (2010b). *What Works in Student Retention? Fourth National Survey. Four-year Colleges and Universities with Twenty Percent or More Black Students Enrolled.* Available from: http://www.act.org/research/policymakers/pdf/droptables/FourYr_BlackEnroll.pdf

ACT (2010c). *What Works in Student Retention? Fourth National Survey. Community Colleges with Twenty Percent or More Hispanic Students Enrolled.* Available from: http://www.act.org/research/policymakers/pdf/droptables/Community_HispanicEnroll.pdf

ACT (2010d). *What Works in Student Retention? Fourth National Survey. Four-year Colleges & Universities with Twenty Percent or More Hispanic Students Enrolled.* Available from: http://www.act.org/research/policymakers/pdf/droptables/FourYr_HispanicEnroll.pdf

Adelman, C. (2004). *Principal Indicators of Student Academic Histories in Postsecondary Education, 1972–2000.* US Department of Education.

Adelphi Research UK (2018). *No Voice, No Choice.* London: Rethink Mental Illness. https://www.adelphiresearchuk.co.uk/no-voice-no-choice/

Adnett, N. (2016). The economic and social benefits of widening participation: Rhetoric or reality? In Shah, M., Bennett, A. & Southgate, E. *Widening Higher Education Participation: A Global Perspective* (pp. 211–24). Hull: Chandos Publishing.

Ahmed, S. (2012). *On Being Included.* Durham, NC: Duke University Press.

Akel, S. (2019). *Insider–Outsider: The Role of Race in Shaping the Experiences of Black and Minority Ethnic Students*. London: Goldsmiths, University of London.

Alexander, J. S. & Gardner, J. N. (2009). Beyond retention: A comprehensive approach to the first college year. *About Campus*, 14(2), 18–26.

Alleman, N. F., Stimpson, R. L. & Holly, L. N. (2009) A Statewide Examination of College Access Services and Resources in Virginia. Virginia: State Council of Higher Education for Virginia.

Allen, J. M., Muragishi, G. A., Smith, J. L., Thoman, D. B. & Brown, E. R. (2015). To grab and to hold: Cultivating communal goals to overcome cultural and structural barriers in first-generation college students' science interest. *Translational Issues in Psychological Science*, 1(4), 331–41.

Allen, L., Cowie, L. & Fenaughty, J. (2020). Safe but not safe: LGBTTIQA+ students' experiences of a university campus. *Higher Education Research & Development*, 39(6), 1075–90.

Allsopp, D. H., Minskoff, E. H. & Bolt, L. (2005). Individualized course-specific strategy instruction for college students with learning disabilities and ADHD: Lessons learned from a model demonstration project. *Learning Disabilities Research & Practice*, 20(2), 103–18.

Altbach, P. G. (ed.) (2013). *The International Imperative in Higher Education*. Berlin: Springer Science & Business Media.

Amis, K. (1960). *Lone Voices*, Encounter XV, 6–11 July.

AMOSSHE (2019). *Annual Benchmarking Data Report*. London: AMOSSHE.

Anders, J. (2012). The link between household income, university applications and university attendance. *Fiscal Studies*, 33(2), 185–210.

Anderson, J., Boyle, C. & Deppeler, J. (2014). The ecology of inclusive education: Reconceptualising Bronfenbrenner. In *Equality in Education* (pp. 23–34). Leiden Netherlands: Brill Sense.

Apple, M. W. (2011). Democratic education in neoliberal and neoconservative times. *International Studies in Sociology of Education*, 21(1), 21–31.

Archer, M. S. (2007). *Making Our Way through the World: Human Reflexivity and Social Mobility*. Cambridge: Cambridge University Press.

Archer, M. S. (2010). *Conversations about Reflexivity*. London and New York: Routledge.

Archer, L., DeWitt, J. & Wong, B. (2014). Spheres of influence: What shapes young people's aspirations at age 12/13 and what are the implications for education policy? *Journal of Education Policy*, 29(1), 58–85.

Archer, L., Hutchings, M. & Ross, A. (2005). *Higher Education and Social Class: Issues of Exclusion and Inclusion*. London and New York: Routledge.

Arday, J. (2020a). Fighting the tide: Understanding the difficulties facing Black, Asian and Minority Ethnic (BAME) doctoral students' pursuing a career in academia. *Educational Philosophy and Theory*, 53(10), 972–9. DOI: 10.1080/00131857.2020.1777640.

Arday, J. (2020b). It's the end of the World as we know it: Racism as a global killer of Black people and their emancipatory freedoms. *Educational Philosophy and Theory*. DOI: 10.1080/00131857.2020.1777640.

Arday, J. (2020c). Race, education and social mobility: We all need to dream the same dream and want the same thing. *Educational Philosophy and Theory* 1, 53(3), 227–32.

Arday, J. & Mirza, H. S. (2018). *Dismantling Race in Higher Education: Racism, Whiteness and Decolonising the Academy*. Cham: Palgrave Macmillan.

Arday, J., Zoe Belluigi, D. & Thomas, D. (2020). Attempting to break the chain: Reimaging inclusive pedagogy and decolonising the curriculum within the academy. *Educational Philosophy and Theory*, 53(3), 298–313.

Atherton, G., Dumangane, C. & Whitty, G. (2016). *Charting Equity in Higher Education: Drawing the Global Access Map*. London: Pearson.

Atherton, M. C. (2014). Academic preparedness of first-generation college students: Different perspectives. *Journal of College Student Development*, 55(8), 824–9.

Atherton and Mazhari (2019). *Understanding Access to Higher Education for White Students from Lower Socio-economic Backgrounds*. London: National Educational Opportunities Network.

Attewell, P. & Jang, S. H. (2013). Summer coursework and completing college. *Research in Higher Education Journal*, 20(4), 1–12.

Augar, P. (2019). *Independent Panel Report to the Review of Post-18 Education and Funding*. HMSO.

Austin, I. & Jones, G. A. (2015). *Governance of Higher Education: Global Perspectives, Theories, and Practices*. London: Routledge.

Baber, K. & Murray, C. (2001). A postmodern feminist approach to teaching human sexuality. *Family Relations*, 50(1), 23–33.

Back, L. (2004). Introduction. In Law, I., Philips, D. & Turney, L. (eds), *Institutional Racism in Higher Education* (pp. 1–24). Stoke on Trent: Trentham Books.

Bae, S. J. (2007). *Self-determination and Academic Achievement of Individuals with Disabilities in Postsecondary Education: A Meta-analysis* (Doctoral dissertation). Lawrence: University of Kansas.

Baez, B. (2000). Race-related service and faculty of color: Conceptualizing critical agency in academe. *Higher Education*, 39(3), 363–91.

Bailey, M. J. & Dynarski, S. M. (2011). *Gains and Gaps: Changing Inequality in US College Entry and Completion* (No. w17633). Cambridge, MA: National Bureau of Economic Research.

Baines, A. D. (2012). Positioning, strategizing, and charming: How students with autism construct identities in relation to disability. *Disability & Society*, 27, 547–61.

Baker, C. (2018). *Mental Health Statistics for England: Prevalence, Services and Funding. Briefing Paper 6988*. London: House of Commons Library.

Baker, K. Q., Boland, K. & Nowik, C. M. (2012). A campus survey of faculty and student perceptions of persons with disabilities. *Journal of Postsecondary Education and Disability*, 25(4), 309–29.

Balchin, P. (ed.) (2013). *Housing Policy in Europe*. London: Routledge.

Ball, S. J., Reay, D. & David, M. (2002). 'Ethnic choosing': Minority ethnic students, social class and higher education choice. *Race Ethnicity and Education*, 5(4), 333–57.

Bamber, J. & Tett, L. (2000). Transforming the learning experiences of non-traditional students: A perspective from higher education. *Studies in Continuing Education*, 22(1), 57–75.

Barad, K. (2007). *Meeting the Universe Halfway: Quantum Physics and the Entanglement of Matter and Meaning*. Durham, NC: Duke University Press.

Barkham, M., Broglia, E. & Dufour, G. (2019). Towards an evidence-base for student wellbeing and mental health: Definitions, developmental transitions and data sets. *Counselling and Psychotherapy. Research*, 19(4), 351–7.

Barnes, L. (2007). Disability, higher education and the inclusive society. *British Journal of Sociology of Education*, 28(1), 135–45.

Barnes, L., McCrea K. & Hill A. (2010). *Teaching Strategies to Use with Deaf Students, Advice for Lecturers in Higher Education*. Preston: University of Central Lancaster Specialised Learning Resource Unit.

Barrable, A., Papadatou-Pastou, M. & Tzotzoli, P. (2018). Supporting mental health, wellbeing and study skills in higher education: An online intervention system. *International Journal of Mental Health Systems*, 12(1), 1–9.

Barraza, B. (2012). *Extended Opportunity Programs and Services (EOPS): A Quantitative Study of Latino Students' Goal Completion*. Michigan: ProQuest LLC.

Bass, M. B. & Halverson, E. R. (2012). Representation radio: Digital art-making as transformative pedagogical practice in the college classroom. *Pedagogies: An International Journal*, 7(4), 347–63.

Bastedo, M. N. & Jaquette, O. (2011). Running in place: Low-income students and the dynamics of higher education stratification. *Educational Evaluation and Policy Analysis*, 33(3), 318–39.

Bauman, Z. (1998). On glocalization: Or globalization for some, localization for some others. *Thesis Eleven*, 54(1), 37–49.

Bauman, Z., (2006). *Liquid Fear*. Cambridge: Polity

Baumann, A. (2014). *User Empowerment in Mental Health – A Statement by the WHO Regional Office for Europe*. [Online] World Health Organization. Available from: http://www.euro.who.int/__data/assets/pdf_file/0020/113834/E93430.pdf

Baxter Magolda, M. B. (2009). The activity of meaning making: A holistic perspective on college student development. *Journal of College Student Development*, 50(6), 621–39.

Beauchamp-Pryor, K. (2013). *Disabled Students in Welsh Higher Education: A Framework for Equality and Inclusion*. Rotterdam: Brill Sense.

Becker, M., Martin, L., Wajeeh, E., Ward, J. & Shern, D. (2002). Students with mental illness in a university setting: Faculty and student attitudes, beliefs, knowledge and experiences. *Psychiatric Rehabilitation Journal*, 25(4), 359–67.

Beilke, J. R. & Yssel, N. (1999). The chilly climate for students with disabilities in higher education. *College Student Journal*, 33(3), 364–71.

Beauchamp-Pryor, K. (2012) From absent to active voices: Securing disability equality within higher education. *International Journal of Inclusive Education*, 16(3), 283–95.

Belfield, C., Britton, J., Buscha, F., Dearden, L., Dickson, M., van der Erve, L., Sibieta, L., Vignoles, A., Walker, I. & Zhu, Y. (2018). *The Relative Labour Market Returns to Different Degrees: Research Report*. London: Institute for Fiscal Studies. https://www.gov.uk/government/publications/undergraduate-degrees-relative-labour-market-returns

Bell, D. (1995). Who's afraid of critical race theory? *University of Illinois Law Review*, 893–910.

Bell, D. & Bansal, P. (1987). The Republican Revival and Racial Politics. *Yale LJ*, 97, 1609.

Bennett, A., Hodges, B., Kavanagh, K., Fagan, S., Hartley, J. & Schofield, N. (2013). 'Hard'and 'soft' aspects of learning as investment: Opening up the neo-liberal view of a programme with 'high' levels of attrition. *Widening Participation and Lifelong Learning*, 14 (3), 141–56.

Bennett, T., Savage, M., Silva, E. B., Warde, A., Gayo-Cal, M. & Wright, D. (2009). *Culture, Class, Distinction*. London: Routledge.

Berger, J. B. & Lyon, S. C. (2005). Past to present: A historical look at retention. In Seidman, A. (ed.), *College Student Retention: Formula for Student Success* (pp. 1–30). Westport, CT: Praeger Publishers.

Berk, M. & Parker, G. (2009). The elephant on the couch: Side-effects of psychotherapy. *Australian & New Zealand Journal of Psychiatry*, 43(9), 787–94.

Bernal, D. D. (2002). Critical race theory, Latino critical theory, and critical raced-gendered epistemologies: Recognizing students of color as holders and creators of knowledge. *Qualitative inquiry*, 8(1), 105–26.

Bernhardt, P. E. (2013). The advancement via individual determination (AVID) program: Providing cultural capital and college access to low-income students. *School Community Journal*, 23(1), 203–22.

Bernstein, B. (1975). Class and pedagogies: Visible and invisible. *Educational Studies*, 1(1), 23–41.

Bernstein, B. & Solomon, J. (1999). 'Pedagogy, identity and the construction of a theory of symbolic control': Basil Bernstein questioned by Joseph Solomon. *British Journal of Sociology of Education*, 20(2), 265–79.

Bernstein, P. L. (1996). *Against the Gods: The Remarkable Story of Risk*. New York: Wiley, 400.

Berrington, A., Roberts, S. & Tammes, P. (2016). Educational aspirations among UK young teenagers: Exploring the role of gender, class and ethnicity. *British Educational Research Journal*, 42(5), 729–55.

Berry, J. & Loke, G. (2011). *Improving the Degree Attainment of Black and Minority Ethnic Students*. Higher Education Academy and Equality Challenge Unit. Available from: http://www.ecu.ac.uk/wp-content/uploads/external/improving-degree-attainment-bme.Pdf

Bewick, B., Koutsopoulou, G., Miles, J., Slaa, E. & Barkham, M. (2010). Changes in undergraduate students' psychological well-being as they progress through university. *Studies in Higher Education*, 35(6), 633–45.

Bhambra, G. K., Gebrial, D. & Nişancıoğlu, K. (2018). *Decolonising the University*. London: Pluto Press.

Bhopal, K. (2020). *Success against the Odds: The Effect of Mentoring on the Careers of Senior Black and Minority Ethnic Academics in the UK*. London: Routledge.

Biggs, D., Hovey, N., Tyson, P. J. & MacDonald, S. (2010). Employer and employment agency attitudes towards employing individuals with mental health needs. *Journal of Mental Health*, 19(6), 505–16.

Binns, C. (2019). *Experiences of Academics from a Working-Class Heritage: Ghosts of Childhood Habitus*. Newcastle upon tyme: Cambridge Scholars Publishing.

Bishop, D. & Rhind, D. J. (2011). Barriers and enablers for visually impaired students at a UK higher education institution. *British Journal of Visual Impairment*, 29(3), 177–95.

Blackburn, L. H., Kadar-Satat, G., Riddell, S. & Weedon, E. (2016). *Access in Scotland: Access to Higher Education for People from Less Advantaged Backgrounds in Scotland*. Edinburgh: Sutton Trust.

Blake, J. & Illingworth, S. (2015). Interactive and interdisciplinary student work: A facilitative methodology to encourage lifelong learning. *Widening Participation and Lifelong Learning*, 17(2), 108–18.

Blicharski, J. (1999). New undergraduates: Access and helping them prosper. *Widening Participation and Lifelong Learning*, 1(1), 34–40.

Boeren, E. & James, N. (2017). *Advancing Theory and Research in Widening Participation*. London and New York: Routledge, 117–19.

Boliver, V. (2013). How fair is access to more prestigious UK universities? *The British Journal of Sociology 2013. Wiley Online Library*, 64(2), 344–64.

Boliver, V. (2016). Exploring ethnic inequalities in admission to Russell Group universities. *Sociology*, 50(2), 247–66.

Boliver, V., Gorard, S. & Siddiqui, N. (2019). Using contextual data to widen access to higher education. *Perspectives: Policy and Practice in Higher Education*, 25(1), 7–13.

Borland, J. & James, S. (1999). The learning experience of students with disabilities in higher education. A case study of a UK university. *Disability & Society*, 14(1), 85–101.

Bourdieu, P. (1986). The forms of capital in Richardson, J. (1986). In *Handbook of Theory and Research for the Sociology of Education* (pp. 241–58). Westport, CT: Greenwood Press.

Bourdieu, P. (1990). *In Other Words: Essays towards a Reflexive Sociology*. Stanford University Press.

Bourdieu, P. (2000). *Pascalian Meditations*. Palo Alto, CA: Stanford University Press.

Bourdieu, P., Passeron, J. C. & Nice, R. (1977). *Education, Society and Culture*. Trans. Richard, Nice. London: Sage.

Bourke, A. B., Strehorn, K. C. & Silver, P. (2000). Faculty members' provision of instructional accommodations to students with LD. *Journal of Learning Disabilities*, 33(1), 26–32.

Bowe, F. G. (2003). Transition for deaf and hard-of-hearing students: A blueprint for change. *Journal of Deaf Studies and Deaf Education*, 8(4), 485–93.

Bowen, W. G., Chingos, M. M. & McPherson, M. S. (2009). *Crossing the Finish Line: Completing College at America's Public Universities*. Princeton, NA: Princeton University Press.

Bowes, L., Jones, S., Thomas, L., Moreton, R., Birkin, G. & Nathwani, T. (2013). *The Uses and Impact of HEFCE Funding for Widening Participation. Report to the Higher Education Funding Council for England*. Ormskirk: CFE and Edge Hill University.

Bowes, L., Tazzyman, S., Sandhu, J., Moreton, R., Birkin, G., McCaig, C. & Wright, H. (2019). The National Collaborative Outreach Programme. End of phase 1 report for the national formative and impact evaluations.

Bowles, S., Gintis, H. & Meyer, P. (1975). The long shadow of work: Education, the family, and the reproduction of the social division of labor. *Insurgent Sociologist*, 5(4), 3–22.

Bowles, H. R. (2013). Psychological perspectives on gender in negotiation. *The Sage Handbook of Gender and Psychology* (pp. 465–83). Newcastle Upon Tyme: Sage.

Braidotti, R. (2016). Posthuman critical theory. In *Critical Posthumanism and Planetary Futures* (pp. 13–32). New Delhi: Springer.

Brennan, J. & Naidoo, R. (2008). Higher education and the achievement (and/or prevention) of equity and social justice. *Higher Education*, 56(3), 287–302.

Brennan, M., Grimes M. & Thoutenhoofd E. (2005) *Deaf Students in Scottish Higher Education*. Coleford: Douglas McLean Publishing, Gloucestershire.

Brohan, E., Henderson, C., Wheat, K., Malcolm, E., Clement, S., Barley, E. A., Slade, M. & Thornicroft, G. (2012). Systematic review of beliefs, behaviours and influencing factors associated with disclosure of a mental health problem in the workplace. *BMC Psychiatry*, 12(1), 1–11, 1–14.

Bronfenbrenner, U. (1979). Contexts of child rearing: Problems and prospects. *American Psychologist*, 34(10), 844.

Bronfenbrenner, U. (2005). *Making Human Beings Human: Bioecological Perspectives on Human Development*. Lonson: Sage.

Brooks, R. & Waters, J. (2010). Social networks and educational mobility: The experiences of UK students. *Globalisation, Societies and Education*, 8(1), 143–57.

Brown, P. (2013). Education, opportunity and the prospects for social mobility. *British Journal of Sociology of Education*, 34(5–6), 678–700.

Brown, P. (2016). *The Invisible Problem?: Improving Students' Mental Health*. Oxford: Higher Education Policy Institute.

Bruce, M. & Bridgeland, J. (2014). *The Mentoring Effect: Young People's Perspectives on the Outcomes and Availability of Mentoring*. Washington, DC: Civic Enterprises with Heart Research Associates.

Buchanan, T. (2011). Attention deficit/hyperactivity disorder and well-being: Is social impairment an issue for college students with ADHD? *Journal of Postsecondary Education and Disability*, 24(3), 193–210.

Bufton, S. (2006). Learning to play the game: Mature, working-class students in higher education. In Jary, D. & Jones, R. (eds), *Perspectives and Practice in Widening Participation in the Social Sciences* (pp. 87–115). Birmingham, UK: University of Birmingham, C-SAP.

Burchard, M. S. & Swerdzewski, P. (2009). Learning effectiveness of a strategic learning course. *Journal of College Reading and Learning*, 40(1), 14–34.

Burgstahler, S. & Doe, T. (2006). Improving postsecondary outcomes for students with disabilities: Designing professional development for faculty. *Journal of Postsecondary Education and Disability*, 18(2), online.

Burke, P. & Hayton, A. (2012). Is widening participation still ethical? *Widening Participation and Lifelong Learning*, 13(1), 8–26.

Burke, P. J. (2002). Accessing education. *Effectively Widening Participation*. Stoke-on-Trent: Trentham Books.

Burke, P. J. (2015). Re/imagining higher education pedagogies: Gender, emotion and difference. *Teaching in Higher Education*, 20(4), 388–401.

Burnell, I. (2015). Widening the participation into higher education: Examining Bourdieusian theory in relation to HE in the UK. *Journal of Adult and Continuing Education*, 21(2), 93–109.

Byrd, R. M and.Adsit, J. (2019). *Writing Intersectional Identities: Keywords for Creative Writers*. Bloomsbury Publishing.

Byrom, N. C. & Murphy, R. A. (2018). Individual differences are more than a gene × environment interaction: The role of learning. *Journal of Experimental Psychology: Animal Learning and Cognition*, 44(1), 36.

Cadge, C., Connor, C. & Greenfield, S. (2019). University students' understanding and perceptions of schizophrenia in the UK: A qualitative study. *BMJ Open*, 9(4), e258–313.

Callender, C. (2011). Widening participation, social justice and injustice: Part-time students in higher education in England. *International Journal of Lifelong Education*, 30(4), 469–87.

Callender, C. & Jackson, J. (2008). Does the fear of debt constrain choice of university and subject of study? *Studies in Higher Education*, 33(4), 405–29.

Calmore, J. O. (1991). Critical race theory, Archie Shepp, and fire music: Securing an authentic intellectual life in a multicultural world. *California Law Review*, 65, 2129.

Calmore, J. O. (1997). Exploring Michael Omi's messy real world of race: An essay for naked people longing to swim free. *Law & Inequality*, 15, 25.

Campbell, L. A. & McKendrick, J. H. (2017). Beyond aspirations: Deploying the capability approach to tackle the under-representation in higher education of young people from deprived communities. *Studies in Continuing Education*, 39(2), 120–37.

Carastathis, A. (2016). *Intersectionality: Origins, Contestations, Horizons*. Lincoln: University of Nebraska Press.

Castillo-Montoya, M. & Reyes, D. (2018). Learning Latinidad: The role of a Latino cultural center service-learning course in Latino identity inquiry and sociopolitical capacity. *Journal of Latinos and Education*. Advance online publication.

Chambers, C. R., Wehmeyer, M. L., Saito, Y., Lida, K. M., Lee, Y. & Singh, V. (2007). Self-determination: What do we know? Where do we go? *Exceptionality*, 15(1), 3–15.

Chowdry, H., Crawford, C., Dearden, L., Goodman, A. & Vignoles, A. (2013). Widening participation in higher education: Analysis using linked administrative data. *Journal of the Royal Statistical Society: Series A (Statistics in Society)*, 176(2), 431–57.

Christie, H., Munro, M. & Fisher, T. (2007). Leaving university early: Exploring the differences between continuing and non-continuing students. *Studies in Higher Education*, 5(29), 617–36.

Clarke, P. & Beech, D. (eds) (2018). *Reaching the Parts of Society Universities Have Missed: A Manifesto for the New Director of Fair Access and Participation*. Oxford: Higher Education Policy Institute.

Cleary, M. (2011). *The Experience of Black and Minority Ethnic Staff in Higher Education in England. Equality Challenge Unity*. London: HMSO.

Clegg, N., Allen, R., Fernandez, S., Freedman, S. & Kinnock, S. (2016). *Commission on Inequality in Education*.

Cobb, B., Lehmann, J., Newman-Gonchar, R. & Alwell, M. (2009). Self-determination for students with disabilities: A narrative metasynthesis. *Career Development for Exceptional Individuals*, 32(2), 108–14.

Cohen, S. & Wills, T. A. (1985). Stress, social support, and the buffering hypothesis. *Psychological Bulletin*, 98(2), 310.

Cole, G. D. H. (1955). *Studies in Class Structure*. London: Routledge & Kegan Paul.

Cole-Hamilton, I. & Vale, D. (2000). *Shaping the Future: The Experiences of Blind and Partially Sighted Children and Young People in the UK (Summary Report)*. London: Royal National Institute for the Blind.

Coleman, J. S. (1966). The possibility of a social welfare function. *The American Economic Review*, 56(5), 1105–22.

Collins, M. E. & Mowbray, C. T. (2005). Understanding the policy context for supporting students with psychiatric disabilities in higher education. *Community Mental Health Journal*, 41(4), 431–50.

Collins, P. H. (1986). Learning from the outsider within: The sociological significance of Black feminist thought. *Social Problems*, 33(6), s14–s32.

Collins, P. H. & Bilge, S. (2020). *Intersectionality*. New Jersey: John Wiley & Sons. Hoboken.

Cominetti, N., Henehan, K. & Clarke, S. (2019). Low Pay Britain. *Resolution Foundation*.

Conley, C. S., Shapiro, J. B., Kirsch, A. C. & Durlak, J. A. (2017). A meta-analysis of indicated mental health prevention programs for at-risk higher education students. *Journal of Counselling Psychology*, 64(2), 121–40.

Connell, J., Barkham, M. & Mellor-Clark J. (2008). The effectiveness of UK student counselling services: An analysis using the CORE System. *British Journal of Guidance & Counselling*, 36(1), 1–18. DOI: 10.1080/03069880701715655.

Connor, H. (2001). Deciding for or against participation in higher education: the views of young people from lower social class backgrounds. *Higher Education Quarterly*, 55(2), 204–24.

Connor, H., Tyers, C., Modood, T. & Hillage, J. (2004). *Why the Difference? A Closer Look at Higher Education Minority Ethnic Students and Graduates* (Research Report No. 552). London: Department for Education and Skills.

Cooke, B. & Kothari, U. (eds) (2001). *Participation: The New Tyranny?* London: Zed Books.

Cooper, C. (2015). Critical pedagogy in higher education. In Cooper, C., Gormally, S. & Hugues, G. (eds), *Socially Just, Radical Alternatives for Education and Youth Work Practice* (pp. 39–64). London: Palgrave Macmillan.

Copestake, J. & Camfield, L. (2010). Measuring multidimensional aspiration gaps: A means to understanding cultural aspects of poverty. *Development Policy Review*, 28(5), 617–33.

Costa, C. & Gilliland, G. (2017). Digital literacies for employability-fostering forms of capital online. *Revista da UIIPS*, 5(2), 186–97.

Costa, C., Taylor, Y., Goodfellow, C. & Ecochard, S. (2020). Estranged students in higher education: Navigating social and economic capitals. *Cambridge Journal of Education*, 50(1), 107–23.

Côté, J. E. & Furlong, A. (eds) (2016). *Routledge Handbook of the Sociology of Higher Education*. London and New York: Routledge.

Cotton, D. R., Joyner, M., George, R. & Cotton, P. A. (2016). Understanding the gender and ethnicity attainment gap in UK higher education. *Innovations in Education and Teaching International*, 53(5), 475–86.

Cowden, S. & Singh, G. (2013). *Acts of Knowing: Critical Pedagogy in, against and beyond the University*. New York: Bloomsbury Publishing USA.

Crawford, C. & Greaves, E. (2015). *Socio-economic, Ethnic and Gender Differences in HE Participation*. Department of Business Skills and Innovation. London: HMSO.

Crenshaw, K., Gotanda, N., Peller, G. & Thomas, K. (1995). Critical race theory. In *The Key Writings That Formed the Movement* (pp. 276–91). New York: The New Press.

Crenshaw, K. W. (2017). *On intersectionality: Essential writings*. New York: The New Press.

Cress, C. M. & Ikeda, E. K. (2003). Distress under duress: The relationship between campus climate and depression in Asian American college students. *Journal of Student Affairs Research and Practice*, 40(2), 260–83.

Crew, T. (2020). *Higher Education and Working-class Academics*. Cham: Palgrave Pivot.

Crocker, J. & Major, B. (1989). Social stigma and self-esteem: The self-protective properties of stigma. *Psychological Review*, 96(4), 608–30.

Crockford, K. (2020). Evaluating widening participation. In *Research Intelligence (Quarterly Magazine)*, 143 (pp. 15–17). London: British Education Research Association.

Crosier, D., Horvath, A., Kerpanova, V., Kocanova, D. & Riihelainen, J. (2015). Modernisation of higher education in Europe: Access, retention and employability. Eurydice brief. *Education, Audiovisual and Culture Executive Agency, European Commission*.

Crozier, G., Reay, D. & Clayton, J. (2019). Working the borderlands: Working-class students constructing hybrid identities and asserting their place in higher education. *British Journal of Sociology of Education*, 40(7), 922–37.

Crozier, G., Reay, D., Clayton, J., Colliander, L. & Grinstead, J. (2008). Different strokes for different folks: Diverse students in diverse institutions–experiences of higher education. *Research Papers in Education*, 23(2), 167–77.

Cummings, C., Laing, K., Law, J., McLaughlin, J., Papps, I., Todd, L. & Woolner, P. (2012). *Can Changing Aspirations and Attitudes Impact on Educational Attainment*. York: Joseph Rowntree Foundation.

Cureton, D. & Gravestock, P. (2019). We belong: Differential sense of belonging and its meaning for different ethnicity groups in higher education. *Compass: Journal of Learning and Teaching*, 12(1), online.

Cusack, C. E., Hughes, J. L. & Nuhu, N. (2013). Connecting gender and mental health to imposter phenomenon feelings. *Journal of Psychological Research*, 18(2), 74–81.

Cuthbert, C. & Hatch, R. (2009). *Educational Aspiration and Attainment amongst Young People in Deprived Communities*. Edinburgh: Centre for Research on Families and Relationships.

DaDeppo, L. M. (2009). Integration factors related to the academic success and intent to persist of college students with learning disabilities. *Learning Disabilities Research & Practice*, 24(3), 122–31.

Dallas, B. K. & Sprong, M. E. (2015). Assessing faculty attitudes toward universal design instructional techniques. *Journal of Applied Rehabilitation Counseling*, 46(4), 18–28.

D'Angelo, R. (2018). *White Fragility: Why It's so Hard for White People to Talk about Racism*. Boston: Beacon Press.

Daughtry, D., Gibson, J. & Abels, A. (2009). Mentoring students and professionals with disabilities. *Professional Psychology: Research and Practice*, 40(2), 201.

David, M., Bathmaker, A. M., Crozier, G., Davis, P., Ertl, H., Fuller, A., Hayward, G., Heath, S., Hockings, C., Parry, G. & Reay, D. (eds) (2009). *Improving Learning by Widening Participation in Higher Education*. London and New York: Routledge.

Davidson, J. & Henderson, V. L. (2010). Coming out'on the spectrum: Autism, identity and disclosure. *Social & Cultural Geography*, 11(2), 155-70.

Davis, K. (2008). Intersectionality as buzzword: A sociology of science perspective on what makes a feminist theory successful. *Feminist theory*, 9(1), 67-85.

De Bruyckere, P. (2018). *The Ingredients for Great Teaching*. London: Sage.

Debrand, C. C. & Salzberg, C. L. (2005). A validated curriculum to provide training to faculty regarding students with disabilities in higher education. *Journal of Postsecondary Education and Disability*, 18(1), 49-61.

Delgado Bernal, D. (2006). Learning and living pedagogies of the home: The Mestiza consciousness of Chicana studies. In Delgado Bernal, D., Elenes, C. A., Godinez, F. & Villenas, S. (eds), *Chicana/Latina Education in Everyday Life: Feminista Perspectives on Pedagogy and Epistemology* (pp. 113-32). Albany, NY: State University of New York Press.

Demack, S. (2020). A convenient paradox: Statistics and white advantage. In *UK Degree Attainment in Research Intelligence (Quarterly Magazine)*, 143 (pp. 15-17). London: British Education Research Association.

Denhart, H. (2008). Deconstructing barriers: Perceptions of students labeled with learning disabilities in higher education. *Journal of Learning Disabilities*, 41(6), 483-97.

Devlin, M. & McKay, J. (2018). Teaching inclusively online in a massified university system. *Widening Participation and Lifelong Learning*, 20(1), 146-66.

Dhanda, M. (2009). Understanding disparities in student attainment: What do Black and minority ethnic students say? Paper presented at the Annual Meeting of the ISPP 32nd Annual Scientific Meeting. Trinity College, Dublin, Ireland.

Dhanda, M. (2010). *Understanding Disparities in Student Attainment: Black and Minority Ethnic Students' Experience*. Wolverhampton: University of Wolverhampton.

Dole, S. (2001). Reconciling contradictions: Identity formation in individuals with giftedness and learning disabilities. *Journal for the Education of the Gifted*, 25(2), 103-37.

Dong, S. & Lucas, M. S. (2013). An analysis of disability, academic performance, and seeking support in one university setting. *Career Development and Transition for Exceptional Individuals*, 20(10), 1–10.

Dong, S. & Lucas, M. S. (2014). Psychological profile of university students with different types of disabilities. *Journal of College Student Development*, 55(5), 481–5.

Donnelly, M. & Evans, C. (2016). Framing the geographies of higher education participation: Schools, place and national identity. *British Educational Research Journal*, 42(1), 74–92.

Donnelly, M. & Gamsu, S. (2018). Regional structures of feeling? A spatially and socially differentiated analysis of UK student im/mobility. *British Journal of Sociology of Education*, 39(7), 961–81.

Doosje, B., Ellemers, N. & Spears, R. (1995). Perceived intragroup variability as a function of group status and identification. *Journal of Experimental Social Psychology*, 31(5), 410–36.

Dougherty, S. J., Campana, K. A., Kontos, R. A., Flores, M. K., Lockhart, R. S. & Douglas, D. S. (1996). Supported education: A qualitative study of the student experience. *Psychiatric Rehabilitation Journal*, 19(3), 59–70.

Douglas, G., McLinden, M., McCall, S., Pavey, S., Ware, J. & Farrell, A. M. (2011). Access to print literacy for children and young people with visual impairment: Findings from a review of literature. *European Journal of Special Needs Education*, 26(1), 25–38.

Dovidio, J. F., Gaertner, S. L., Niemann, Y. F. & Snider, K. (2001). Racial, ethnic, and cultural differences in responding to distinctiveness and discrimination on campus: Stigma and common group identity. *Journal of Social Issues*, 57(1), 167–88.

Dowrick, P. W., Anderson, J., Heyer, K. & Acosta, J. (2005). Postsecondary education across the USA: Experiences of adults with disabilities. *Journal of Vocational Rehabilitation*, 22(1), 41–7.

Doyle, M. & Griffin, M. (2012). Raised aspirations and attainment? A review of the impact of Aimhigher (2004–2011) on widening participation in higher education in England. *London Review of Education*, 10(1), 75–88 and 105–15.

Duffy, A., Keown-Stoneman, C., Goodday, S., Horrocks, J., Lowe, M., King, N. & Saunders, K. E. A. (2020). *Predictors of Mental Health and Academic Outcomes in First-year University Students: Identifying Prevention and Early-intervention Targets*. Cambridge: Cambridge University Press.

Dunn, D. S. & Burcaw, S. (2013). Disability identity: Exploring narrative accounts of disability. *Rehabilitation Psychology*, 58(2), 148–57.

Eddy, S. L. & Hogan, K. A. (2014). Getting under the hood: How and for whom does increasing course structure work? *CBE—Life Sciences Education*, 13(3), 453–68.

Elliott, D. C. (2014). Trailblazing: Exploring first-generation college students' self-efficacy beliefs and academic adjustment. *Journal of the First-Year Experience & Students in Transition* 26(2), 29–49.

Engle, J. & Theokas, C. (2010). *Top Gainers: Some Public Four-year Colleges and Universities Have Madegood Progress in Closing Graduation-rate Gaps. College Results Online.* Available from: http://www.edtrust.org/sites/edtrust.org/files/publications/files/CRO%20Brief%20Top%20Gainers.pdf

Evans, N. J., Assadi, J. L. & Herriott, T. K. (2005). Encouraging the development of disability allies. *New Directions for Student Services*, 2005(110), 67–79.

Fabri, M., Andrews, P. & Pukki, H. (2016). *Best Practice for Professionals Supporting Autistic Students within or outside HE Institutions*. Leeds: Autism and Uni.

Faine, M., Plowright, S. & Seddon, T. (2016). Higher education and social cohesion: Universities, citizenship, and spaces of orientation. In *Creating Social Cohesion in an Interdependent World* (pp. 205–19). New York: Palgrave Macmillan.

Farrar, V. & Young, R. (2007). *Supervising Disabled Research Students. Issues in Postgraduate Education: Management, Teaching and Supervision*. London: Society for Research into Higher Education.

Faulkner, B. & Burdenski, T. K., Jr (2011). Empowering lower-income developmental math students to satisfy Glasser's five basic needs. *International Journal of Choice Theory and Reality Therapy*, 31(1), 128–42.

Field, J. & Morgan-Klein, T. (2010). Studenthood and identification: Higher education as liminal transitional space. Paper presented at 40th Annual Conference of Standing Conference on University Teaching and Research in the Education of Adults (SCUTREA), University of Warwick.

Finesilver, C., Leigh, J. S. & Brown, N. (2020). Invisible Disability, Unacknowledged Diversity. Canterbury: Kent University.

Fiorenza, E. S. (1993). *But She Said: Feminist Practices of Biblical Interpretation.* Boston, MA: Beacon Press.

Fisher, P. & Goodley, D. (2007). The linear medical model of disability: Mothers of disabled babies resist with counter-narratives. *Sociology of Health & Illness*, 29(1), 66–81.

Fisher, S. & Hood, B. (1987). The stress of the transition to university: A longitudinal study of psychological disturbance, absent mindedness and vulnerability to homesickness. *British Journal of Psychology*, 78(4) (November), 425–41.

Fleischer, D. Z. & Zames, F. (2001). *The Disability Rights Movement: From Charity to Confrontation*. Philadelphia: Temple University Press.

Forsyth, A. & Furlong, A. (2003). Access to higher education and disadvantaged young people. *British Educational Research Journal*, 29(2), 205–25.

Foster, S., Long, G. & Snell, K. (1999). Inclusive instruction and learning for deaf students in postsecondary education. *Journal of Deaf Studies and Deaf Education*, 4(3), 225–35.

Fowler, C. H., Konrad, M., Walker, A. R., Test, D. W. & Wood, W. M. (2007). Self-determination interventions' effects on the academic performance of students with developmental disabilities. *Education and Training in Developmental Disabilities*, 42(3), 270–85.

Freire, P. (1996). *Pedagogy of the Oppressed (Revised)*. New York: Continuum.

Freire, P. (2000). *Pedagogy of Freedom: Ethics, Democracy, and Civic Courage*. Washington, DC: Rowman & Littlefield Publishers.

Friedman, S. & Laurison, D. (2020). *The Class Ceiling: Why It Pays to Be Privileged*. Bristol: Policy Press.

Furlong, A. & Cartmel, F. (2009). *Higher Education and Social Justice*. London: McGraw-Hill Education (UK).

Gair, S. & Baglow, L. (2018). 'We barely survived': Social work students' mental health vulnerabilities and implications for educators, universities and the workforce. *Aotearoa New Zealand Social Work*, 30(1), 32.

Galderisi, S., Heinz, A., Kastrup, M., Beezhold, J.& Sartorius, N. (2015). Toward a new definition of mental health. *World Psychiatry*, 14(2), 231.

Galdi, L. L. (2007). *Factors That Enable Graduate Students with Visual Disabilities to Succeed in Their Educational Pursuits* (Doctoral dissertation). Available from ProQuest Dissertation and Theses database. (UMI No. 3272639).

Gale, T. & Hodge, S. (2014). Just imaginary: Delimiting social inclusion in higher education. *British Journal of Sociology of Education*, 35(5), 688–709.

Gale, T. & Parker, S. (2014). Navigating change: A typology of student transition in higher education. *Studies in Higher Education*, 39(5), 734–53.

Gall, T. L., Evans, D. R. & Bellerose, S. (2000). Transition to first-year university: Patterns of change in adjustment across life domains and time. *Journal of Social and Clinical Psychology*, 19(4), 544–67.

Gamoran, A. (2001). American schooling and educational inequality: A forecast for the 21st century. *Sociology of Education*, 74, 135–53.

Garritzmann, J. L. (2017). The partisan politics of higher education. *PS: Political Science & Politics*, 50(2), 413–17.

Gaskell, S. & Lingwood, R. (2019). *Widening Opportunity in Higher Education: The Third Phase: Beyond Graduation*. London: Universities UK.

Giddens, Anthony. (1984). *The Constitution of Society: Outline of the Theory of Structuration*. University of California Press.

Giddy, D. (1807). *Parochial Schools Bill*. London: HMSO.

Gillborn, D. (2015). Intersectionality, critical race theory, and the primacy of racism: Race, class, gender, and disability in education. *Qualitative Inquiry*, 21(3), 277–87.

Gillian-Daniel, D. L. & Kraemer, S. B. (2015). Faculty development to address the achievement gap. *Change: The Magazine of Higher Learning*, 47(6), 32–41.

Giri, A., Aylott, J., Giri, P., Ferguson-Wormley, S. & Evans, J. (2021). Lived experience and the social model of disability: Conflicted and inter-dependent ambitions for employment of people with a learning disability and their family carers. *British Journal of Learning Disabilities*.

Giroux, H. A. (2017). Neoliberalism's war against higher education and the role of public intellectuals. In Izak, M., Kostera, M. & Zawadzki, M. (eds), *The Future of University Education* (pp. 185–206). Cham: Palgrave Macmillan.

Goldstein, S. B. & Johnson, V. A. (1997). Stigma by association: Perceptions of the dating partners of college students with physical disabilities. *Basic and Applied Social Psychology*, 19(4), 495–504.

Gonzalez, L. M., Borders, L. D., Hines, E. M., Villalba, J. A. & Henderson, A. (2013). Parental involvement in children's education: Considerations for school counselors working with Latino immigrant families. *Professional School Counseling*, 16(3), online.

Goode, J. (2007). 'Managing' disability: Early experiences of university students with disabilities. *Disability & Society*, 22(1), 35–48.

Goodenow, C. (1993a). The psychological sense of school membership among adolescents: Scale development and educational correlates. *Psychology in the Schools*, 30(1), 70–90.

Goodenow, C. & Grady, K. E. (1993). The relationship of school belonging and friends' values to academic motivation among urban adolescent students. *The Journal of Experimental Education*, 62(1), 60–71.

Gorard, S., See, B. H. & Davies, P. (2012). *The Impact of Attitudes and Aspirations on Educational Attainment and Participation*. York: Joseph Rowntree Foundation.

Gorard, S. & Smith, E. (2006). Beyond the 'learning society': What have we learnt from widening participation research? *International Journal of Lifelong Education*, 25(6), 575–94.

Gos, M. W. (1995). Overcoming social class markers: Preparing working class students for college. *The Clearing House*, 69(1), 30–4.

Gotanda, N. (1991). A Critique of 'Our Constitution Is Color-Blind' *Stanford Law Review*, 44(1) (November), 1–68

Gover, J. P., Garcia, J., Purdie-Vaughns, V., Binning, K. R., Cook, J. E., Reeves, S. L., Apfel, N., Taborsky-Barba, S., Sherman, D. K. & Cohen, G. L. (2017). Self-affirmation facilitates minority middle schoolers' progress along college trajectories. *Proceedings of the National Academy of Sciences of the United States of America*, 114(29), 7594–9.

Grange, L. L., Du Preez, P., Ramrathan, L. & Blignaut, S. (2020). Decolonising the university curriculum or decolonial-washing? A multiple case study. *Journal of Education (University of KwaZulu-Natal)*, 80, 25–48.

Grant, A. M. & Schwartz, B. (2011). Too much of a good thing: The challenge and opportunity of the inverted U. *Perspectives on Psychological Science*, 6(1), 61–76.

Griffin, E. & Pollak, D. (2009). Student experiences of neurodiversity in higher education: Insights from the BRAINHE project. *Dyslexia*, 15(1), 23–41.

Griffith, A. L. & Rask, K. N. (2014). Peer effects in higher education: A look at heterogeneous impacts. *Economics of Education Review*, 39, 65–77.

Griffith, G. M., Totsika, V., Nash, S. & Hastings, R. P. (2012). 'I just don't fit anywhere': Support experiences and future support needs of individuals with Asperger syndrome in middle adulthood. *Autism*, 16(5), 532–46.

Grodsky, E. & Pager, D. (2001). The structure of disadvantage: Individual and occupational determinants of the black-white wage gap. *American Sociological Review*, 66(4), 542–67.

Grosz, E. (2020). *Volatile Bodies: Toward a Corporeal Feminism*. London and New York: Routledge.

Guiffrida, D. A., Boxell, O., Hamell, S., Ponicsan, I. & Akinsete, R. (2018a). Supporting black British university students. Part one: Understanding students' experiences with peers and academic staff. *University and College Counselling*, 6(3), 4–11.

Guiffrida, D. A., Boxell, O., Hamell, S., Ponicsan, I. Akinsete, R. (2018b). Supporting black British university students: Understanding students' experiences with family members. *University and College Counselling*, November, 6(4), 4–12.

Guthrie, S., Lichten, C., van Belle, J., Ball, S., Knack, A. & Hofman, J. (2017). *Understanding Mental Health in the Research Environment a Rapid Evidence Assessment*. London: RAND Europe Royal Society and the Wellcome Trust.

Gutiérrez-Jones, C. (2001). *Critical Race Narratives: A Study of Race, Rhetoric, and Injury* (Vol. 42). New York: NYU Press.

Gutman, L. & Akerman, R. (2008). *Determinants of Aspirations [Wider Benefits of Learning Research Report No. 27]*. London: Centre for Research on the Wider Benefits of Learning, Institute of Education, University of London.

Hackman, H. W. & Rauscher, L. (2004). A pathway to access for all: Exploring the connections between universal instructional design and social justice education. *Equity & Excellence in Education*, 37(2), 114–23.

Hagerty, B. M., Williams, R. A., Coyne, J. C. & Early, M. R. (1996). Sense of belonging and indicators of social and psychological functioning. *Archives of Psychiatric Nursing*, 10(4), 235–44.

Haggis, T. (2003). Constructing images of ourselves? A critical investigation into 'approaches to learning' research in higher education. *British Educational Research Journal*, 29, 89–104.

Hale, S. (2021). The class politics of foundation years. *Journal of the Foundation Year Network*, 3, 91–100.

Hall, J. & Teresa, T. *Students First: The Experiences of Disabled Students in Higher Education. SCRE Research Report Series.* Scottish Council for Research in Education. Available from: http://www.scre.ac.uk

Hanafin, J., Shevlin, M., Kenny, M. & Mc Neela, E. (2007). Including young people with disabilities: Assessment challenges in higher education. *Higher Education: The International Journal of Higher Education and Educational Planning*, 54, 435–48.

Hannam-Swain, S. (2017). Safe with self-injury: A practical guide to understanding, responding and harm-reduction, by Kay Inckle, Monmouth. *PCCS Books*, 265, 1–3.

Hannam-Swain, S. (2018). The additional labour of a disabled PhD student. *Disability & Society*, 33(1), 138–42.

Hannon, C., Faas, D. & O'Sullivan, K. (2017). Widening the educational capabilities of socio-economically disadvantaged students through a model of social and cultural capital development. *British Educational Research Journal*, 43(6), 1225–45.

Harackiewicz, J. M., Canning, E. A., Tibbetts, Y., Priniski, S. J. & Hyde, J. S. (2016). Closing achievement gaps with a utility-value intervention: Disentangling race and social class. *Journal of Personality and Social Psychology*, 111(5), 745–65.

Harris, A. (2019). *Finding Our Own Way* (Rep). Online: Centre for Mental Health.

Harris, C. & Oppenheim, C. (2003). The provision of library services for visually impaired students in UK further education libraries in response to the Special Educational Needs and Disability Act (SENDA). *Journal of Librarianship and Information Science*, 35(4), 243–57.

Harrison, N. (2012). The mismeasure of participation: How choosing the 'wrong' statistic helped seal the fate of aimhigher. *Higher Education Review*, 45(1), 30–61.

Harrison, N. (2020). Patterns of participation in higher education for care-experienced students in England: Why has there not been more progress? *Studies in Higher Education*, 45(9), 1986–2000.

Harrison, N. & McCaig, C. (2015). An ecological fallacy in higher education policy: The use, overuse and misuse of 'low participation neighbourhoods'. *Journal of Further and Higher Education*, 39(6), 793–817.

Harrison, N. & Waller, R. (2017). Success and impact in widening participation policy: What works and how do we know? *Higher Education Policy*, 30(2), 141–60.

Hartman-Hall, H. M. & Haaga, D. A. F. (2002). College students' willingness to seek help for their learning disabilities. *Learning Disability Quarterly*, 25(4), 263–74.

Hartrey, L., Denieffe, S. & Wells, J. S. G. (2017). A systematic review of barriers and supports to the participation of students with mental health difficulties in higher education. *Mental Health & Prevention*, 6, 26–43.

Harvey, J., Lévesque, M. & Donnelly, P. (2007). Sport volunteerism and social capital. *Sociology of Sport Journal*, 24(2), 206–23.

Harvill, E. L., Maynard, R. A., Nguyen, H. T., Robertson-Kraft, C. & Tognatta, N. (2012). Effects of college access programs on college readiness and enrollment: A meta-analysis. *Society for Research on Educational Effectiveness*. Evanston.

Hattie, J. (2008). *Visible Learning*. London: Routledge.

Healey, M., Flint, A. & Harrington, K. (2014). *Engagement through Partnership: Students as Partners in Learning and Teaching in Higher Education*. [Online] Higher Education Academy.

Hedrick, B., Dizen, M., Collins, K., Evans, J. & Grayson, T. (2010). Perceptions of college students with and without disabilities and effects of STEM and non-STEM enrollment on student engagement and institutional involvement. *Journal of Postsecondary Education and Disability*, 23(2), 129–36.

HEFCE (2016). *UK Review of the Provision of Information about Higher Education: National Student Survey Results and Trends Analysis 2005–2013*. Available from: https://webarchive.nationalarchives.gov.uk/20160106171010/http://www.Hefce.ac.uk/pubs/year/2014/201413/

HEFCE (2018). *HEFCE Annual Report and Accounts 2017 to 2018*. London: HMSO

Hennessey, M. L., Roessler, R., Cook, B., Unger, D. & Rumrill, P. (2006). Employment and career development concerns of postsecondary students with disabilities: Service and policy implications. *Journal of Postsecondary Education and Disability*, 19(1), 39–55.

Hennessey, M. L., Rumrill, P. D., Jr, Roessler, R. T. & Cook, B. G. (2006). Career development needs among college and university students with learning disabilities and attention deficit disorder/attention deficit hyperactivity disorder. *Learning Disabilities: A Multidisciplinary Journal*, 14(1), 57–66.

Henry, W. J., Fuerth, K. & Figliozzi, J. (2010). Gay with a disability: A college student's multiple cultural journey. *College Student Journal*, 44(2), 377–88.

Herz, M. & Johansson, T. (2015). The normativity of the concept of heteronormativity. *Journal of Homosexuality*, 62(8), 1009–20.

HESA (2021) Higher Education Student data. https://www.hesa.ac.uk/data-and-analysis/students

Hewett, R., Douglas, G., McLinden, M. & Keil, S. (2017). Developing an inclusive learning environment for students with visual impairment in higher education: Progressive mutual accommodation and learner experiences in the United Kingdom. *European Journal of Special Needs Education*, 32(1), 89–109.

Hewitt, L. E. (2011). Perspectives on support needs of individuals with autism spectrum disorders: Transition to college. *Topics in Language Disorders*, 31(3), 273–85.

Hewitt, R. (2019). *Measuring Well-being in Higher Education*. HEPI Policy Note 13. London: Higher Education Policy Institute.

Heyward, S. (2011). Legal challenges and opportunities. In Harbour, W. S. & Madaus, J. W. (eds), New directions for higher education: No. 154. *Disability Services and Campus Dynamics* (pp. 55–64). San Francisco: Jossey-Bass.

Hicks, T. & Wood, J. L. (2016). What do we know about diverse college students in STEM? A meta-synthesis of academic and social characteristic studies. *Journal for Multicultural Education*, 10(2), 107–23.

Higginbotham, H. K. (2012). *A Psychoeducational Approach to Improving College Student Mental Health* (Thesis). Wright State University.

Higher Education Statistics Agency (HESA) (2019). *Higher Education Student Statistics: UK, 2017/18 – Student Numbers and Characteristics*. Cheltenham: HESA.

Hill, E., Posey, T., Gomez, E. & Shapiro, S. L. (2018). Student readiness: Examining the impact of a university outdoor orientation program. *Journal of Outdoor Recreation, Education, and Leadership*, 10(2), 109–23.

Hill, S. & Roger, A. (2016). The experience of disabled and non-disabled students on professional practice placements in the United Kingdom. *Disability & Society*, 31(9), 1205–25.

Hillman, N. (2017). Introduction: Running to stand still in. *Where Next for Widening Participation and Fair Access*, 7–16. New Insights from Leading Thinkers, HEPI Report 98.

Hillman, N. & Corral, D. (2017). The equity implications of paying for performance in higher education. *American Behavioral Scientist*, 61(14), 1757–72.

Hindes, Y. & Mather, J. (2007). Inclusive education at the post-secondary level: Attitudes of students and professors. *Exceptionality Education Canada*, 17(1), 107–28.

Hinton-Smith, T. (ed.) (2012). *Widening Participation in Higher Education: Casting the Net Wide?* London: Palgrave Macmillan.

Hinton-Smith, T., Danvers, E. & Jovanovic, T. (2018). Roma women's higher education participation: Whose responsibility? *Gender and Education*, 30(7), 811–28.

Hitchings, W. E., Johnson, K. K., Luzzo, D. A., Retish, P., Hinz, C. & Hake, J. (2010). Identifying the career development needs of community college student with and without learning disabilities. *Journal of Applied Research in the Community College*, 18(1), 22–9.

Hitchings, W. E., Luzzo, D. A., Ristow, R., Horvath, M., Retish, P. & Tanners, A. (2001). The career development needs of college students with learning disabilities: In their own words. *Learning Disabilities Research & Practice*, 16(1), 8–17.

Hockings, C. S., Cooke, S. & Bowl, M. (2008). *Learning and Teaching for Social Diversity and Difference: Full Research Report. ESRC End of Award Report, RES - 139-25-0222*. Swindon: ESRC.

Hofmann, S. & Mühlenweg, A. (2018). Learning intensity effects in students' mental and physical health – Evidence from a large scale natural experiment in Germany. *Economics of Education Review*, 67, 216–34.

Hollinrake, S., Hunt, G., Dix, H. & Wagner, A. (2019). Do we practice (or teach) what we preach? Developing a more inclusive learning environment to better prepare social work students for practice through improving the exploration of their different ethnicities within teaching, learning and assessment opportunities. *Social Work Education*, 38(5), 582–603.

Holt, E. & McKay, D. R. (2000, December). Access and success: Issues affecting post-graduate students with disabilities at the University of Otago, New Zealand. In *Pathways V Conference*, University of Canberra, Canberra, Australia. Retrieved from http://www.adcet.edu.au/StoredFile.Aspx

Holzer, M. L., Madaus, J. W., Bray, M. A. & Kehle, T. J. (2009). The test-taking strategy intervention for college students with learning disabilities. *Learning Disabilities Research & Practice*, 24(1), 44–56.

hooks, b. (2014). *Teaching to Transgress*. London: Routledge.

Hordósy, R. & Clark, T. (2018). Beyond the compulsory: A critical exploration of the experiences of extracurricular activity and employability in a northern red brick university. *Research in Post-Compulsory Education*, 23(3), 414–35.

Horowitz, G. (2017). First-generation college students: How to recognize them and be their ally and advocate. *Journal of College Science Teaching*, 46(6), 8.

Hosking, D. L. (2008). Critical disability theory. A paper presented at the 4th Biennial Disability Studies Conference at Lancaster University, UK, 4 September 2008. *Journal of Consulting and Clinical Psychology*, 72(3), 467–78.

Houghton, A.-M. & Anderson, J. (2017). *Embedding Mental Wellbeing in the Curriculum: Maximising Success in Higher Education*. York: Higher Education Academy.

Howlin, P., Goode, S., Hutton, J. & Rutter, M. (2004). Adult outcome for children with autism. *Journal of Child Psychology and Psychiatry*, 45(2), 212–29.

Hua, Y., Hendrickson, J. M., Therrien, W. J., Woods-Groves, S., Ries, P. S. & Shaw, J. J. (2012). Effects of combined reading and question generation on reading fluency and comprehension of three young adults with autism and intellectual disability. *Focus on Autism and Other Developmental Disabilities*, 27(3), 135–46.

Hua, Y., Woods-Groves, S., Kaldenberg, E. R. & Scheidecker, B. J. (2013). Effects of vocabulary instruction using constant time delay on expository reading of young adults with intellectual disability. *Focus on Autism and Other Developmental Disabilities*, 28(2), 89–100.

Hubble, S. & Bolton, P. (2020). Support for students with mental health issues in higher education in England. *UK Parliament Briefing Paper*.

Huffman, M. L. & Cohen, P. N. (2004). Racial wage inequality: Job segregation and devaluation across US labor markets. *American Journal of Sociology*, 109(4), 902–36.

Hughes, G., Panjwani, M., Tulcidas, P. & Byrom, N. (2018). *Student Mental Health: The Role and Responsibilities of Academics*. Oxford: Student Minds.

Hughes, G. & Spanner, L. (2019). *The University Mental Health Charter*. Leeds: Student Minds.

Hughes, G. & Wilson, C. (2017). From transcendence to general maintenance: Exploring the creativity and wellbeing dynamic in higher education. In Reisman, F. (ed.), *Creativity, Innovation and Wellbeing* (pp. 23–65). London: KIE Conference Publications.

Hughes, G. J. & Byrom, N. C. (2019). Managing student mental health: The challenges faced by academics on professional healthcare courses. *Journal of Advanced Nursing*, 75(7), 1539–48.

Huntly, H. & Donovan, J. (2009). Supporting the development of persistence: Strategies for teachers of first year undergraduate students. *International Journal of Teaching and Learning in Higher Education*, 21(2), 210–20.

Hurst, R. (1999). Disabled people's organisations and development: Strategies for change. *Disability and Development*, 25–35.

Hurtado, S. (2001). Linking Diversity and Educational Purpose: How Diversity Affects the Classroom Environment and Student Development. In Orfield, Gary, (ed.), *Diversity Challenged: Evidence on the Impact of Affirmative Action* (pp. 187–203). Cambridge: Harvard Education Publishing Group.

Hurtado, S., Alvarez, C. L., Guillermo-Wann, C., Cuellar, M. & Arellano, L. (2012). A model for diverse learning environments. In Smart, J. C. (ed.), *Higher Education: Handbook of Theory and Research* (pp. 41–122). Dordrecht: Springer.

Hutcheon, E. J. & Wolbring, G. (2012). Voices of 'disabled' post secondary students: Examining higher education 'disability' policy using an ableism lens. *Journal of Diversity in Higher Education*, 5(1), 39–49.

Hutchings, M. & Archer, L. (2001). 'Higher than Einstein': Constructions of going to university among working-class non-participants. *Research Papers in Education*, 16(1), 69–91.

Huws, J. C. & Jones, R. S. P. (2008). Diagnosis, disclosure, and having autism: An interpretative phenomenological analysis of the perceptions of young people with autism. *Journal of Intellectual and Developmental Disability*, 33, 99–107.

Hysenbegasi, A., Hass, S. L. & Rowland, C. R. (2005). The impact of depression on the academic productivity of university students. *Journal of Mental Health Policy and Economics*, 8(3), 145.

Israilov, S. & Cho, H. J. (2017). How co-creation helped address hierarchy, overwhelmed patients, and conflicts of interest in health care quality and safety. *AMA J Ethics*, 19(11), 1139–45.

Iverson, S. V. & Jaggers, D. (2015). Racial profiling as institutional practice: Theorizing the experiences of Black male undergraduates. *Journal of Student Affairs Research and Practice* 52(1), 38–49.

Ives, J. & Castillo-Montoya, M. (2020). First-generation college students as academic learners: A systematic review. *Review of Educational Research*, 90(2), 139–78.

Izard, C. E. (1992). Basic emotions, relations among emotions, and emotion-cognition relations. *Psychological Review*, 99(3), 561–5.

Jackson, B. & Marsden, D. (2012). *Education and the Working Class* (RLE Edu L Sociology of Education). London: Routledge.

Jacobs, B. & van Wijnbergen, S. J. G. (2007). Capital-market failure, adverse selection, and equity financing of higher education. *FinanzArchiv/Public Finance Analysis*, 1–32.

Jacobs, N. & Harvey, D. (2005). *Do Parents Make a Difference to Children's Academic Achievement? Differences between Parents of Higher and Lower Achieving Students*. London: Routledge.

James, S., Swan, K. & Daston, C. (2016). Retention, progression and the taking of online courses. *Online Learning*, 20(2), 75–96.

Janiga, S. J. & Costenbader, V. (2002). The transition from high school to postsecondary education for students with learning disabilities: A survey of college service coordinators. *Journal of Learning Disabilities*, 35(5), 463–70.

Jarvis, J. & Knight, P. (2003). Supporting deaf students in higher education. In *Special Teaching in Higher Education: Successful Strategies for Access and Inclusion* (pp. 54–75). London and Stirling, VA: Kogan.

Jehangir, R. (2009). Cultivating voice: First-generation students seek full academic citizenship in multicultural learning communities. *Innovative Higher Education*, 34(1), 33–49.

Jehangir, R. (2010). *Higher Education and First-generation Students: Cultivating Community, Voice, and Place for the New Majority*. Berlin: Springer.

Jehangir, R., Williams, R. D. & Jeske, J. (2012). The influence of multicultural learning communities on the intrapersonal development of first-generation college students. *Journal of College Student Development*, 53(2), 267–84.

Jehangir, R., Williams, R. D. & Pete, J. (2011). Multicultural learning communities: Vehicles for developing self-authorship in first-generation college students. *Journal of the First-Year Experience & Students in Transition*, 23(1), 53–74.

Jencks, C., Smith, M., Acland, H., Bane, M. J. & Cohen, D. (1972). *Inequality Reassessment of the Effect of Family and Schooling in America* (No. 305.5073 I5).

Jennes-Coussens, M., Magill-Evans, J. & Koning, C. (2006). The quality of life of young men with Asperger syndrome: A brief report. *Autism*, 10(4), 403–14.

Jensen, J. M., McCrary, N., Krampe, K. & Cooper, J. (2004). Trying to do the right thing: Faculty attitudes toward accommodating students with learning disabilities. *Journal of Postsecondary Education and Disability*, 17(2), 81–90.

Johnson, C., Rossiter, K., Cartmell, B., Domingos, M. & Svanaes (2019). *Evaluation of Disabled Students' Allowances: Research Report*, Department of Education. London: HMSO.

Johnson-Bailey, J. & Cervero, R. M. (2004). Mentoring in black and white: The intricacies of cross-cultural mentoring. *Mentoring & Tutoring: Partnership in Learning*, 12(1), 7–21.

Jones, M. M. & Goble, Z. (2012). Creating effective mentoring partnerships for students with intellectual disabilities on campus: Mentoring partnerships. *Journal of Policy and Practice in Intellectual Disabilities*, 9(4), 270–8.

Jones, S. R. (2009). Constructing identities at the intersections: An autoethnographic exploration of multiple dimensions of identity. *Journal of College Student Development*, 50(3), 287–304.

Junco, R. & Salter, D. W. (2004). Improving the campus climate for students with disabilities through the use of online training. *NASPA Journal*, 41(2), 263–76.

Kahu, E. R. & Nelson, K. (2018). Student engagement in the educational interface: Understanding the mechanisms of student success. *Higher Education Research & Development*, 37(1), 58–71.

Kamatuka, N. (2016). 2 Marching in the rain: The TRIO programme and the civil rights legacy in the United States. *Access to Higher Education: Understanding Global Inequalities*, 29.

Kantzara, V. (2011). The relation of education to social cohesion. *Social Cohesion and Development*, 6(1), 37–50.

Kapilashrami, A. (2021) *Intersectionality-informed Framework for Tackling Racism and Embedding Inclusion and Diversity in Teaching & Learning*. Colchester: Essex University.

Karchmer M. & Mitchell R. (2003). Demographic and achievement characteristics of deaf and hard of hearing students. In Marschark, M. & Spencer, P. (eds), *Oxford Handbook of Deaf Studies, Language, and Education* (pp. 21–37). New York: Oxford University Press.

Kelly, K. & Cook, S. (2007). *Full-time Young Participation by Socio-economic Class: A New Widening Participation Measure in Higher Education*. London: Department for Education and Skills, HMSO.

Kemp, H., Lefroy, A. & Callan, N. (2013). Three-tiered support: Individual, school and institution-wide initiatives through a first year advisor network through a first year advisor network. *The International Journal of the First Year in Higher Education*, 4(2), 75–86.

Keohane, N. & Petrie, K. (2017). *On Course for Success? Student Retention at University*. London: Social Market Foundation.

Kessler, R. C., Berglund, P. A., Foster, C. L., Saunders, W. B., Stang, P. E. & Walters, E. E. (1997). Social consequences of psychiatric disorders, II: Teenage parenthood. *American Journal of Psychiatry*, 154(10), 1405–11.

Kessler, R. C., Walters, E. E. & Forthofer, M. S. (1998). The social consequences of psychiatric disorders, III: Probability of marital stability. *American Journal of Psychiatry*, 155(8), 1092–6.

Kettley, N. (2007). The past, present and future of widening participation research. *British Journal of Sociology of Education*, 28(3), 333–47.

Keynes, M. (2005). The personality and health of King Henry VIII (1491–1547). *Journal of Medical Biography*, 13(3), 174–83.

Kift, S. (2008). The next, great, first year challenge: Sustaining, coordinating and embedding coherent institution-wide approaches to enact the FYE as 'everybody's business'. Keynote. *11th Pacific Rim First Year Experience in Higher Education (FYHE) Conference 2008* (19).

Kift, S. (2015). A decade of transition pedagogy: A quantum leap in conceptualising the first year experience. *HERDSA Review of Higher Education*, 2, 51–86.

Kift, S., Nelson, K. & Clarke, J. (2010). Transition pedagogy: A third generation approach to FYE – A case study of policy and practice for the higher education sector. *The International Journal of the First Year in Higher Education*, 1(1), 1–20.

Kim, Y. K. & Sax, L. J. (2009). Student–faculty interaction in research universities: Differences by student gender, race, social class, and first-generation status. *Research in Higher Education*, 50(5), 437–59.

Kimball, E. W., Wells, R. S., Ostiguy, B. J., Manly, C. A. & Lauterbach, A. A. (2016). Students with disabilities in higher education: A review of the literature and an agenda for future research. In Paulsen, M. B. & Perna, L. W. (eds), *Higher Education: Handbook of Theory and Research* (pp. 91–156). New York: Springer.

Kinnell, M. & Creaser, C. (2001). A new outlook: Services to visually impaired people in UK public libraries. *Journal of Librarianship and Information Science*, 33(1), 5–14.

Kleiber, P., Whillans, A. V. & Chen, F. S. (2018). Long-term health implications of students' friendship formation during the transition to university. *Applied Psychology: Health and Well-being*, 10(2), 290–308.

Knis-Matthews, L., Bokara, J., DeMeo, L., Lepore, N. & Mavus, L. (2007). The meaning of higher education for people diagnosed with a mental illness: Four students share their experiences. *Psychiatric Rehabilitation Journal*, 31(2), 107–14.

Krause, K. L., Hartley, R., James, R. & McInnis, C. (2005). *The First-year Experience in Australian Universities: Findings from a Decade of National Studies*. Melbourne: University of Melbourne, Centre for the Study of Higher Education.

Kuh, G. D., Cruce, T. M., Shoup, R., Kinzie, J. & Gonyea, R. M. (2008). Unmasking the effects of student engagement on first-year college grades and persistence. *The Journal of Higher Education*, 79(5), 540–63.

Kuh, G. D., Kinzie, J., Schuh, J. H. & Whitt, E. J. (2005). Never let it rest lessons about student success from high-performing colleges and universities. *Change: The Magazine of Higher Learning*, 37(4), 44–51.

Kumashiro, K. (2002). *Troubling Education: Queer Activism and Anti-Oppressive Pedagogy*. New York: Routledge Falmer.

Kurth, N. & Mellard, D. (2006). Student perceptions of the accommodation process in postsecondary education. *Journal of Postsecondary Education and Disability*, 19(1), 71–84.

Kutscher, E. L. & Tuckwiller, E. D. (2019). Persistence in higher education for students with disabilities: A mixed systematic review. *Journal of Diversity in Higher Education*, 12(2), 136–55.

Lang H. (2002). Higher education for deaf students: Research priorities in the new millennium. *J Studies in Deaf Education*, 7(4), 267–80.

Lardner, E. & Malnarich, G. (2008). A new era in learning-community work. *Change*, 40(4), 30.

Law, I., Philips, D. & Turney, L. (2004). *Institutional Racism in Higher Education*. Stoke on Trent: Trentham Books.

Lawson, R. (1995). Critical race theory as praxis: A view from outside to the outside. *Howard Law Journal*, 38, 353–70.

Layer, G. (2005). *The Final Year Experience. Keynote Address at the Course Directors' Conference*. Kingston upon Thames: Kingston University.

Le, T. D., Robinson, L. J. & Dobele, A. R. (2020). Understanding high school students use of choice factors and word-of-mouth information sources in university selection. *Studies in Higher Education*, 45(4), 808–18.

Leading Routes (2019). *The Broken Pipeline: Barriers to Black PhD Students Accessing Research Council Funding*. UCL/Leading Routes.

Leatherwood, C. & O'Connell, P. (2003). It's a struggle: The construction of the 'New Student' in higher education. *Journal of Education Policy*, 18(6), 597–615.

Leicester, M. & Lovell, T. (1994). Equal opportunities and university practice; race, gender and disability: A comparative perspective. *Journal of Further and Higher Education*, 18(2), 43–51.

Lench H. C., Darbor K. E. & Berg, L. A. (2013). Functional perspectives on emotion, behavior, and cognition. *Behavioral Sciences*, 3(4), 536–40.

Leslie, D. (2005). Why people from the UK's minority ethnic communities achieve weaker degree results than whites. *Applied Economics* 37(6), 619–32.

Levecque, K., Anseel, F., De Beuckelaer, A., van der Heyden, J. & Gisle, L. (2017). Work organization and mental health problems in PhD students. *Research Policy*, 46(4), 868–79.

Levinson, E. M. (1998). *Transition: Facilitating the Post School Adjustment of Students with Disabilities*. Boulder, CO: Westview Press.

Liasidou, A. (2014). Critical disability studies and socially just change in higher education. *British Journal of Special Education*, 41(2), 120–35.

Lieberman, D. A. & Remedios, R. (2007). Do undergraduates' motives for studying change as they progress through their degrees? *British Journal of Educational Psychology*, 77(2), 379–95.

Lipp, E. & Jones, B. A. (2010/11). Bilingual Hispanic and Southeast Asian students' challenges in a freshman history course. *CATESOL Journal*, 22(1), 64–86.

Lizotte, M. C. & Simplican, S. C. (2017). Doctoral students with disabilities: Challenges in academic programs and research methodology. *Journal for the Study of Postsecondary and Tertiary Education*, 2, 181–93.

Lizzio, A. (2011). *Succeeding@ Griffith: Next Generation Partnerships across the Student Lifecycle*. Queensland, brisbane: Griffith University.

Lizzio, A. & Wilson, K. (2010, June). Strengthening commencing students' sense of purpose: Integrating theory and practice. *13th Pacific Rim First Year in Higher Education Conference*. Adelaide: Australia.

Loewen, G. & Pollard, W. (2010). The social justice perspective. *Journal of Postsecondary Education and Disability*, 23(1), 5–18.

Lombardi, A. R. & Murray, C. (2011). Measuring university faculty attitudes toward disability: Willingness to accommodate and adopt universal design principles. *Journal of Vocational Rehabilitation*, 34(1), 43–56.

Lombardi, A. R., Murray, C. & Gerdes, H. (2012). Academic performance of first-generation college students with disabilities. *Journal of College Student Development*, 53(6), 811–26.

Macaskill, A. (2013). The mental health of university students in the United Kingdom. *British Journal of Guidance*, 41(4), 426–41.

Machell, J. (1996). *Library and Information Services for Visually Impaired People: National Guidelines.* London: Library Association Publishing.

Madaus, J. W., Gelbar, N., Dukes, L. L., III, Lalor, A. R., Lombardi, A., Kowitt, J. & Faggella-Luby, M. N. (2018). Literature on postsecondary disability services: A call for research guidelines. *Journal of Diversity in Higher Education*, 11, 133–45.

Madaus, J. W. & Shaw, S. F. (2006). The impact of the IDEA 2004 on transition to college for students with learning disabilities. *Learning Disabilities Research & Practice*, 21(4), 273–81.

Madriaga, M. (2007). Enduring disablism: Students with dyslexia and their pathways into UK higher education and beyond. *Disability & Society*, 22(4), 399–412.

Madriaga, M. (2010). 'I avoid pubs and the student union like the plague': Students with Asperger syndrome and their negotiation of university spaces. *Children's Geographies*, 8(1), 39–50.

Major, L. E. & Machin, S. (2018). *Social Mobility and Its Enemies*. London: Penguin UK.

Malik, T. (2011). *College Success: First Year Seminar's Effectiveness on Freshmen Academic and Social Integration, Impact on Academic Achievement and Retention at a Southern Institution.* Providence Rhode Island: Johnson & Wales University.

Mamiseishvili, K. & Koch, L. C. (2011). First-to-second-year persistence of students with disabilities in postsecondary institutions in the United States. *Rehabilitation Counseling Bulletin*, 54(2), 93–105.

Mamiseishvili, K. & Koch, L. C. (2012). Students with disabilities at 2-year institutions in the United States: Factors related to success. *Community College Review*, 40(4), 320–39.

Manuel, M., Hanson, K., Heaton, C., Kay, H., Newitt, S. & Walker, A. (2010). Confronting similar challenges? Disabled and non-disabled students' learning and assessment experiences. *Studies in Higher Education*, 647–58.

Markoulakis, R. & Kirsh, B. (2013). Difficulties for university students with mental health problems: A critical interpretive synthesis. *The Review of Higher Education*, 37(1), 77–100.

Marschark, M., Leigh, G. & Sapere, P. (2009). Benefits of sign language interpreting and text alternatives for deaf students' classroom learning. *Journal of Deaf Studies and Deaf Education*, 11(4), 421–37.

Marshak, L., van Wieren, T., Ferrell, D. R., Swiss, L. & Dugan, C. (2010). Exploring barriers to college student use of disability services and accommodations. *Journal of Postsecondary Education and Disability*, 22(3), 151–65.

Martin, J. M. (2010). Stigma and student mental health in higher education. *Higher Education Research and Development*, 29(3), 259–74.

Martinez Dy, A. Martin, L.& Marlow, S. (2014). Developing a critical realist positional approach to intersectionality. *Journal of Critical Realism*, 13(5), 447–66.

Maseti, T. (2018). The university is not your home: Lived experiences of a Black woman in academia. *South African Journal of Psychology*, 48(3), 343–50.

Matthews, N. L., Ly, A. R. & Goldberg, W. A. (2015). College students' perceptions of peers with autism spectrum disorder. *Journal of Autism and Developmental Disorders*, 45(1), 90–9.

May, A. L. & Stone, C. A. (2010). Stereotypes of individuals with learning disabilities: Views of college students with and without learning disabilities. *Journal of Learning Disabilities*, 43(6), 483–99.

May, H. & Bridger, K. (2010). *Developing and Embedding Inclusive Policy and Practice in Higher Education*. York: Higher Education Academy.

Mayhew, M. J., Vanderlinded, K. & Kim, E. K. (2010). A multi-level assessment of the impact on orientation programs on student learning. *Research in Higher Education*, 51(4), 320–45.

Maylor, U. (2010). Widening participation: A worthwhile strategy? In Weekes-Bernard, D. (ed.), *Widening Participation and Race Equality*, Runnymede Perspectives Series (pp. 1–14). London: Runnymede.

McBurnie, J. E., Campbell, M. & West J. M. (2012). Avoiding the second year slump: A transition framework for students progressing through university. *International Journal of Innovation in Science and Mathematics Education*, 20(2), 14–24.

McCune, P. (2001). What do disabilities have to do with diversity? *About Campus*, 6(2), 5–12.

McGrath, S. M. & Burd, G. D. (2012). A success course for freshmen on academic probation: Persistence and graduation outcomes. *NACADA Journal*, 32(1), 43–52.

McKay, J. & Devlin, M. (2015). 'Low income doesn't mean stupid and destined for failure': Challenging the deficit discourse around students from low SES backgrounds in higher education. *International Journal of Inclusive Education*, 20(4), 347–63.

McKnight, O., Paugh, R., Waltz, J. & McKnight, J. (2015). Retrenchment in higher education: Public perceptions and marketing implications. *Journal of Higher Education Theory & Practice*, 15(5), online.

Meekosha, H. & Shuttleworth, R. (2009). What's so 'critical' about critical disability studies? *Australian Journal of Human Rights*, 15(1), 47–75.

Megivern, D., Pellerito, S. & Mowbray, C. (2003). Barriers to higher education for individuals with psychiatric disabilities. *Psychiatric Rehabilitation Journal*, 26(3), 217.

Melguizo, T. (2008). Quality matters: Assessing the impact of attending more selective institutions on college completion rates of minorities. *Research in Higher Education*, 49(3), 214–36.

Mellifont, D., Smith-Merry, J., Dickinson, H., Llewellyn, G., Clifton, S., Ragen, J. & Williamson, P. (2019). The ableism elephant in the academy: A study examining academia as informed by Australian scholars with lived experience. *Disability & Society*, 34(7–8), 1180–99.

Mercer, L., Evans, L. J., Turton, R. & Beck, A. (2018). Psychological therapy in secondary mental health care: Access and outcomes by ethnic group. *Journal of Racial and Ethnic Health Disparities*, 6(2), 419–26.

Metcalfe, J., Wilson, S. & Levecque, K. (2018). *Exploring Wellbeing and Mental Health and Associated Support Services for Postgraduate Researchers*. Cambridge: Vitae.

Meuleman, A., Garrett, R., Wrench, A. & King, S. (2015). 'Some people might say I'm thriving but … ': Non-traditional students' experiences of university. *International Journal of Inclusive Education*, 19(5), 503–17.

Milem, J. F. & Astin, H. S. (1993). The changing composition of the faculty: What does it really mean for diversity? *Change: The Magazine of Higher Learning*, 25(2), 21–7.

Milem, J. F., Umbach, P., Ting, M., Sherlin, J., Liang, C., Kelly, R. D. & Alimo, C. (2001). Educating students for their roles as citizens in a diverse democracy: Assessing the democratic outcomes of diversity. *Maryland Student Affairs Conference*, University of Maryland, College Park, MD, September, 23.

Millburn, A. (2012). *University Challenge: How Higher Education Can Advance Social Mobility a Progress Report by the Independent Reviewer on Social Mobility and Child Poverty*. Cabinet Office, London: HMSO.

Miller, M. (2016). *The Ethnicity Attainment Gap Literature Review*. Sheffield: Widening Participation Unity, University of Sheffield.

Milligan, N. V. (2010). Effects of training about academic accommodations on perceptions and intentions of health science faculty. *Journal of Allied Health*, 39(1), 54–61.

Mitchell Jr, D., Marie, J. & Steele, T. L. (2019). *Intersectionality & Higher Education: Research, Theory, & Praxis*. Peter Lang Publishing Group. 29 Broadway 18th Floor, New York, NY 10006.

Mole, J. & Peacock D. (2005a). *Learning, Teaching and Assessment. A Guide to Good Practice for Staff Teaching Deaf Students in Art, Design*. Wolverhampton: University of Wolverhampton.

Mole J. & Peacock D. (2005b). *Learning, Teaching and Assessment: A Guide to Good Practice for Lecturers Teaching Science or Engineering to Deaf Students*. Wolverhampton: University of Wolverhampton.

Montacute, R. & Holt-White, E. (2020). Covid-19 and Social Mobility Impact Brief# 2: University Access and Student Finance. Sutton Trust.

Moody, J. (2020). *Designing Inclusive Curricula Teaching and Learning*. London: London Advance HE.

Moore, J. & Dunworth, F. (2011). Review of evidence from Aimhigher area partnerships of the impact of Aimhigher. *Manchester: Aim Higher Research Network*.

Moore, J., Sanders, J. & Higham, L. (2013). Literature review of research into widening participation to higher education. *Report to HEFCE and OFFA. AimHigher Research & Consultancy Network*.

Moore, R. (1996). Back to the future: The problem of change and the possibilities of advance in the sociology of education. *British Journal of Sociology of Education*, 17(2), 145–61.

Moorish, F. (2019) 'Pressure Vessels': The Epidemic of Poor Mental Health among Higher Education Staff, London, Higher Education Policy Institute.

Morales, E. E. (2012). Learning as liberation: How liberal arts education transforms first-generation/low socio-economic college students. *Journal of College Student Retention*, 13(4), 499–518.

Morales, E. E. (2014). Learning from success: How original research on academic resilience informs what college faculty can do to increase the retention of low socioeconomic status students. *International Journal of Higher Education*, 3(3), 92–102.

Morgan, C. (2011). Constructing the OECD programme for international student assessment. *PISA under Examination* (pp. 47–59). Leiden Netherlands: Brill Sense.

Morgan, M. (2011a). Reorientation and reinduction. In Morgan, M. (ed.), *Improving the Student Experience* (pp. 105–25). London: Routledge.

Morgan, M. (2011b). The student experience practitioner model. In Morgan, M. (ed.), *Improving the Student Experience*. London: Routledge.

Morgan, W. (2016). Why is my professor still not black? Winston Morgan explores what his career might reveal about the position of ethnic minority academics. *Times Higher Education*, 14 March 2016. https://www.timeshighereducation.com/blog/why-my-professor-still-not-black?page=0 (accessed 8 January 2022).

Morningstar, M. E., Frey, B. B., Noonan, P. M., Ng, J., Clavenna-Deane, B., Graves, P., et al. (2010). A preliminary investigation of the relationship of transition preparation and selfdetermination for students with disabilities in postsecondary educational settings. *Career Development for Exceptional Individuals*, 33(2), 80–94.

Morrice, L. (2013). Managing difference and diversity in higher education: The limitations of widening participation discourses. *Mobilities and Transitions: Learning, Institutions, Global and Social Movements*, 179.

Morrish, L. (2019). *Pressure Vessels: The Epidemic of Poor Mental Health among Higher Education Staff*. London: Higher Education Policy Institute.

Murray, C. (2006). Rediscovering the underclass. *The American Enterprise*, 17(1), 29–30.

Murray, C., Lombardi, A. & Wren, C. T. (2011). The effects of disability-focused training on the attitudes and perceptions of university staff. *Remedial and Special Education*, 32(4), 290–300.

Myers, K. A. & Bastian, J. J. (2010). Understanding communication preferences of college students with visual disabilities. *Journal of College Student Development*, 51(3), 265–78.

Naylor, R. & James, R. (2016). Systemic equity challenges: An overview of the role of Australian universities in student equity and social inclusion. *Widening Higher Education Participation*, 1–13.

Neary, M. (2016). Student as producer: The struggle for the idea of the university. *Other Education*, 5(1), 89–94.

Ness, B. M. (2013). Supporting self-regulated learning for college students with Asperger syndrome: Exploring the "Strategies for College Learning" model. *Mentoring & Tutoring: Partnership in Learning*, 21(4), 356–77.

Neves, J. & Hillman, N. (2016). The 2016 Student Academic Experience Survey. *Higher Education Academy*.

Nevill, R. E. & White, S. W. (2011). College students' openness toward autism spectrum disorders: Improving peer acceptance. *Journal of Autism and Developmental Disorders*, 41(12), 1619–28.

NICHE (1997). (Dearing Report), *Higher Education in the Learning Society, National Committee of Inquiry into Higher Education*. London: HMSO.

Nichols, S. & Stahl, G. (2019). Intersectionality in higher education research: A systematic literature review. *Higher Education Research & Development*, 38(6), 1255–68.

Nicholson, S. & Cleland, J. A. (2017). 'It's making contacts': Notions of social capital and implications for widening access to medical education. *Advances in Health Sciences Education*, 22(2), 477–90.

Nixon, J. & McDermott, D. (2010). Teaching race in social work education. *Enhancing Learning in the Social Sciences*, 2(3), 1–14.

Noble, H. (2010). Improving the experience of deaf students in higher education. *British Journal of Nursing*, 19(13), 851–4.

Noden, P., Shiner, M. & Modood, T. (2014). *University Offer Rates for Candidates from Different Ethnic Categories*. London: Routledge.

Norman, K., Caseau, D. & Stefanich, G. P. (1998). Teaching students with disabilities in inclusive science classrooms: Survey results. *Science Education*, 82(2), 127–46.

Norwich, B. (2009). How compatible is the recognition of dyslexia with inclusive education? In Reid, G. (ed.), *The Routledge Companion to Dyslexia* (pp. 177–92). New York: Routledge/Taylor & Francis Group.

Norwich, B. & Lewis, A. (2005). How specialized is teaching pupils with disabilities and difficulties? *Special Teaching for Special Children? Pedagogies for Inclusion*, 1–14.

Nosaka, T. & Novak, H. (2014). Against the odds: The impact of the key communities at Colorado State University on retention and graduation for historically underrepresented students. *Learning Communities Research and Practice*, 2(2), Article 3.

Nuñez, A. (2011). Counterspaces and connections in college transitions: First-generation Latino students' perspectives on Chicano studies. *Journal of College Student Development*, 52(6), 639–55.

NUS and Universities UK (2019). Black, Asian and minority ethnic student attainment at UK universities: Case studies. London: NUS and Universities UK

OfS (2019a). Equality and diversity data. Available from: www.officeforstudents.org.uk/data-and-analysis/equality-anddiversity/equality-and-diversity-data/.

OfS (2019b). How do student outcomes vary by disability status? https://www.officeforstudents.org.uk/data-and-analysis/differences-in-student-outcomes/disability/ (accessed 8 January 2022).

OfS (2019c). *Beyond the Bare Minimum: Are Universities Doing Enough for Disabled Students*. London: OfS.

OfS (2019d). Official statistic: Key performance measure 5. Available from: gap-in-degree-outcomes-1sts-or-21s-between-disabledstudents-and-non-disabled-students-hesa/

OfS (2020). *Topic Briefing: Black and Minority Ethnic (BME) Students*. London: OFS.

OfS (2021). *English Higher Education 2020: The Office for Students Annual Review*. London: OfS. https://www.officeforstudents.org.uk/annual-review-2021/improving-students-experience-of-higher-education/ (accessed 6 January 2021).

Olivas, M. A. (1990). Breaking the law on principle: An essay on lawyers' dilemmas, unpopular causes, and legal regimes. *University of Pittsburgh Law Review*, 52, 815.

Oliver, C., Petty, J., Ruddick, L. & Bacarese-Hamilton, M. (2012). The association between repetitive, self-injurious and aggressive behavior in children with severe intellectual disability. *Journal of Autism and Developmental Disorders*, 42(6), 910–19.

Olney, M. F. & Brockelman, K. F. (2005). The impact of visibility of disability and gender on the self-concept of university students with disabilities. *Journal of Postsecondary Education and Disability*, 18(1), 80–91.

O'Neill, R. & Jones, M. (2007). The experience of d/Deaf FE students moving to HE: A tale of transition. In Barnes, L., Harrington, F., Williams, J. & Atherton, M. (eds), *Deaf Students in Higher Education, Current Research and Practice* (pp. 53–74). Coleford, Gloucestershire: McLean.

Orellana, M. L., Darder, A., Pérez, A. & Salinas, J. (2016). Improving doctoral success by matching PhD students with supervisors. *International Journal of Doctoral Studies*, 11, 87–103.

Orne, J. (2013). Queers in the line of fire: Goffman's stigma revisited. *The Sociological Quarterly*, 54(2), 229–53.

Osberg, L. (2015). *Economic Inequality in the United States*. New York: Routledge.

Osborne, T. Department of Education, Communication and Learning, Faculty of Education (2019). Not lazy, not faking: Teaching and learning experiences of university students with disabilities. *Disability & Society*, 34(2), 228–52.

O'Shea, S. (2016). First-in-family learners and higher education: Negotiating the 'silences' of university transition and participation. *HERDSA Review of Higher Education*, 3, 5–23.

Osterman, K. F. (2000). Students' need for belonging in the school community. *Review of Educational Research*, 70(3), 323–67.

O'Sullivan, K., Robson, J. & Winters, N. (2019). *'I feel like I have a Disadvantage': How Socio-economically Disadvantaged Students Make the Decision to Study at a Prestigious University*. London and New York: Routledge.

Owen-hutchinson, J. S., Atkinson, K. & Orpwood, J. (1998). *Breaking Down Barriers: Access to Further and Higher Education for Visually Impaired Students*. Cheltenham: Stanley Thornes Publishers Ltd., in collaboration with the Royal National Institute for the Blind.

Ozga, J. (1999). *Policy Research in Educational Settings: Contested Terrain*. United Kingdom: McGraw-Hill Education.

Page, L. C. & Scott-Clayton, J. (2016). Improving college access in the United States: Barriers and policy responses. *Economics of Education Review*, 51, 4–22.

Pakenham, K. I. & Viskovich, S. (2019). Pilot evaluation of the impacts of a personal practice informed undergraduate psychotherapy curriculum on student learning and wellbeing. *Australian Psychologist*, 54(1), 55–67.

Palmer, M., O'Kane, P. and Owens, M. (2009). Betwixt spaces: Student accounts of turning point experiences in the first-year transition. *Studies in Higher Education*, 34(1), 37–54.

Papasotiriou, M. & Joel Windle, J. (2012). The social experience of physically disabled Australian university students. *Disability & Society*, 27(7), 935–47.

Parkes, S., Mathias, L. & Seal, M. (2018). Becoming a Newman foundation year student: Conscientization to promote democratic engagement, meaningful dialogue and co-operative working. *Journal of the Foundation Year Network*, 1.

Parkes, S., Young, J. B., Cleaver, E. & Archibald, K. (2014). Academic and professional services in partnership literature review and overview of results. *Higher Education Academy and Leadership Foundation for Higher Education*. Retrieved from: https://www.heacademy.ac.uk/sites/default/files/Prof_Service_Partnership_report_final_200214_updated_1.Pdf

Parsons, S. & Platt, L. (2017). The early academic progress of children with special educational needs. *British Educational Research Journal*, 43(3), 466–85.

Patterson, M. (1976). Governmental policy and equality in higher education: The junior collegization of the French university. *Social Problems*, 24(2), 173–83.

Patton, L. D., McEwen, M., Rendón, L. & Howard-Hamilton, M. F. (2007). Critical race perspectives on theory in student affairs. *New Directions for Student Services*, (120), 39–53.

Pelco, L. E., Ball, C. T. & Lockeman, K. S. (2014). Student growth from service learning: A comparison of first-generation and non-first-generation college students. *Journal of Higher Education Outreach and Engagement*, 18(2), 49–66.

Pennacchia, J., Jones, E. & Aldridge, F. (2018). *Barriers to Learning for Disadvantaged Groups: Report of Qualitative Findings*. London: Department of the Environment, HMSO.

Pennington, C. R., Bates, E. A., Kaye, L. K. & Bolam, L. T. (2018). Transitioning in higher education: An exploration of psychological and contextual factors affecting student satisfaction. *Journal of Further and Higher Education*, 42(5), 596–607.

Perna, L. W. (2006). Studying college access and choice: A proposed conceptual model. In *Higher Education* (pp. 99–157). Dordrecht: Springer.

Perry, A. (2011). Outduction – preparing to leave, graduation and beyond. In Morgan, M. (ed.), *Improving the Student Experience*. London: Routledge.

Pettersen, K. T. & Fugletveit, R. (2015). 'should we talk about it?': A study of the experiences business leaders have of employing people with mental health problems. *Work*, 52(3), 635–41.

Pino, M. & Mortari, L. (2014). The inclusion of students with dyslexia in higher education: A systematic review using narrative synthesis. *Dyslexia*, 20(4), 346–69.

Piper, R. & Emmanuel, T. (2019). *Co-producing Mental Health Strategies with Students: A Guide for the Higher Education Sector*. Leeds: Student Minds.

Postareff, L., Mattsson, M., Lindblom-Ylänne, S. & Hailikari, T. (2016). The complex relationship between emotions, approaches to learning, study success and study progress during the transition to university. *Higher Education*, 73(3), 441–5.

Powell, J. J. & Pfahl, L. (2019). Disability and inequality in educational opportunities from a life course perspective. In Becker, R. (ed.), *Research Handbook on the Sociology of Education*. Cheltenham: Edward Elgar Publishing.

Purcell, M. (2013). *The Down-deep Delight of Democracy*. Hoboken, NJ: John Wiley & Sons.

Putnam, R. D. (2000). *Bowling Alone: The Collapse and Revival of American Community*. Columbia: Simon and Schuster.

Quinn, G. & Nunn, N. (2007). Year zero for deaf students: An access course for deaf students. In Barnes, L., Harrington, F., Williams, J. & Atherton, M. (eds), *Deaf Students in Higher Education, Current Research and Practice* (pp. 75–88). Coleford, Gloucestershire: McLean.

Quinn, J. (2004). Understanding working-class 'drop-out' from higher education through a sociocultural lens: Cultural narratives and local contexts. *International Studies in Sociology of Education*, 14(1), 57–74.

Quinn, N., Wilson, A., MacIntyre, G. & Tinklin, T. (2009). 'People look at you differently': Students' experience of mental health support within higher education. *British Journal of Guidance & Counselling*, 37(4), 405–18.

Raffe, D. & Croxford, L. (2015). How stable is the stratification of higher education in England and Scotland? *British Journal of Sociology of Education*, 36(2), 313–35.

Rao, S. & Gartin, B. C. (2003). Attitudes of university faculty toward accommodations to students with disabilities. *Journal of Vocational Special Needs Education*, 25(2), 47–54.

Rashed, M. A. (2019). In defense of madness: The problem of disability. *The Journal of Medicine and Philosophy: A Forum for Bioethics and Philosophy of Medicine*, 44(2), (April), 150–74.

Reardon, S. F. (2011). The widening academic achievement gap between the rich and the poor: New evidence and possible explanations. *Whither Opportunity*, 1(1), 91–116.

Reay, D. (2017). *Miseducation: Inequality, Education and the Working Classes* (1st ed.) Bristol: Policy Press.

Reay, D. (2021). The working classes and higher education: Meritocratic fallacies of upward mobility in the United Kingdom. *European Journal of Education*, 56(1), 53–64.

Reay, D., Crozier, G. & Clayton, J. (2010). 'Fitting in' or 'standing out': Working-class students in UK higher education. *British Educational Research Journal*, 36(1), 107–24.

Reino, V. & Byrom, N. (2017). *Graduate Mental Wellbeing in the Workplace*. Oxford: Student Minds.

Richardson, E., Fenton, L., Parkinson, J., Pulford, A., Taulbut, M., McCartney, G. & Robinson, M. (2020). The effect of income-based policies on mortality inequalities in Scotland: A modelling study. *The Lancet Public Health*, 5(3), e150–6.

Richardson, J. T. (2018). Understanding the under-attainment of ethnic minority students in UK higher education: The known knowns and the known unknowns. In *Dismantling Race in Higher Education* (pp. 87–102). Cham: Palgrave Macmillan.

Richardson, J. T., Roy, A. W. (2002). The representation and attainment of students with a visual impairment in higher education. *British Journal of Visual Impairment*, 20(1), 37–48.

Riddell, S., Tinklin, T. & Wilson, A. (2005). *Disabled Students in Higher Education: Perspectives on Widening Access and Changing Policy*. London: Routledge.

Riddell, S. & Weedon, E. (2014). European higher education, the inclusion of students from under-represented groups and the Bologna Process. *International Journal of Lifelong Education*, 33 (1), 26–44.

Riddell, S. & Weedon, E. (2016). Higher education in Europe: Widening participation. In Shah, M., Bennett, A. & Southgate, E. (2015). *Widening Higher Education Participation: A Global Perspective* (pp. 49–62). Hull: Chandos Publishing.

Roberts, K. & Atherton, G. (2011). Career development among young people in Britain today: Poverty of aspiration or poverty of opportunity? *International Journal of Educational Administration and Policy Studies*, 3(5), 59–67.

Robinson, D. & Salvestrini, V. (2020). *The Impact of Interventions for Widening Access to Higher Education: A Review of the Evidence*. University of Strathclyde.

Roessler, R. T., Hennessey, M. L. & Rumrill, P. D. (2007). Strategies for improving career services for postsecondary students with disabilities: Results of a focus group study of key stakeholders. *Career Development for Exceptional Individuals*, 30(3), 158–70.

Roessler, R. T., Neath, J., McMahon, B. T. & Rumrill, P. D. (2007). Workplace discrimination outcomes and their predictive factors for adults with multiple sclerosis. *Rehabilitation Counseling Bulletin*, 50(3), 139–52.

Rollock, N. (2012). Unspoken rules of engagement: Navigating racial microaggressions in the academic terrain. *International Journal of Qualitative Studies in Education*, 25(5), 517–32.

Rollock, N. & Dixson, A. D. (2016). Critical race theory. *The Wiley Blackwell Encyclopedia of Gender and Sexuality Studies*, 1–6.

Rosado, D. & David, M. (2006). 'A massive university or auniversity for the masses?' Continuity and change in higher education in Spain and England. *Journal of Education Policy*, 21(03), 343–65.

Rumrill, P. D., Jr (1999). Effects of a social competence training program on accommodation request activity, situational self-efficacy, and Americans with disabilities act knowledge among employed people with visual impairments and blindness. *Journal of Vocational Rehabilitation*, 12(1), 25–31.

Russell, K. K. (1992). Development of a black criminology and the role of the black criminologist. *Justice Quarterly*, 9(4), 667–83.

Rydberg, E., Gellerstedt, L. C. & Danermark, B. (2009). Toward an equal level of educational attainment between deaf and hearing people in Sweden? *Journal of Deaf Studies and Deaf Education*, 14(3), 312–23.

Sahlin, R. (2009). Reasonable accommodation for faculty with psychosocial impairment: A legal analysis of the university's duty in the US, the UK and Sweden. *International Journal of Discrimination and the Law*, 10(2), 57–94.

Salzer, M. S., Wick, L. C. & Rogers, J. A. (2008). Familiarity with and use of accommodations and supports among postsecondary students with mental illnesses. *Psychiatric Services*, 59(4), 370–5.

Sargent, J., Williams, R. A., Hagerty, B., Lynch-Sauer, J. & Hoyle, K. (2002). Sense of belonging as a buffer against depressive symptoms. *Journal of the American Psychiatric Nurses Association*, 8(4), 120–9.

Saunders, J. (2013). The support of deaf students in the transition between further education and school into higher education. *Deafness & Education International*, 14(4), 199–216.

Scharp, K. M. & Dorrance-Hall, E. (2017). Family marginalization, alienation, and estrangement: Questioning the nonvoluntary status of family relationships. *Annals of the International Communication Association*, 41(1), 28–45.

Schmid, M. E., Gillian-Daniel, D. L., Kraemer, S. & Kueppers, M. (2016). Promoting student academic achievement through faculty development about inclusive teaching. *Change: The Magazine of Higher Learning*, 48(5), 16–25.

Scott, D., Hughes, G., Burke, P., Evans, C., Watson, D. & Walter, C. (2013). *Learning Transitions in Higher Education*. London: Palgrave Macmillan.

Scott, J. & Cashmore, A. (2012). Fragmented transitions: Moving to the 2nd year. *Proceedings STEM Annual Conference*. Available from: https://www.heacademy.ac.uk/system/files/jon_scott_1.pdf

Scott, S. S. (1997). Accommodating college students with learning disabilities: How much is enough? *Innovative Higher Education*, 22(2), 85–99.

Seal, M. (2009). *Not about Us without Us: Client Involvement in Supported Housing*. Lyme Regis: Russell House Publishing.

Seal, M. (2018). *Participatory Pedagogic Impact Research: Co-production with Community Partners in Action*. London and New York: Routledge.

Seal, M. (2019). *The Interruption of Heteronormativity in Higher Education, Queer and Critical Pedagogies*. London: Palgrave Macmillan.

Seal, M. (2020). No homo: Reactions to the interruption of heteronormativity on a youth and community work course. *Journal of LGBT Youth*, 18(4), 1–31.

Seal, M. (ed.) (2021). *Hopeful Pedagogies in Higher Education*. New York and London: Bloomsbury.

Seal, M. & Frost, S. (2014). *Philosophy in Youth and Community Work*. Lyme Regis: Russell House Publishing.

Seal, M. & Parkes, S. (2019). Pedagogy as transition: Student directed tutor groups on foundation years. *Journal of the Foundation Year Network*, 2, 7–20.

Seal, M. & Smith, A. (2021). *Enabling Critical Pedagogies in Higher Education*. St Albans: Critical Publishing.

Senior, N. (2013). *Exploring the Retention and Attainment of Black and Minority Ethnic (BME) Students on Social Policy Pathways in Higher Education*. London: Advance HE.

Shah, M., Bennett, A. & Southgate, E. (2015). *Widening Higher Education Participation: A Global Perspective*. Hull: Chandos Publishing.

Shakespeare, T. & Watson, N. (2010). Beyond models: Understanding the complexity of disabled people's lives. In Scambler, G. & Scambler, S. (eds), *New Directions in the Sociology of Chronic and Disabling Conditions* (pp. 57–76). London: Palgrave Macmillan.

Shattuck, P. T., Narendorf, S. C., Cooper, B., Sterzing, P. R., Wagner, M. & Taylor, J. L. (2012). Postsecondary education and employment among youth with an autism spectrum disorder. *Pediatrics*, 129(6), 1042–9.

Sheppard-Jones, K., Krampe, K. M., Danner, F. & Berdine, W. H. (2002). Investigating postsecondary staff knowledge of students with disabilities using a web based survey. *Journal of Applied Rehabilitation Counseling*, 33, 1.

Shifrer, D. (2013). Stigma of a label: Educational expectations for high school students labeled with learning disabilities. *Journal of Health and Social Behavior*, 54(4), 462–80.

Shildrick, M. (2012). Critical disability studies: Rethinking the conventions for the age of postmodernity. In Watson, N., Thomas, C. & Roulstone, A. (eds), *Routledge Handbook of Disability* (pp. 32–44). London and New York: Routledge.

Shildrick, T., MacDonald, R. & Furlong, A. (2016). Not single spies but in battalions: A critical, sociological engagement with the idea of so-called 'troubled families'. *The Sociological Review*, 64(4), 821–36.

Shogren, K. A., McCart, A. B., Lyon, K. J. & Sailor, W. S. (2015). All means all: Building knowledge for inclusive schoolwide transformation. *Research and Practice for Persons with Severe Disabilities*, 40(3), 173–91.

Simcock, P. (2010). A case study into the experience of a Deaf social worker during his studies at Staffordshire University – Poster Presentation Innovative Practice in Higher Education. *Innovative Practice in Higher Education*, 1(1).

Simkiss, P., Garner, S. & Dryden, G. (1998). *What Next? The Experience of Transition: Visually Impaired Students, Their Education and Preparation for Employment*. London: Royal National Institute for the Blind.

Simmons, L. (2008). *Think Differently ñ Act Positively: Public Perceptions of Autism*. London: The National Autistic Society.

Sims, J. M. (2007). *Not Enough Understanding? Student Experiences of Diversity in UK Universities*. The Runnymede Trust. Available from: https://www.runnymedetrust.org/uploads/publications/pdfs/NotEnoughUnderstanding-2007.pdf

Simui, F., Kasonde-Ngandu, S., Cheyeka, A. M., Simwinga, J. & Ndhlovu, D. (2018). Enablers and disablers to academic success of students with visual impairment: A 10-year literature disclosure, 2007–2017. *The British Journal of Visual Impairment*, 36(2), 163–74.

Sinclair, S., McKendrick, J. H. & Scott, G. (2010). Failing young people? Education and aspirations in a deprived community. *Education, Citizenship and Social Justice*, 5(1), 5–20.

Singh, G. (2011). *Black and Minority Ethnic (BME) Students' Participation in Higher Education: Improving Retention and Success. A Synthesis of Research Evidence*. London: Higher Education Academy.

Slate, J. R., LaPrairie, K., Schulte, D. P. & Onwuegbuzie, A. J. (2009). A mixed analysis of college students' best and poorest college professors. *Issues in Educational Research*, 19(1), 61–78.

Slay, J. & Stephens, L. (2013). *Co-production in Mental Health: A Literature Review*. London: New Economics Foundation.

Smith, B. L., MacGregor, J., Matthews, R. S. & Gabelnick, F. (2004). *Learning Communities: Reforming Undergraduate Education*. San Francisco, CA: Wiley.

Smith, J. M. & Lucena, J. C. (2016). Invisible innovators: How low-income, first-generation students use their funds of knowledge to belong in engineering. *Engineering Studies*, 8(1), 1–26.

Smith, L. T. (1999). *Decolonising Methodologies: Researching and Indigenous Peoples*. London: Zed Books.

Smith, S., Joslin, H. & Jameson, J. (2015). Progression of college students in England to higher education. BIS research paper number 239.

Smith, W. & Zhang, P. (2010). The impact of key factors on the transition from high school to college among first-and second-generation students. *Journal of the First-Year Experience & Students in Transition*, 22(2), 49–70.

Smithies, D. & Byrom, N. (2018). *LGBTQ+ Student Mental Health: The Challenges and Needs of Gender, Sexual and Romantic Minorities in Higher Education*. Leeds: Student Minds. https://www.studentminds.org.uk/uploads/3/7/8/4/3784584/180730_lgbtq_report_final.pdf (4)

Sniatecki, J. L., Perry, H. B. & Snell, L. H. (2015). Introductory biology course reform: A tale of two courses. *Journal of Post Secondary Education and Disability*, 28(3), 259–75.

Social Sciences Feminist Network Research Interest Group (2017). The burden of invisible work in academia: Social inequalities and time use in five university departments. *Humboldt Journal of Social Relations*, 39, 228–45.

Solnit, R. (2016). *Hope in the Dark: Untold Histories, Wild Possibilities*. Haymarket Books.

Solórzano, D. G. (1997). Images and words that wound: Critical race theory, racial stereotyping, and teacher education. *Teacher Education Quarterly*, 24(3), 5–19.

Solórzano, D. G. (1998). Critical race theory, race and gender microaggressions, and the experience of Chicana and Chicano scholars. *International Journal of Qualitative Studies in Education*, 11(1), 121–36.

Solórzano, D. G. & Bernal, D. D. (2001). Examining transformational resistance through a critical race and LatCrit theory framework: Chicana and Chicano students in an urban context. *Urban Education*, 36(3), 308–42.

Soria, K. M. & Stebleton, M. J. (2012). First-generation students' academic engagement and retention. *Teaching in Higher Education*, 17(6), 673–85.

Soria, K. M. (2013). *What Happens Outside of the College Class (ed) Room? Examining College Students' Social Class and Social Integration in Higher Education*. A Dissertation submitted to the faculty of the graduate school of the University of Minnesota.

Sotardi, V. A. & Dubien, D. (2019). Perfectionism, wellbeing, and university performance: A sample validation of the Frost Multidimensional Perfectionism

Scale (FMPS) in New Zealand. *Personality & Individual Differences*, 143, 103–6.

Sparks, R. L. & Lovett, B. J. (2009). Objective criteria for classification of postsecondary students as learning disabled: Effects on prevalence rates and group characteristics. *Journal of Learning Disabilities*, 42(3), 230–9.

Spohrer, K. (2015). Opening doors or narrowing opportunities? The coalition's approach to widening participation, social mobility and social justice. In Finn, M. (ed.), *The Gove Legacy: Education in Britain after the Coalition* (pp. 101–15). Basingstoke: Palgrave Macmillan.

St Clair, R. & Benjamin, A. (2011). Performing desires: The dilemma of aspirations and educational attainment. *British Educational Research Journal*, 37(3), 501–17.

Stage, F. K. & Milne, N. V. (1996). Invisible scholars: Students with learning disabilities. *The Journal of Higher Education*, 67(4), 426–45.

Stallman, H. M. (2010). Psychological distress in university students: A comparison with general population data. *Australian Psychologist*, 45(4), 249–57.

Stanley, N., Mallon, S., Bell, J. & Manthorpe, J. (2009). Trapped in transition: Findings from a UK study of student suicide. *British Journal of Guidance & Counselling*, 37(4), 419–33.

Stanley, N. & Manthorpe, J. (2001). Responding to students' mental health needs: Impermeable systems and diverse users. *Journal of Mental Health*, 10, 41–52.

Stefancic, J. & Delgado, R. (eds) (2000). *Critical Race Theory: The Cutting Edge*. Harvard: Temple University Press.

Stephen, C. O. L. E. & Barber, E. G. (2003). *Increasing Faculty Diversity*. Cambridge, MA: Harvard University Press.

Stephens, N. M., Hamedani, M. G. & Destin, M. (2014). Closing the social-class achievement gap: A difference-education intervention improves first-generation students' academic performance and all students' college transition. *Psychological Science*, 25(4), 943–53.

Stevenson, J. (2012). *Black and Minority Ethnic Student Degree Retention and Attainment*. York: Higher Education Academy.

Stevenson, J. & Lang, M. (2010). *Social Class and Higher Education: A Synthesis of Research*. York: Higher Education Academy.

Stevenson, J., O'Mahony, J., Khan, O., Ghaffar, F. & Stiell, B. (2019). *Understanding and Overcoming the Challenges of Targeting Students from Under-represented and Disadvantaged Ethnic Backgrounds*. London: Office for Students.

Stevenson, J. & Whelan, B. (2013). *Synthesis of US Literature Relating to the Retention, Progression, Completion and Attainment of Black and Minority Ethnic (BME) Students in HE*. London: Advance HE.

Stitch, A. E. (2012). *Access to Inequality: Reconsidering Class, Knowledge, and Capital in Higher Education*. Maryland, MA: Lexington Books.

Stones, S. & Glazzard, J. (2019). *Supporting Student Mental Health in Higher Education*. St Albans: Critical Publishing.

Story, A. E., Carpenter–Song, E. A., Acquilano, S. C., Becker, D. R. & Drake, R. E. (2019). Mental health leaves of absence in college and therapy: A qualitative study of student experiences. *Journal of College Student Psychotherapy*, 33(1), 38–46.

Strand, S. (2012). The White British–Black Caribbean achievement gap: Tests, tiers and teacher expectations. *British Educational Research Journal*, 38(1), 75–101.

Strike, T. & Toyne, J. (2015). *Widening Access to Postgraduate Study and Fair Access to the Professions: Working Together to Ensure Fair Access to Postgraduate Taught Education*. University of Sheffield.

Stubb, J., Pyhalto, K. & Lonka, K. (2018). Balancing between inspiration and exhaustion: PhD students' experienced sociopsychological well-being. *Studies in Continuing Education*, 33(7), Vitae.

Student Minds (2017). *Student Voices*. Oxford: Student Minds.

Swinney, P. & Williams, M. (2016). *The Great British Brain Drain*. London: Centre for Cities.

Taylor, E., Gillborn, D. & Ladson-Billings, G. (2009). *Foundations of Critical Race Theory in Education*. London and New York: Routledge.

Taylor, Y. & Costa, C. (2019). *Estranged Students in Higher and Further Education*. Strathclyde: University of Stratclyde.

Test, D. W., Fowler, C. H., Wood, W. M., Brewer, D. M. & Eddy, S. (2005). A conceptual framework of self-advocacy for students with disabilities. *Remedial and Special Education*, 26(1), 43–54.

Tett, L., Cree, V. E. & Christie, H. (2016). From further to higher education: Transition as an on-going process. *Higher Education*, 73(3), 389–406.

Thomas, L. (2002). Student retention in higher education: The role of institutional habitus. *Journal of Education Policy*, 17(4), 423–42.

Thomas, L. (2012). Building student engagement and belonging in Higher Education at a time of change. *Paul Hamlyn Foundation*, 100, 1–99.

Thomas, L. & May, H. (2011). Student engagement to improve retention and success model. In Thomas, L. & Jamieson- Ball, C. (eds), *Engaging Students to Improve*

Student Retention and Success in Higher Education in Wales. London: Higher Education Academy.

Thomas, L. & Jones, R. (2017). Student engagement in the context of commuter students. London: The Student Engagement Partnership.

Thomas, L. J. & Asselin, M. (2018). Promoting resilience among nursing students in clinical education. *Nurse Education in Practice*, 28, 231–4.

Thomas, S. L., Rothschild, P. C. & Donegan, C. (2015). Social networking, management responsibilities, and employee rights: The evolving role of social networking in employment decisions. *Employee Responsibilities and Rights Journal*, 27 (4), 307–23.

Thompson, D. W. (2012). Widening participation from a historical perspective: Increasing our understanding of higher education and social justice. *Social Inclusion and Higher Education*, 41–64.

Thompson, S., Milsom, C., Zaitseva, E., Stewart, M., Darwent, S. & Yorke, M. (2013). The forgotten year? Tackling the second year slump, London, Advance HE.

Thompson, T., Burgstahler, S. & Moore, E. J. (2010). Web accessibility: A longitudinal study of college and university home pages in the northwestern United States. *Disability and Rehabilitation: Assistive Technology*, 5(2), 108–14.

Thorley, C. (2017). Not by Degrees: Improving Student Mental Health in the UK's Universities. London, UK: IPPR.

Tibbetts, Y., Harackiewicz, J. M., Priniski, S. J. & Canning, E. A. (2016). Broadening participation in the life sciences with social-psychological interventions. *CBE – Life Sciences Education*, 15(4), 1–10.

Tight, M. (1998). Bridging the 'learning divide': The nature and politics of participation. *Studies in the Education of Adults*, 30(2), 110–19.

Tinklin, T., Riddell, S. & Wilson, A. (2004). *Disabled Students in Higher Education: A Centre for Higher Educational Sociology (CES) Briefing*. Edinburgh: Centre for Educational Sociology.

Tinto, V. (1975). Dropout from higher education: A theoretical synthesis of recent research. *Review of educational research*, 45(1), 89–125.

Tinto, V. (1993). Building community. *Liberal Education*, 79(4), 16–21.

Tinto, V. (2003). Learning better together: The impact of learning communities on student success. *Higher Education Monograph Series*, 1(8), 1–8.

Tinto, V. (2005). Moving from theory to action. *College Student Retention: Formula for Student Success*, 3, 317–33.

Tinto, V. (2006). *Research and practice of student retention: What next? Journal of College Student Retention: Research, Theory & Practice*, 8(1), 1–19.

Tomlinson, M. (2018). Student perceptions of themselves as 'consumers' of higher education. *British Journal of Sociology of Education*, 38(4), 450–67.

Tomlinson, S. (2017). A sociology of special and inclusive education. In *Exploring the Manufacture of Inability*. Abingdon: Routledge.

Toor, N., Hanley, T. & Hebron, J. (2016). The facilitators, obstacles and needs of individuals with Autism Spectrum Conditions accessing further and higher education: A systematic review. *Journal of Psychologists and Counsellors in Schools*, 26(2), 166–90.

Torgerson, C., Gascoine, L., Heaps, C., Menzies, V. & Younger, K. (2014). Higher Education Access: Evidence of Effectiveness of University Access Strategies and Approaches. London: Sutton Trust, 47–64.

Trammell, J. (2009). Postsecondary students and disability stigma: Development of the postsecondary student survey of disability-related stigma. *Journal of Postsecondary Education and Disability*, 22(2), 106–16.

Triandis, H. C. (1989). Cross-cultural studies of individualism and collectivism. *Nebraska Symposium on Motivation*, 37(1), 41–133.

Troiano, P. F. (2003). College students and learning disability: Elements of self-style. *Journal of College Student Development*, 44(3), 404–19.

Truong, K. A. (2010). Exploring racism and racial trauma in doctoral study. In *Invited Presentation to Tara L. Parker's Access and Equity course*. Boston, MA: University of Massachusetts, College of Education and Human Development.

Tsai, T. (2012). Coursework-related information horizons of first-generation college students. *Information Research*, 17(4), Article 542.

Tudge, J. R., Mokrova, I., Hatfield, B. E. & Karnik, R. B. (2009). Uses and misuses of Bronfenbrenner's bioecological theory of human development. *Journal of Family Theory & Review*, 1(4), 198–210.

Tuitt, F. (2012). Black like me: Graduate students' perceptions of their pedagogical experiences in classes taught by Black faculty in a predominantly White institution. *Journal of Black Studies*, 43(2), 186–206.

Umbach, P. D. & Kuh, G. D. (2006). Student experiences with diversity at liberal arts colleges: Another claim for distinctiveness. *The Journal of Higher Education*, 77(1), 169–92.

vanBergeijk, E. O., Klin, A. & Volkmar, F. (2008). Supporting more able students on the autism spectrum: College and beyond. *Journal of Autism and Developmental Disorders*, 38(7), 1359–70.

Vasek, D. (2005). Assessing the knowledge base of faculty at a private, four-year institution. *College Student Journal*, 39(2), 307–15.

Vaughn, W. P. (2015). *Schools for All: The Blacks and Public Education in the South, 1865–1877*. Lexington, KY: University Press of Kentucky.

Vickerman, P. & Blundell, M. (2010). Hearing the voices of disabled students in higher education. *Disability & Society*, 25(1), 21–32.

Vincent, C., Rollock, N., Ball, S. & Gillborn, D. (2012). Being strategic, being watchful, being determined: Black middle-class parents and schooling. *British Journal of Sociology of Education*, 33(3), 337–54.

Vuong, M., Brown-Welty, S. & Tracz, S. (2010). The effects of self-efficacy on academic success of first-generation college sophomore students. *Journal of College Student Development*, 51(1), 50–64.

Wachelka, D. & Katz, R. C. (1999). Reducing test anxiety and improving academic self-esteem in high school and college students with learning disabilities. *Journal of Behavior Therapy and Experimental Psychiatry*, 30(3), 191–8.

Walker, B., Holling, C. S., Carpenter, S. R. & Kinzig, A. (2004). Resilience, adaptability and transformability in social–ecological systems. *Ecology and Society*, 9(2), online.

Walker, L., Matthews, B. & Black, F. (2004). Widening access and student noncompletion: An inevitable link? Evaluating the effects of the top-up programme on student completion. *International Journal of Lifelong Education*, 23(1), 43–59.

Wampold, B. E. & Brown, G. S. (2005). Estimating variability in outcomes attributable to therapists: A naturalistic study of outcomes in managed care. *Journal of Consulting and Clinical Psychology*, 73(5), 914–23.

Warmington, P. (2020). Critical race theory in England: Impact and opposition, identities. *Global Studies in Culture and Power*, 27(1), 20–37.

Waterfield, B. & Whelan, E. (2017). Learning disabled students and access to accommodations: Socioeconomic status, capital, and stigma. *Disability & Society*, 32(7), 986–1006.

Waters, J. & Brooks, R. (2010). Accidental achievers? International higher education, class reproduction and privilege in the experiences of UK students overseas. *British Journal of Sociology of Education*, 31(2), 217–28.

Watson, J. (2013). Profitable portfolios: Capital that counts in higher education. *British Journal of Sociology of Education*, 34(3), 412–30.

Weale, S. (2018). Bristol University faces growing anger after student suicides. *The Guardian*, 26 May 2018. Available from: https://www.theguardian.com/education/2018/may/26/bristoluniversity-faces-growing-anger-after-student-suicides

Weale, S. (2019) Levels of distress and illness among students in the UK 'alarmingly high'. [Online] *The Guardian*, 5 March. Available at: https://www.theguardian.com/education/2019/mar/05/levels-of-distress-and-illness-among-students-in-uk-alarmingly-high (accessed 20 September 2019).

Webb, O., Wyness, L. & Cotton, D. (2017). *Enhancing Access, Retention, Attainment and Progression in Higher Education: A Review of the Literature Showing Demonstrable Impact*. London: Higher Education Academy.

Webb, O. J. & Cotton, D. R. E. (2019). *Deciphering the Sophomore Slump: Changes to Student Perceptions during the Undergraduate Journey*. England: Plymouth University.

Webb, S. N., Chonody, J. M. & Kavanagh, P. S. (2017). Attitudes toward same-sex parenting: An effect of gender. *Journal of Homosexuality*, 64(11), 1583–95.

Weedon, E. & Riddell, S. (2016). Higher education in Europe: Widening participation. In Shah, M., Bennett, A. & Southgate, E. (eds), *Widening Higher Education Participation* (pp. 49–61). Witney Oxfordshire: Chandos Publishing.

Wehmeyer, M. L. (2004). Beyond self-determination: Causal agency theory. *Journal of Developmental and Physical Disabilities*, 16(4), 337–59.

Wehmeyer, M. L. (2005). Self-determination and individuals with severe disabilities: Re-examining meanings and misinterpretations. *Research and Practice for Persons with Severe Disabilities*, 30(3), 113–20.

Wehmeyer, M. L., Morningstar, M. E. & Husted, D. (1999). *Family Involvement in Transition Planning and Program Implementation*. Austin, TX: ProEd.

Weidman, J. (1989). Undergraduate socialization: A conceptual approach. *Higher Education: Handbook of Theory and Research*, 5(2), 289–322.

Weiner, E. (1999). The meaning of education for university students with a psychiatric disability: A grounded theory analysis. *Psychiatric Rehabilitation Journal*, 22(4), 403–9.

Weiner, E. & Weiner, J. (1996). Concerns and needs of university students with psychiatric disabilties. *Journal of Postsecondary Education and Disability*, 12(1), 403–9.

Wessel, R. D., Jones, J. A., Markle, L. & Westfall, C. (2009). Retention and graduation of students with disabilities: facilitating student success. *Journal of Postsecondary Education and Disability*, 21(3), 116–25.

White, J. W. (2011). Resistance to classroom participation: Minority students, academic discourse, cultural conflicts, and issues of representation in whole class discussion. *Journal of Language, Identity, and Education*, 10(4), 250–65.

White, S. W., Ollendick, T. H. & Bray, B. C. (2011). College students on the autism spectrum: Prevalence and associated problems. *Autism: The International Journal of Research and Practice*, 15(6), 683–701.

Whittle, S. R. (2018). The second-year slump – now you see it, now you don't: Using DREEM-S to monitor changes in student perception of their educational environment. *Journal of Further and Higher Education*, 42(1), 92–101.

Whitty, G., Hayton, A. & Tang, S. (2015). Who you know, what you know and knowing the ropes: A review of evidence about access to higher education institutions in England. *Review of Education*, 3(1), 27–67.

Whitty, G., et al. (2018). Diversity and complexity: Becoming a teacher in England in 2015–16. *Review of Education*, 6(1), 69–96.

Williams, M., Pollard, E., Takala H. & Houghton, E. (2019). *Review of Support for Disabled Students in Higher Education in England*. Bristol: Institute for Employment Studies.

Woodrow, M., Lee, M. F., McGrane, J., Osborne, B., Pudner, H. & Trotman, C. (1998). *From Elitism to Inclusion: Good Practice in Widening Access to Higher Education, Executive Summary*. London: Committee of Vice-Chancellors and Principals of the Universities of the United Kingdom.

Wu, G., Feder, A., Cohen, H., Kim J., Calderon, S., Charney, D. & Mathé, A. (2013). Understanding resilience. *Frontiers in Behavioral Neuroscience*, 7(10), online.

Yee, A. (2016). The unwritten rules of engagement: Social class differences in undergraduates' academic strategies. *Journal of Higher Education*, 87(6), 831–58.

Yeh, T. L. (2010). Service-learning and persistence of low-income, first-generation college students: An exploratory study. *Michigan Journal of Community Service Learning*, 16(2), 50–65.

Yorke, M. (2015). Why study the second year? In Milson, C., Stewart, M., Yorke, M. & Zaitseva, E. (eds), *Stepping up to the Second Year at University* (pp. 1–13). London: Routledge.

Yorke, M. & Longden, B. (2004). *Retention and Student Success in Higher Education*. London: Society for Research into Higher Education.

Yorke, M. & Longden, B. (2008). *The First-year Experience of Higher Education in the UK: Final Report*. York: The Higher Education Academy.

Yosso, T. J. (2005). *Whose Culture Has Capital? A Critical Race Theory Discussion of Community Cultural Wealth*. London, United Kingdom: Taylor and Francis.

Younger, K., Gascoine, L., Menzies, V. & Torgerson, C. (2019). A systematic review of evidence on the effectiveness of interventions and strategies for widening participation in higher education. *Journal of Further and Higher Education*, 43(6), 742–73.

Zaitseva, E., Darwent, S. & Thompson, S. (2015). Implications for student support. In Milson, C., Stewart, M., Yorke, M.& Zaitseva, E. (eds), *Stepping up to the Second Year at University* (pp. 23–38). London: Routledge.

Zandy, J. (ed.) (1990). *Calling Home: Working-class Women's Writings: An Anthology*. New Brunswick, NJ: Rutgers University Press.

Zepke, N., Leach, L., Prebble, T., Campbell, A., Coltman, D., Dewart, B. & Wilson, S. (2005). *Improving Tertiary Student Outcomes in the First Year of Study*. Final Report. Wellington, New Zealand: Teaching and Learning Research Initiative.

Zhang, D. & Katsiyannis, A. (2002). Minority representation in special education: A persistent challenge. *Remedial and Special Education*, 23(3), 180–7.

Zipin, L., Sellar, S., Brennan, M. & Gale, T. (2015). Educating for futures in marginalized regions: A sociological framework for rethinking and researching aspirations. *Educational Philosophy and Theory*, 47(3), 227–46.

Index

ableism 10, 129, 130, 153
access and participation plans 15, 53, 54, 60, 62, 64, 68, 190
accessibility 106, 135, 144, 154, 172
advance HE 9, 113, 139
affirmative model 139
agency 5, 6, 14, 23, 29, 55, 81, 82, 87, 89, 121, 139, 155
aim Higher 36, 41, 113
alliances 7, 8
  importance of 4, 7
anti-oppressive practice 16, 100, 101, 102, 130
archetypes 11, 29, 30, 31, 186
Arday, J. 12, 107, 119, 121, 124, 125, 185
aspiration 21, 29, 30, 41, 70, 72, 73, 74, 80, 109, 116, 187, 192
  Low aspiration 73
  poverty of 14, 25, 40
assessment 16, 17, 34, 55, 128, 132, 187, 188
  and disability 136, 143, 151, 158
  and global majority students 100
  and mental health 18, 163, 170, 177, 183
asset-based approaches 80, 184
assimilation models 10, 11, 14, 16, 29, 71–2, 78, 80, 87, 96, 114, 130
attainment 9, 15, 16, 41, 42, 43, 47, 53, 54, 56, 57, 58, 66, 69, 71, 73, 74, 90, 100, 111, 114, 115, 144, 145, 147, 167
attitudes 128, 129, 138, 143
  of employers 181
  of management 61, 135
  of other students 16, 72, 134, 170
  of staff 75, 134, 146, 152, 165, 170
  toward HE 85
autism 17, 127, 131, 144, 148

Bell Curve 101
belonging 14, 16, 23, 32, 33, 48, 51, 86, 92, 93, 100, 116, 118, 163
'Black Lives Matter' 5, 7
Black and Minority Ethnic (BAME) 15, 28, 54, 58, 65, 66, 82, 125
Bologna Process 3, 14, 45
Bourdieu 12, 23, 24, 28, 72, 74, 77, 78, 97, 130
bridging capital 83, 89

citizen 27, 44, 48, 121
civic 5, 18, 188
class 2, 7
  middle class 12
    access to Russell Group universities 40
    anxiety 46
    asking for help 79
    doctoral advantage 95
    expansion of university to 38
    schooling 21
  upper class 12
    gatekeeping 47, 78
    schooling 21
  working class
    achievement 15
    representation at university 15
    participation
    progression 15
complicity 8, 17, 157
community 18, 26, 33, 73, 81, 82, 95, 109, 110, 112, 113, 117, 118, 123, 137, 159, 169, 174, 190, 192 193
  business community 11
  Community Cultural Wealth 109
  youth and community 22
Conceptual Model of College Choice 128
Conceptual Model of Undergraduate Socialization 128

continuation 14, 15, 33, 53, 56, 57, 70, 72, 90, 100, 114, 144, 145, 167
co-production 108, 121, 144, 189, 190, 191
critical disability theory (CDT) 129, 157
critical pedagogy 4, 5, 9, 21, 22, 102, 109
critical race theory 8, 16,25, 100, 102, 125
critical realism 5, 6
cultural capital 11, 24, 31, 44, 51, 87, 88, 131, 137
curriculum 9, 21, 34, 188
  and class 74
  decolonizing 121, 123, 126
  and disability 17, 128, 135, 132, 155
  liberating/decolonizing 16, 60, 120, 121, 125, 126
  and mental health 18, 158, 161, 167, 168, 174, 176, 177, 178, 183
  and race 5, 7, 25, 46, 100, 106, 107

dearing report 14, 38, 40
debt 85, 86, 111
decolonizing 11–12, 16, 120, 121–6
depression 67, 89, 89, 147, 160, 164, 166, 178, 179
disability
  models of 17, 128, 139
disabled student commission (DSC) 50, 139
Disabled Students Allowance (DSA) 49, 50, 60, 141, 174
disclosure 17, 18, 128, 132, 135, 136, 147, 155, 157, 160, 162, 166, 182
discrimination 7, 9, 10, 49, 61, 95, 100, 104, 106, 107, 120, 123, 126, 127, 134, 138, 153, 158, 160, 169, 183, 186, 191
disadvantaged students
  deficit views of 10, 13, 15
also see outreach
distress 68, 148, 159, 164, 173, 184
doctoral study 16, 18, 49, 69, 95, 96, 100, 158
double consciousness 76
dyslexia 2, 17, 67, 89, 127, 136, 142, 146, 147
dyspraxia 2, 17, 67, 127

employability 2, 27, 45
employers 18, 47, 60, 95, 123, 157, 158, 181, 182, 183, 188, 192
epistemology 7, 8, 16, 102, 107, 121, 188, 184
Equality Act 49, 67, 139, 158
Europe 3, 14, 32, 37, 44, 45, 54
evaluation 3, 54, 60, 62, 63, 84, 108, 184, 189
evidence based policy 7, 8
extrinsic motivation 10, 28, 114, 115, 176, 186

family 22, 24, 76, 77, 99, 105, 111, 112, 114, 115, 131, 133, 180, 187
feminism 20, 23, 94, 119
finance 7, 17, 41, 43, 89, 96, 126, 141, 187, 188
first year experience 16, 55, 71, 80, 90, 97, 123, 140, 160
foundation years 16, 72
Freire, Paulo 1, 4, 86–8, 122

gender 2, 8, 21, 45, 57, 66, 73, 93, 96, 103, 107, 118, 121, 131, 132, 136, 137, 145
global majority 15, 27, 38, 46, 66, 72, 76, 99, 100, 106, 110, 116, 184
  aspirations 26
  barriers 117
  communities 11
  Debt 111
  decolonizing 121
  doctoral experience 124–5
  entering HE 55
  initiative for 107, 108, 113
  parents 112, 115
  progression 123
  senses of belonging 116, 118
  staff 118, 119, 120, 190
  students 10, 12, 14, 16, 100, 104, 126, 172, 191
  success 114
  which universities 39, 48, 81, 95, 106, 110, 111

habitus 22, 23, 24, 28, 68, 76, 88, 137
higher Education

Index

Access, Participation and Progression Plans 10, 15
  assumption it is a good thing 10, 13
  civic purpose of 5
  engagement in 11
  expectations 97, 187
    of disabled students 139, 152, 158
    of global majority students 118, 123, 124
  higher education as site for liberation 4
  participation in 11
  reproducing existing privileges 5, 13
  site of transformation 4
  source of progression and regression 1
higher education opportunity act 43
Higher Education Funding Council for England (HEFCE) 33, 42, 49, 56, 57, 59, 66, 84, 101, 145, 152
Higher Education Participation and Partnership Programme (HEPPP) 3, 14
Hinton-Smith 1, 15, 27, 29, 30, 31, 34

identity 5, 33, 131, 137, 138, 143, 155, 159, 182, 184
  academic 34, 138
  class 12, 24, 77, 92, 189
  disability 17, 132, 134, 135
  mental health 128
  and race 76, 77, 115
  student 72, 138
IMD 84
inclusive practice 35, 49, 119, 129, 135
inequality 4, 9, 12, 13, 24, 27, 28, 30, 32, 40, 47, 51, 74, 78, 82, 104, 106, 108, 113, 123
integration 14, 16, 19, 28, 37, 38, 46, 48, 49, 71–2, 76, 115, 121, 131, 136, 155, 163, 174, 183
intersectionality 7, 8, 16, 93, 115,116, 118, 119, 121
  Anuj Kapilashrami 8, 9
isolation 9, 51, 82, 124, 126, 132, 134, 144, 146, 147, 164, 168, 176, 177, 189

knowledge creation 1, 5, 18, 188
kyriarchy 8, 105

LGBTQAI+ 127, 172
Liquid Modernity 77
low socio-economic 46, 111

marginalization 15, 16, 17, 19, 31, 32, 54, 64, 77, 78, 82, 100, 107, 108, 121, 122, 127, 186
Marxism 7, 20, 25, 33, 189
massification 22, 37
mechanics institute 20
meritocracy 22, 25, 29, 47, 78, 103, 109
morphogenic approach 6
motivation 1, 2, 9, 10, 28, 34, 37, 43, 81, 114, 115, 142, 163, 164, 176, 186

National Health Service 160, 171, 173
National Union of Students (NUS) 50, 116, 117, 153, 160, 175
neo-liberal 19, 25, 37, 45, 48, 52, 54, 69
New Labour 14, 37, 38, 47
neuro-typical 17, 127, 136, 153, 183, 184
new universities 22, 31, 49, 73, 80, 163
'no place like home' initiative 192

office for fair access (OFFA) 9, 36, 42, 53, 60, 114
office for students 9, 15, 50, 53, 56, 60, 65, 66, 90, 165
ontology 5
Open Method of Co-ordination 3, 14
othering 13, 14, 31, 102, 106
outreach for disadvantaged students 4, 11, 16, 39, 41, 51, 71, 84, 85, 97, 99, 113, 153, 186

participatory research 109, 189, 190
pedagogy 9, 16, 18, 24, 92, 93, 100, 122, 123, 126, 143, 162, 176
  anti-racist pedagogy 121
  critical pedagogy 4, 9, 15, 16, 89, 106, 109
  queer pedagogy 106
  transitional pedagogy 163
peer support 116, 149, 171
personal tutoring 17, 128, 183
placements 57, 145, 163, 168

POLAR 64, 65, 78, 84
polytechnics 39
postgraduate 3, 11, 16, 50, 57, 58, 59, 71, 96, 124, 145, 152, 165, 172, 178, 179, 186
progressive education 4, 7, 10
psychoeducational 12, 158, 174, 178

queer 2, 102

race 8
  primacy of 8
  racism 16, 10, 12, 25, 82, 99, 101, 103, 104, 112, 115, 117, 119, 123, 125, 155
  structural 7, 16
reasonable adjustment 49, 50, 129, 139, 147, 149, 153, 158, 189
Reay, D. 12, 24, 26, 31, 76, 77, 78, 84
Robbins Committee 20, 39, 185
Russell Group 22, 39, 55, 73, 78, 103, 110, 141, 191

safe space 116, 177
schizophrenia 170
segregation 44, 49
self-advocacy 17, 128, 131, 132, 133, 152
self-determination 17, 128, 130, 132, 133, 152
simultaneity 7
social capital 11, 18, 23, 27, 77, 78, 83, 95, 109, 137, 162, 177
social constructionism 6, 10
social expectations 32
social good 10, 105, 185
social justice 1, 10, 102, 104, 106, 121, 123, 126, 130, 154
social mobility 1, 2, 10, 6, 8, 14, 18, 45, 51, 83, 137, 155, 188, 191
  antithesis of 3
  global majority student 46
  and higher education 22, 29, 37, 38, 41, 47, 48, 77, 188, 189
  working class 15, 46, 94
social policy 14
  higher education 4, 5, 10, 13
standpoint epistemology 8
STEM 7
stereotyping 14, 30, 112, 117, 118, 122

stigma 17, 75, 128, 130, 131, 132, 134, 135, 137, 146, 147, 155, 162, 169, 170, 175
stress 50, 68, 92, 131, 140, 147, 163, 165, 166, 178, 179, 180, 182
students
  ideal types 11, 31, 78, 89, 130, 155, 188
  elite 1
  expectations 16, 30, 59, 72, 83, 169, 183; *of disabled students* 148; *of global majority students* 125, 130
structuration 6
student voice 118, 122, 184
summer schools 40, 91

targets 10, 15, 42, 43, 45, 54, 60, 61, 68, 69, 187
Teaching Excellence Framework (TEF) 42, 64, 69
Tinto, V. 24, 28, 78, 115, 163, 164
transfactual 6
transition 14, 53, 81, 142, 143, 160, 167
  academic 88
  in HE 18, 31, 32, 33, 34, 86, 113, 115, 144, 156, 183
  to HE 163–4, 166, 168
  institutional 88
  out of HE 152, 158, 180
  transition as becoming
Trio Programme 4, 14

unconscious bias 109
underclass 26
United States 4, 11, 13, 14, 21, 30, 37, 43, 44, 45, 47, 49, 74, 97, 105, 111, 113, 115, 118, 124, 132, 133, 152, 169

visual impairment 138, 153

well-being 10, 15, 17, 27, 54, 68, 92, 157, 159, 160, 161, 163, 164, 167, 168, 169, 171, 175–8, 180, 183
'What works' 5, 6, 34, 62, 149, 154, 187
white supremacy 103, 126
whole institutional approach 9, 11, 12, 100, 116, 117, 128, 135, 154, 157, 159, 160, 183
  Also see widening participation

'Why is my curriculum white' 5
widening participation 11
   agenda item for governments 2
   failure of 2
   initiatives 1
   key studies 13
   Theoretical perspectives 13

tinkering approach 9
training, limitations of 9
universal design for learning 17, 123, 128, 150
whole institutional approach 9
Yerevan Communiqué 14
Workers Educational Association 20

www.ingramcontent.com/pod-product-compliance
Lightning Source LLC
Chambersburg PA
CBHW062137300426
44115CB00012BA/1958